ITALIAN GARDENS
A CULTURAL HISTORY

ITALIAN GARDENS
A CULTURAL HISTORY

HELENA ATTLEE

SPECIAL PHOTOGRAPHY BY ALEX RAMSAY

F

FRANCES LINCOLN LIMITED
PUBLISHERS
www.franceslincoln.com

ACKNOWLEDGEMENTS

I am grateful to several people for their enthusiasm and practical help during the research and writing of this book. In particular I would like to thank Andrea Bianchi Bandinelli for supplying photographs of the frescoes at Geggiano, The Authors' Foundation for the generous grant that supported my research, New York University for the loan from their archive of photographs of Villa La Pietra and its garden, Nick Dakin-Elliott for his help at La Pietra, Ada Segre for a careful reading of the manuscript and helpful suggestions, Silvia Bonacossa Sella for the loan of pictures of Villa San Remigio and finally David Wheeler for the perpetually open door of the Bryan's Ground library.

The photograph on the title-page was taken at Isola Bella, that on the frontispiece at Villa d'Este and the painting opposite is *Park of a Villa* by Marco Ricci (1676-1730)

Frances Lincoln Ltd
4 Torriano Mews
Torriano Avenue
London NW5 2RZ
www.franceslincoln.com

Italian Gardens: a cultural history
Copyright © Frances Lincoln Ltd 2006
Text copyright © Helena Attlee 2006
Photographs copyright © Alex Ramsay
unless otherwise stated on page 233
Illustrations copyright: see page 233

First Frances Lincoln edition 2006
First paperback edition 2012

British Library Cataloguing-in-Publication data
A catalogue record for this book is available from the British Library.

978-0-7112-3392-8

Commissioned and edited by Jane Crawley
Picture editor Julia Brown
Designed by Ian Hunt

Printed in China

9 8 7 6 5 4 3 2 1

FOR ROSEMARY AND DAVID ATTLEE

Contents

Padiglione Chinese per un Giardino

I | Cultivated ideas
Early Renaissance 1450-1504

ON A CLOUDY AFTERNOON IN FEBRUARY 1349 Francesco Petrarch decided to move a mature apple tree from one end of his garden to the other. He uprooted it from a shady corner at the far end of the garden and brought it to a sunny position near the house. Gardening was Petrarch's hobby, a distraction from desk and library. His approach to it was experimental and often unsuccessful. In gardening, as in every other aspect of his life, he looked to the ancient world for guidance. Classical treatises were his gardening manuals, and he noted his successes and failures in their margins. The apple tree died quite quickly.

Despite his use of classical methods of cultivation, Petrarch was a medieval man in the garden. He created four gardens during his life, and all of them were built to a traditional medieval design. High walls protected and isolated them from the outside world, and they were used predominantly for growing culinary and medicinal herbs, fruit and vegetables. At his desk, however, Petrarch was one of the first of a new generation of modern scholars whose devotion to rediscovering the ideas of classical authors, artists, architects, mathematicians and philosophers triggered the Renaissance. These 'humanists', as we now call them, sought out classical texts, many of them forgotten for centuries in monastery libraries or cathedral archives, and read and translated them properly for the first time. As they read, they realized that the natural landscape and the garden were of great cultural significance in the ancient world. They became immersed in the imaginary landscape of groves, grottoes and pools that Ovid conjured up in the *Metamorphoses*. They re-read Pliny the Younger's letters, written between AD100 and 105, where they discovered vivid descriptions of the gardens surrounding the author's villas at Laurentum in Tuscany and on the coast near Ostia, south-west of Rome. For an early humanist reader, in love with the classical world, Pliny's descriptions were a vision of earthly paradise:

LEFT *Francesco Cossa (1435-78) painted this traditional scene of vines being pruned for the month of March in the Room of the Months, Palazzo Schifanoia, Ferrara.*

ABOVE *Andrea del Castagno's* Portrait of Petrarch *from the* Famous Men and Women *series of frescoes (1449-51) from Villa Carducci Pandalfini, Legnaia.*

At the upper end … [there] is a curved dining seat of white marble, shaded by a vine trained over four slender pillars of Carystian marble. Water gushes out through pipes from under the seat as if pressed out by the weight of people sitting there, is caught in a stone cistern, and then held in a polished marble basin which is regulated by a hidden device so as to remain full without overflowing. The preliminaries and main dishes for dinner are placed on the edge of the basin, while the lighter ones float about in vessels shaped like birds or little boats.

Pliny the Elder's *Naturalis historia* (AD77), a thirty-seven book encyclopaedia on natural science, introduced the idea of garden gazebos and summerhouses, and the custom of cladding the inside of these buildings with pumice stone, 'so as to create an artificial imitation of a cave'. Treatises on agriculture were also full of information about gardens and the practicalities of classical villa life. *Rerum rusticarum* (Of rustic matters) was one such example. It was written by Varro, the Roman scholar, for his wife in about 36BC. In it he described his own

garden, with its aviary, outdoor dining room and fish pool, and the gardens of Julius Caesar, Cicero and other great figures of the day.

When Petrarch died, still gardening, in 1379, the design of the traditional medieval garden remained unchanged. Within fifty years, however, the Renaissance had gathered force and the influence of classical thought was evident in every aspect of art and architecture, including the architecture of gardens. The humanist gardens of the early Renaissance were generally quite simple structures, and yet they represented a revolutionary change in the purpose of the garden and its place in contemporary culture. The practical enclosed space of the traditional medieval garden gave way to a new idiom: a garden designed to embrace the view and to integrate the villa with the countryside that surrounded it, so that villa, garden and landscape appeared to be part of a single design. Although fruit, vegetables and herbs continued to be cultivated, the aesthetic aspect of the garden became increasingly important. By the middle of the fifteenth century the garden already occupied an important position in cultural life and garden making

L'ARCHITETTVRA
DI LEONBATISTA
ALBERTI

Tradotta in lingua Fiorentina da Cosimo
Bartoli Gentil'huomo & Accade-
mico Fiorentino.

Con la aggiunta de
Disegni.

11039

IN FIRENZE.   M. D. L.
Appresso Lorenzo Torrentino Impressor Ducale.

LEFT *A traditional, medieval* hortus conclusus, *screened from the surrounding landscape by protective walls. Medicinal herbs and flowers are cultivated in small beds, and fruit bushes grow against the walls. This illustration was made for a fifteenth-century edition of Pietro de' Crescenzi's* Liber ruralium commodorum *(1306).*

RIGHT *Almost a century after he completed his groundbreaking treatise,* De re aedificatoria, *Leon Battista Alberti's ideas were still highly influential.*

De re aedificatoria (On the art of building), was written over a period of eight years and completed in 1453 by Leon Battista Alberti (1404-72). A prodigious writer, Alberti also produced plays, poems and treatises on subjects ranging from the minutiae of domestic management (including some riveting advice regarding the correct conditions for the conception of children), to architecture, engineering and philosophy. Alberti also wrote about gardens in an essay on villa life included in a treatise entitled *Della famiglia* (On the family). On this occasion he compares gardens to children, 'One is too few', he says, 'two are plenty, and three are too many' – a maxim that was clearly ignored by Alberti's aristocratic readers, as they were often patrons of several gardens apiece.

In *De re aedificatoria* Alberti practised the typically humanist writing technique of creating a mosaic of ideas drawn from a variety of different classical sources and then cementing them together with his own prose. The *tesserae*, or tiles, of Alberti's 'mosaic' consisted of quotations from Vitruvius and snippets from Ovid, Horace, and Theophrastus. The majority of the specific references to gardens were drawn from the two Plinys, Elder and Younger.

One of the earliest humanist gardens to have survived in Italy is that of the Villa Medici in Fiesole, north of Florence. It is thought to have been designed and built by Michelozzi Michelozzo (1396-1472) between *c.* 1455 and 1461, shortly after Alberti completed his treatise, although there is no documentary proof of this attribution. The architect's patron was Giovanni de' Medici (1421-63), the son of Cosimo the Elder de' Medici, ruler of Florence and founder of the powerful Medici dynasty. The portrait of Giovanni in Benozzo Gozzoli's *The Journey of the Magi*, a fresco in the chapel of the Palazzo Medici Riccardi in Florence, shows a balding man with a wide forehead, narrow lips and a bony, intelligent face. It was painted only five years before Giovanni died at the age of forty-three. Gozzoli's flattering image seems to contradict the cause of death, which is said to have been obesity. It also diminishes the odd lump of flesh above Giovanni's nose which is clearly visible in other portraits.

In his working life Giovanni was the director of the Medici family bank, both at home and abroad, and the family's ambassador to Rome, Naples and Milan. By the sixteenth century a man in this powerful position would automatically commission a garden, or even a series of gardens to surround his urban palaces and country villas. This was not the case in the fifteenth century, and therefore the garden at Villa Medici can be read as the expression of a genuine and personal interest in both gardens and plants. Like a clever biographer, or a carefully placed mirror, the garden reflected the true personality behind the public figure of Giovanni de' Medici, banker, politician and diplomat. The garden was also an intellectual statement, for Giovanni was a renowned humanist scholar. His magnificent library, for which the architect is thought to have designed a special room in the villa, included a collection of classical and humanist texts. Among them were the treatise on plants

had became extremely fashionable among cardinals, princes, popes and other members of Italy's educated aristocratic élite.

The earliest surviving humanist gardens are to be found in Tuscany, at the heart of early Renaissance culture. It is no coincidence that the most important humanist treatise on architecture, including some aspects of the architecture of gardens, was written in Florence.

and botany by Theophrastus (c.372-c.287 BC), and *De re rustica*, twelve books on farming, gardening and the care of domestic animals by Columella (*fl.*1st century AD). Alberti wrote *De re aedificatoria* for just such a man.

Villa Medici is built on a hill high above Florence, a site originally occupied by a fortified farmhouse called the Villa Belcanto. Giovanni's decision to build on a rocky hillside was a test of the architect's ingenuity. The site was awkward and both the villa and the garden terraces had to be shored up and underpinned by massive foundations driven into the rock. The immense difficulty and expense of this operation alert us to a new phase in the history of garden and villa design. Previous generations built country houses and enclosed gardens on practical sites, generally surrounded by their own land. The two earliest Medici villas of Il Trebbio and Cafaggiolo, for example, were built in the fertile Mugello Valley north of Florence, where the family had owned agricultural land since the mid-fourteenth century. Giovanni chose to build his new villa on the steep, stony ground of Fiesole, which had no agricultural value, and did not in any case belong to his family. He selected the site purely on the grounds of its beauty. Giovanni's father, Cosimo the Elder de' Medici, belonged to an earlier generation, and it is said that he could not understand his son's motivation for building in Fiesole. Although he was steeped in classical learning himself, he told Giovanni that he preferred his own villa at Cafaggiolo, because all of its windows overlooked his own farmland. The contrast between the attitudes of these two men from successive generations demonstrates the ongoing effect of humanist thought on even the most practical aspects of life. Villa Medici and its garden reflect the ideals of a new generation of young humanists.

Giovanni de' Medici would have perceived his new villa as a mid-fifteenth century version of a classical *villa suburbana*. Literally, a suburban villa, the *villa suburbana* was associated with a classical way of life that the humanists sought to emulate. Giovanni would have been familiar with Pliny's description of the life that he led at Laurentum, his villa on the seashore, not far from Rome. He describes it as:

> A good life and a genuine one, a seclusion which is happy and honourable, more rewarding than any 'business' can be. ...You should take the first opportunity to leave the din, the futile bustle and useless occupations of the city and devote yourself to literature or to leisure.

There was a strong association between the word *otium*, translated in the quotation above as 'seclusion', and the humanist villa and garden. Although it translates into English simply as 'seclusion', 'serenity' or 'relaxation', Giovanni would have understood the full classical connotation of *otium*, perceiving it as a finely balanced combination of physical well-being and relaxation with great intellectual alertness. Following the example of 'the Ancients' he would have substituted the 'futile bustle' of the city with the intellectual activities that delighted him – reading, writing, listening to music and conversing with like-minded friends. The garden was an important part of this lifestyle. Pliny himself set a precedent by making use of the garden as a place to meditate and write, and long before that Plato had used a garden surrounded by trees as the classroom for his philosophy lessons.

LEFT *A detail from Benozzo Gozzoli's* Journey of the Magi *fresco, c.1460. Giovanni de' Medici, with his unmistakable profile, is included in the magnificent procession of pilgrims on their way to Bethlehem.*

RIGHT *Alberti said that a villa should both 'see' and 'be seen'. This detail from a fresco by Ghirlandaio (c.1486) reveals Villa Medici's elevated position in the landscape, and also shows the monastery that stood immediately behind it.*

Despite the practical difficulties encountered by the architect and his workmen, the villa's position had much to recommend it to a humanist patron, for it corresponded exactly to Alberti's advice in *De re aedificatoria*. Alberti instructed his reader to choose an elevated site for a villa 'that would enjoy all the benefit and delight of breeze, sun and view'. The position of Villa Medici also satisfies Alberti's vision of a view that 'overlooks the city, the owner's land, the sea or a great plain and familiar hills and mountains'. The villa commands a view of Florence and the great plain of the Arno valley backed by hills. Finally, and most significantly, Alberti suggests that the foreground of this view should be filled by 'the delicacy of gardens'.

Michelozzo, if he was in fact the architect, designed two garden terraces for Giovanni. The main terrace extends from the east-facing

LEFT *The east-facing loggia links the reception rooms on the* piano nobile *of the villa to the main garden, with its ravishing view over Florence.*

ABOVE *In the main garden the original box-lined compartments have been replaced with lawns on which ancient paulownia trees grow. Roses and pots of lemons line the paths.*

façade, and corresponds to the first floor of the villa. The other terrace is on the west side of the building, at ground-floor level. A sixteenth-century architect would undoubtedly have found some impressive architectural solution to link these two terraces – ramps, perhaps, or a grand balustraded staircase. However, Villa Medici demonstrates the simplicity characteristic of the humanist garden in the early Renaissance. Michelozzo made no formal architectural link between the terraces, and today the lower terrace can only be reached from the upper garden by a circuitous path that runs through the modern pergola built against the retaining wall of the upper terrace.

By building the villa into the hillside, Michelozzo created a *piano nobile*, or first floor, that was on the same level as the main garden terrace. This meant that the family and their visitors could move from the reception rooms of the *piano nobile* into the loggia on the main façade, which opened in turn on to the garden beyond. Michelozzo was one of the earliest Renaissance architects to revive this ancient Roman custom of fusing interior and exterior space, making the garden into a seamless extension of the house. Long before building work was complete the Medici family began to use the garden as an outdoor

room. In July 1455 Ginevra degli Alessandri, Giovanni's wife, threw an impromptu party in the garden. She and her friends were entertained by a troupe of dancing girls, whose performance was so moving that they became 'almost delirious' with pleasure. Nobody returned to Florence until two o'clock in the morning.

To the north the upper garden terrace is bounded by a retaining wall. To the south only a low brick wall divides the terrace from the breathtaking view. The villa's west façade was again faced by a loggia. The terrace on this side corresponded to the ground floor. An inventory of 1492 referred to this area as a vegetable garden – a convenient arrangement as it was on the same level as the kitchen and other service rooms.

Any knowledge that we have of the layout and planting of Villa Medici's gardens comes from the inventory of 1492, which lists all the 'contiguous pieces of land', including 'a garden behind said villa with various small walled gardens or with surrounding walls and a piece of

land in the grounds with cypresses and trees in a wood'. It was made on the death of Lorenzo de' Medici, who had owned the villa. The 'small walled gardens' were probably enclosed beds on the upper garden terrace. Something about the planting of these beds can be gleaned from a letter that Giovanni de' Medici received from an acquaintance called Giovanni di Luca Rossi in April 1455. It was written to inform him that a certain Bartolommeo Serragli was to travel to Naples in eight days time, where he could be commissioned to buy pomegranate, orange and lemon trees. There is no written evidence to prove that these purchases were ever made. However, an *Annunciation* by Biagio d'Antonio suggests that the trees may have been bought. The Virgin is shown sitting in front of an open window. Behind her the view opens out over the Villa Medici and its terraces. Small bush-like trees are shown growing against the retaining wall of the terrace. Italian garden historian Giorgio Galletti, who has worked on the restoration of many Medici gardens both in Florence and Rome, believes that these bushes could represent espaliered oranges. Citrus trees were unusual in Tuscany in the fifteenth century, and it is possible that Giovanni was one of the first people to grow them in central Italy. During the sixteenth and seventeenth centuries aristocrats all over Italy made citrus cultivation their hobby. The Medici citrus collection, housed at Castello and Boboli, was one of the largest and most diverse collections in Europe (see Chapter 7).

Another letter to Giovanni, this time dated 10 March 1456, furnishes us with further botanical information about the garden. The letter was sent from Ferrara where Giovanni had once worked for a branch of the Medici bank. It was written by a certain Francesco della Torre, who must have visited Giovanni's garden in the past because he makes some very specific requests. He asks to be sent cuttings of a sweet-scented white rose with a pink flush. Giorgio Galletti suggests that this was the highly scented *Rosa* x *alba* 'incarnata', the flower that is scattered across the canvas of Botticelli's *Birth of Venus*. Francesco della Torre also wanted plants or seeds of the pink and red dianthus that grew in the villa garden.

Giovanni left the makings of a garden that really came into its own under his nephew, Lorenzo ('the Magnificent') de' Medici (1449-92), who was the ruler of Florence, a humanist and a poet. Lorenzo's grandfather, Cosimo the Elder, had founded an academy devoted to the study of Plato. Lorenzo continued this tradition, inviting scholars, artists and writers to join his Platonic academy. The garden in Fiesole became an outdoor salon. Lorenzo's guests read aloud to him, discussed classical texts and philosophy and listened to music. Alberti himself was often present on these occasions. In November each year the academy celebrated Plato's birthday with an informal banquet.

The Florentine scholar and poet Angelo Poliziano was engaged by Lorenzo as tutor to his children. In 1479 he wrote a letter from Fiesole

LEFT *The ceiling of Villa Medici's loggia is decorated with these frescoes* alla grottesca, *a style inspired by the classical decorations rediscovered during the excavations at the end of the fifteenth century.*

RIGHT Rosa *x* alba 'incarnata' *drift on the wind in this detail from Botticelli's* Birth of Venus. *It is thought that this rose also flowered in the fifteenth century at Villa Medici.*

to Marsilio Ficino, another humanist, currently engaged as scholar in residence to the Medici in their villa at Careggi. His words show how successful Villa Medici and its garden were as a realization both of the humanist aesthetic and of Alberti's practical advice in *De re aedificatoria*:

> When you are incommoded with the heat of the season in your retreat at Careggi, you will perhaps think the shelter of Fiesole not undeserving notice. Seated between the sloping sides of the mountain we have here water in abundance and being constantly refreshed with moderate winds find little inconvenience from the glare of the sun. As you approach the house it seems embosomed in the wood, but when you reach it you find it commands a full prospect of the city. Populous as the vicinity is, yet I can enjoy the solitude so gratifying to my disposition.

In 1459, when work was already begun on the challenging commission at Villa Medici, another ambitious and profoundly humanist building project was underway in southern Tuscany. Imagine a garden suspended between earth and sky; a tiny, light-filled box hanging above the vast spaces of the Val d'Orcia. This is the garden that Bernardo Rossellino (1409-64) designed for Aenius Silvius Piccolomini (1405-64).

Piccolomini began his career as a Latin poet and diplomat, he was a free thinker, an opponent of the papacy and a notorious womanizer. Eventually he settled his differences with the Roman church, becoming first a priest and then, quite rapidly, a cardinal. When he was elected as Pope Pius II in 1458, he became the first humanist scholar to occupy the papal throne.

Within a year of his accession Pius II embarked upon transforming his obscure birthplace, a little village called Corsignano, into an ideal city that he planned to rename Pienza. He commissioned Rossellino, the Tuscan sculptor turned engineer, to design the central piazza and the cluster of buildings around it. The most important structures were the cathedral, the town hall and the Piccolomini palace with its small hanging garden. Pius instructed the cardinals who followed his court to build palaces of their own around this nucleus.

Pienza is built on a high plateau. The Piccolomini palace stands on the edge of the cliff that runs along the southern side of the town. Its garden occupies the narrow space between the palace and the cliff edge. Originally the garden site was uneven and the ground sloped steeply towards the cliff edge. Rossellino found an extraordinary architectural solution to this problem that is carefully described by Pius II in his *Commentaries*:

> Very thick walls were built on a stone base and between columns of brick or stone it had arched openings which could provide stabling for 100 horses and workshops for blacksmiths. Above them was left some twelve feet of solid wall and above that a second row of arches. On these was heaped earth deep enough to make a hanging garden with vines and trees….

This proved a successful solution to the physical problems of the site, although several men were killed when the excavation collapsed, trapping them in a hole thirty metres (100 feet) deep. In order to keep the stables and workshops dry, Rossellino made raised beds in the garden.

Rossellino's design represents another perfect realization of Leon Battista Alberti's vision of a garden. This is no casual coincidence, for Rossellino came to Pienza directly from Florence, where he had been working with Alberti on the construction of the façade for Palazzo Rucellai. He designed the palace garden in Pienza to be seen from the triple-tiered loggia that occupies the building's south-facing garden façade. Today it is a room enclosed by the palace on one side, two walls and a tall box hedge at its far end. This enclosed garden is an invention

LEFT *Aenius Silvius Piccolomini served as court poet to the Holy Roman Emperor, Frederick III. Bernardino Pintoricchio's fresco (c.1504) shows him kneeling at the emperor's feet to receive the crown of poet laureate in 1442.*

RIGHT *The triple, south-facing loggia of Palazzo Piccolomini incorporates three of the four classical orders. The fountain in the foreground of the picture was not part of Rossellino's original design.*

of the early twentieth century. In the *Commentaries*, Pius II describes a garden that is open to the town, the palace and the view. The only enclosure was a 'breast-high' balustrade. It is clear that the garden was designed to be seen and enjoyed by all comers, as Pius explains that the balustrade is decorated with painted pinnacles, 'which from a distance presented a very gay appearance'.

The garden creates a foreground for the magnificent view that Pius II described in his *Commentaries*. Originally the *Commentaries* were composed in elegant humanist Latin, and, although Pius chose to write in the third person, they are the only autobiography ever written by a pope. Pius's description makes it clear that most of Alberti's essential

elements – a great plain, distant hills and mountains, the owner's land – were encompassed in the view from the loggia of his new palace:

> The view from the three loggias to the south is bounded by…towering and wooded Monte Amiata. You look down the valley of the Orcia and green meadows and hills covered with grass in season and fruited fields and vineyards, towns and citadels and precipitous cliffs and Bagni di Vignoni and Montepescali, which is higher than Radicofani and is the portal of the winter sun.

At ground level the garden is like a small sun-filled room. The modern hedge on the cliff edge serves the double purpose of screening and framing the view, for it is pierced by three arches. This contrast between the enclosed space of the garden and the infinite space beyond adds drama to Rossellino's original design.

Rossellino employed each of the three classical orders – Ionic, Doric and Corinthian – in the triple loggia of the Piccolomini palace. This was an overt allusion to the architecture of the ancient world, but Rossellino had no intention of reproducing a genuinely classical building in fifteenth-century Italy. It was not until the following century that Donato Bramante took the revival of the ancient Roman garden beyond the realms of intellectual exercise to physical reality. In 1504 he was commissioned by Pope Julius II to re-create a classical pleasure garden in the heart of Renaissance Rome. Bramante's response to this challenge triggered a revolution that changed the whole concept of the garden in Italy and then Europe. His design was a watershed between the simple early humanist gardens of the fifteenth century, and the extravagant inventions that followed.

The site at Bramante's disposal was a rough patch of sloping ground that separated the papal palace from a fifteenth-century building called Villa Belvedere. The Pope was fond of the villa, and liked to use it as a retreat from the papal palace. He wanted the garden to link the two buildings, making it easier for him to move from one to the other.

Bramante made his plans, drawing inspiration directly from classical ruins. His main inspiration is thought to have been the Temple of Fortune at Praeneste, or Palestrina as it is now called. He worked like a classical architect, introducing the rules of proportion, perspective and symmetry into the garden, and devising a central axis that would create a muscular link between garden, villa and palace.

During the fifteenth century garden architects had never looked beyond the surface of a site. Bramante's approach was far more invasive. He created powerful architectural forms from the landscape itself, moulding the gentle slope between the palace and villa into a courtyard and a series of dramatic open terraces linked by two sets of double ramps inspired by the ancient layout of Palestrina. This was the Cortile del Belvedere.

Between the terraces and the palace, Bramante created a vast level courtyard enclosed by triple-tiered loggias. This was a theatrical space,

an ideal setting for pageants, jousting matches and other courtly entertainments. The audience sat on a massive flight of semicircular steps built against the papal palace, an imitation of an ancient Roman theatre.

Villa Belvedere stood at an odd angle on its hilltop. It could have threatened the symmetry of Bramante's design. He resolved this problem by partially concealing the building with a wall and a central exedra. The exedra formed the climax of a magnificent perspective up the centre of the courtyard and the ramps and staircases of the terraces.

Pope Julius II was a passionate collector of antique statues, and the Cortile served as an open-air gallery where his collection could be beautifully displayed among fountains, flowers and trees. By the time of his death in 1513, the garden was almost complete. A description written in 1523 by a Venetian ambassador creates a vivid impression:

One enters a very beautiful garden, of which half is filled with growing grass and bays and mulberries and cypresses, while the other half is paved with squares of bricks laid upright, and in every square a beautiful orange tree grows out of the pavement, of which there are a great many, arranged in perfect order. . . . At the main entrance of this garden on the left there is a sort of chapel built into the wall where, on a marble base, stands the Apollo. . . . Somewhat further on. . . . opposite a most perfect well, is the Laocoön, not far from this, mounted in similar fashion, is the Venus. . . . On one side of the garden is a most beautiful loggia, at one end of which is a lovely fountain that irrigates the orange trees and the rest of the garden by a little canal in the centre of the loggia.

By the end of the sixteenth century the Vatican Library had been built across the middle of this breathtakingly beautiful garden, wrecking its proportions. Verbal descriptions, prints and drawings are all that is left of the Cortile del Belvedere today. However, Bramante's work was done. His original design was so dynamic, so revolutionary and exciting, that it made an immediate and indelible impression. The Cortile del Belvedere opened the way for a new and exciting chapter in the history of garden design. It was a blueprint for the Italian Renaissance garden.

LEFT AND ABOVE *The view over the Val d'Orcia from the first floor loggia has changed very little since Pius II described it in his autobiography. The garden was designed to be seen from this level.*

OVERLEAF *The upper terrace and the exedra of Bramante's Cortile del Belvedere are just visible beyond the trees in this painting by Henrick van Cleef III of 1550. The gardens attracted artists and scholars, who were invited to study and draw the statues.*

II | Medici gardeners
Renaissance 1518-1550

THE DESIRE TO MAKE GARDENS is like a hereditary disease. It may lie dormant for many years, but sooner or later it will break out. The Medici displayed all the usual symptoms. Giovanni de' Medici (1421-63) and his nephew, Lorenzo the Magnificent (1449-92), were the gene holders in the fifteenth century. They created the garden of the Medici villa in Fiesole that is described in the previous chapter. During the sixteenth century, when the Medici became one of the most powerful dynasties in Europe, there were gardeners in every generation. They were the brave patrons of extraordinarily ambitious gardens, fountains, statues and grottoes, and the owners of some of the greatest plant collections in Europe.

The garden-making gene was taken into the sixteenth century by Cardinal Giulio de' Medici (1478-1534). In 1518 he became patron of Villa Madama, Raphael's revolutionary attempt to reproduce a classical villa and garden on the slopes of Monte Mario, overlooking Rome. Raphael was originally commissioned in 1516 by Giulio's cousin, Pope Leo X, but by the autumn of 1518, when construction work began, Giulio's name replaces Leo's on the documents relating to the villa and garden. Giulio was already a keenly intelligent, discerning and well-established patron. Unlike many of his contemporaries he took a great interest in his commissions, visiting building sites, workshops and studios, and asking searching questions about the practical details of every project.

In 1516 Raphael was at the height of his career. He responded to the commission for Villa Madama with a long letter, devoting the bulk of it to a description of a house and garden that was already fully formed in his brilliant imagination. His vision was a fusion of two principal

LEFT *The elaborate interior of Villa Madama's north-west loggia, which Raphael began to decorate before his death. The stucco work was completed by Giovanni da Udine and scenes from Ovid's* Metamorphoses *were painted by Giulio Romano. Much of the lower portion of the decoration was destroyed by rain, or damaged*

when the villa was used first as a farmhouse and then as a military barracks before the arches were eventually glazed.

RIGHT *Raphael's portrait of Pope Leo X, with his cousin Cardinal Giulio de' Medici to the left, and Cardinal Luigi Rossi behind him.*

sources, Vitruvius's *De architectura* – the only complete treatise on architecture to have survived from antiquity – and the letters of Pliny the Younger. Raphael's letter and the architectural drawings, many of them by members of the Sangallo family rather than Raphael himself, combine to create a vivid image of the architect's original plans for the site. He describes a building with a vast, open, circular courtyard at its heart, perhaps modelled on the 'two colonnades, rounded like the letter 'D' in Pliny's Laurentine villa. The building is divided into summer and winter apartments, as Vitruvius suggests, and Raphael writes in detail about the orientation of the villa in relation to the sun and the prevailing winds. For example, a round tower at the eastern corner of the courtyard is designated for use as a garden room during the winter. Its upper windows are glazed, creating a warm sun-filled space overlooking wonderful views of the valley. In Raphael's imagination this was already 'a most delightful place to be in the winter to converse with gentlemen'.

The drawings show passages leading from the central courtyard to a series of magnificent garden loggias, creating a truly classical fusion between interior and exterior space. The loggia on the south-west façade opens on to the entrance courtyard. A small garden to one side of the entrance is both described by Raphael in his letter and shown in a plan executed by Francesco da Sangallo. A rectangular space, it is neatly planted with bitter orange trees arranged around a central fountain. To the south-east the loggia overlooks three garden terraces perched above the magnificent view that François Maximilian Misson described in the seventeenth century as:

> A Prospect of Rome, with several Gardens and many pleasant Seats; and on the other the Eye is ravish'd with a beautiful Landskip of little and well cultivated Hills: over-against it the Tiber creeps thro' the Fields and Meadows…

Raphael's own drawing of the terraces shows that he planned to make each one a different geometric shape – a square, a circle and an oval. The 68 metre (30 Renaissance *canne*, or canes) measurement of the square terrace was to be repeated in the diameter of the circular terrace immediately below, and the lowest, oval terrace was to be exactly double their width. Some years later Francesco da Sangallo made drawings for two more terraces, linking them with double flights of steps. He jotted down planting suggestions on the plan. The upper terrace – a huge space – was to be planted with chestnut trees and firs. The narrow space between the two terraces was designated an orange grove. On the lower terrace he drew numerous square beds, labelling it simply *giardino*, or 'garden'. Had his plan ever been realized, these parterres would probably have been filled with flowering plants and herbs.

Of the three projected loggias, only the one on the north-west façade of the villa exists today. It was conceived by Raphael as the perfect garden room for summer as 'it is always shady, and has water and green things to make it beautiful'. Beyond the loggia was another enclosure, described by Raphael as a *xystus*, the classical term used to describe a long walk bordered by colonnades or trees, and below it there was a fish pool dug into the slope. The slope behind the loggia was to be excavated to create the most dramatic feature of all: a vast semicircular theatre inspired by a description in Vitruvius's *De architectura*.

Building work began in about 1518, but in 1520 Raphael unexpectedly died at the age of thirty-seven, leaving Rome shocked and bereaved by the loss of its finest and best loved artist. In the last years of his life he had been employed on so many different commissions for the Pope that he was accustomed to relying heavily on assistants to execute his designs. Various members of the Sangallo family, Giulio Romano and Giovanni da Udine were already in place to continue his work on the villa and gardens, although a letter from Giulio de' Medici to his friend Bishop Maffei indicates that there was some squabbling between the artists about their responsibilities after Raphael's death. Eventually it was agreed that Giovanni da Udine would be responsible for all the stucco work, and Giulio Romano would focus on the frescoes inside the loggias.

Unfortunately Raphael's death proved to be only the first in a series of setbacks. The following year Pope Leo X also died. This should not have affected the progress on site, but Giulio had been convinced that he would succeed his cousin as Pope. When the conclave elected Adrian Dedel of Utrecht as Pope Adrian VI he abandoned Rome and retreated to the Medici heartlands in Tuscany, where he took over the government of Florence. In his absence building work ground to a halt. It was not until 1523, when Giulio was finally elected as Pope Clement VII, that the workmen returned.

While his men were busy at Villa Madama, Clement VII was embroiled in a series of political manoeuvres and unstable alliances, first with the Habsburg Emperor Charles V and then with François I, King of France. In the words of the court poet Francesco Berni (c.1497-1535), his papacy was composed:

Of much consideration and discussion,
Of 'wells' and 'yes buts', of 'maybe' and 'also',
Of scores of words without effect.

This indecisiveness was eventually to have disastrous consequences for the city of Rome, and for the villa and garden that had already been a decade in the making. However this was all in the future and by the beginning of 1527 real progress had been made at Villa Madama. The workmen had completed the structure that stands today: one side of the villa, half of its circular courtyard and the north-west loggia, which was frescoed with exquisite 'grotesque' decorations by Giulio Romano and stucco work by Giovanni da Udine, with assistance from Baldassare Peruzzi. Work had also progressed in the garden. A 'private garden' or *giardino segreto* occupied the space beyond the north-west loggia, its gateway flanked by two gigantic, stucco figures made by Baccio Bandinelli. Giovanni da Udine had already made his lovely elephant-head fountain with water pouring from its trunk. He chose white marble for the fountain – perhaps because his model was the white Indian elephant presented to Pope Leo X by King Emanuel I of Portugal in 1514. Leo had named the animal Hanno after the Carthaginian sailor who founded colonies on the west coast of Africa in the sixth century BC. Hanno soon endeared himself to Leo by learning to genuflect three

FAR LEFT *Beyond the north-west façade of the Villa Madama, Baccio Bandinelli's gigantic stucco figures flank the entrance to the* giardino segreto.

LEFT *Giovanni da Udine's elephant-head fountain, set into the west wall of the* giardino segreto.

times at the sight of him, and simultaneously making a noise that onlookers described as 'bar, bar, bar!' Giovanni da Udine also built an elaborate grotto in the garden. It was an exact copy of the Temple of Neptune that had just been discovered among the classical ruins on the Palatine. Vasari describes the grotto as being 'wrought excellently well, and . . . all adorned with lifelike products of the sea, . . . with various ornaments in stucco'.

At this stage in the history of the garden Clement's indecisive political manoeuvres finally backfired and the entire force of Charles V's imperial army was turned upon Rome. In the half light of a foggy dawn on 6 May 1527 a savage and mutinous troop of forty thousand soldiers poured into the city. Twelve thousand of them were German Lutherans who expressed their antipathy to Catholicism by robbing and desecrating every Catholic church, convent and monastery that they could find, raping nuns and torturing priests. For eight days Charles's soldiers rampaged, committing every conceivable crime against the unprotected population of Rome. Barricaded inside Castel Sant'Angelo, Clement and his cardinals escaped physical harm. However the soldiers sought out the Pope's property for special attention. They found their way to the half-built villa on Monte Mario and set light to it with burning torches. From his window in Castel Sant'Angelo, Clement could see the smoke from the villa drifting across the wooded hillside.

The imperial army reduced Rome to a wilderness. News of the sacking and the Pope's humiliation spread all over the peninsula. Although the workmen returned to Monte Mario, they did no more than restore the villa and garden to the stage that they had reached before the arrival of Charles's troops. Had Raphael's plans ever been fully realized, Villa Madama would have been both the bravest and the most successful attempt ever made to revive the classical *villa suburbana*. However in 1534 Clement VII died, and the great scheme was abandoned forever.

In 1537, only three years after Pope Clement VII's death, another member of the Medici clan embarked upon the first of a series of massive garden-building projects in Florence. Cosimo de' Medici (1519–74) was only seventeen years old in January 1537 when he was unexpectedly elected as the new head of the Florentine Republic. In the same year he took over his grandmother's villa on the family estate at Castello outside Florence, and immediately commissioned Niccolò Tribolo (1500–50) to design a new garden. Tribolo was also the architect of Cosimo's other gardens, the Giardino dei Semplici (1545), a garden dedicated to 'simples' or medicinal herbs, and the preliminary structure and decoration of the Boboli Garden (1550). Cosimo's three gardens were a genuine expression of their patron's fascination for rare and medicinal plants, his love of ingenious hydraulic devices and bold sculpture. However Cosimo's enthusiasm extended beyond personal pleasure. He was one of many dukes, princes, cardinals and kings to use the garden as a means of bolstering their public image and expressing the political power that they had won and hoped to retain in the volatile political climate of sixteenth-century Italy. During the first half of

ABOVE *Cosimo I in a portrait by Agnolo Bronzino, c.1550.*

the sixteenth century magnificence came to be perceived as a princely virtue, and all over the Italian peninsula architects, sculptors, painters, poets, historians and humanist scholars were commissioned to concoct a magnificent image for their powerful patrons. Magnificence had a purpose, it impressed the ruler's citizens, helping to secure their allegiance and reducing the danger of insurrection, or even assassination. Tribolo's grand gardens found their place within the cult of magnificence, enhancing Cosimo's image and nourishing an impressive reputation that rapidly spread beyond the boundaries of Tuscany to the courts of foreign rulers.

A magnificent garden conveyed a blatant message about the wealth, power and artistic sensibilities of its patron. However the Renaissance garden also carried a cargo of symbolic associations that Cosimo de' Medici was bound to find extremely useful. Intellectual life was shaped by humanism during the Renaissance, and in the humanist imagination gardens were associated with the classical Golden Age, with Arcadia and the Garden of the Hesperides. This tradition served Cosimo and many other garden-making rulers well. It imbued them with dignity, and triggered the helpful suggestion that they might be heirs to the classical virtues of the Golden Age. The Renaissance garden was also perceived as a microcosm of the patron's kingdom. Its sheltering walls excluded all danger. Through skill, virtue and hard work the landscape had been tamed, cleared, organized and irrigated with an abundant supply of fresh water. The plants thriving in the warm soil became a metaphor for the happy citizens of this well managed kingdom.

As well as these general associations, the garden incorporated a complex iconographic programme designed for Cosimo by Benedetto Varchi. In his hands fountains, statues and plants became the words in a silent visual language that he used to encode the garden with flattering messages about Cosimo's political and military prowess, about Florence and the achievements of the entire Medici dynasty.

Varchi took on the task of glorifying the Medici at a rather inauspicious moment in the family's history and an awkward phase in its relationship with Florence. It was only ten years since the Sack of Rome, when Pope Clement VII (Giulio de' Medici) was defeated and humiliated by Charles V. The Florentines had taken this opportunity to free themselves from Medici government and to draw up a new republican constitution. Within two years of the Sack of Rome Clement had made an alliance with his old enemy Charles V, largely because Charles promised to restore Florence to the Medici. It is hard to imagine the mind of Clement VII. He had witnessed the atrocities committed in Rome by Charles's troops, and yet he sanctioned their use against his own home, the city of Florence. The city suffered a ten-month siege at his command, and the countryside around it was laid waste. Clement then made Alessandro de' Medici, whom many believed to be his illegitimate son, head of state. He proved cruel, corrupt, tyrannical and so unpopular that he was eventually murdered by a cousin who felt obliged to release the city from his grasp. This was the context in which Tribolo set to work at Castello. Cosimo, his new patron, was then an untried seventeen year old, a naïve country boy selected as head of state because Florence's chief senators planned to dominate him and keep power safely in their own hands. While Castello's new garden was slowly taking shape, Cosimo was defying these expectations by growing into a ruthless and effective leader. His early achievements were soon reflected in the iconography of Castello's statues and fountains.

Castello was the first and far the most elaborate garden that Tribolo ever created. It was laid out on the site of the old walled garden that occupied sloping ground between the villa and the hill of Monte Morello. According to Giorgio Vasari's description in *Lives of the Painters, Sculptors and Architects* (1568) it was a promising position:

> It stretches so well clear of the palace as it rises, that the midday sun searches it out and bathes it all with its rays, as if there were no palace in front; and at the upper end it stands so high that it commands a view not only of the whole palace, but also of the plain that is in front and around it.

Tribolo took the dimensions of his new design from the existing site. His first task was to divide the space up into separate areas and he began by building a new wall across the slope, separating the old walled garden into two parts. The largest space lay closest to the villa, and this was to be the main garden. Tribolo planned an orange garden to occupy the smaller space that lay between the dividing wall and the side of Monte Morello. The garden's central axis ran the length of the site, passing though a gate in the dividing wall and stopping only when it reached the retaining wall at the base of Monte Morello. He trained orange and lemon trees to grow against the old garden wall and divided the main garden up with hedges, rows of trees and scented tunnels of cedar, olive and citron so that he created a series of vistas and small garden rooms. Tribolo was the first garden architect to manipulate space in this way, concealing the true proportions of the site and preparing a series of visual surprises for the garden visitor.

Between 1599 and 1602 Ferdinando I de' Medici commissioned the Flemish artist Giusto Utens to paint seventeen lunettes of Medici villas and gardens in Florence and the surrounding countryside. The lunette of Castello shows a series of square box-lined beds in the main garden. The edge of each bed is planted with an alternating pattern of fruit trees and clipped shrubs. These decorative compartments would have served as showcases for the rare specimens that made up Cosimo's extensive plant collection.

Tribolo designed two fountains to stand in prominent positions on the garden's central axis. Carved from pale marble, the first fountain was made to be seen against the dark leaves of the cypresses that formed a labyrinth at the centre of the garden. Its slender, richly ornamented shaft supports two simple basins. It is crowned by two bronze figures representing Hercules and Antaeus, depicted in the final frenzied moment before Antaeus's death. Crushed between Hercules's forearms, Antaeus makes one last desperate attempt to escape, head flung back, legs flailing, and one arm pushing down on Hercules's head. The hero's body is bathed in the water that shoots from his victim's upturned mouth. Hercules has arrived at this moment of triumph through intelligence, not brute force, for he has realized that the source of Antaeus's superhuman strength is his mother, the Earth. By lifting his feet clear of the ground, Hercules deprives Antaeus of all his power and is able to defeat him. The Medici already had a long established tradition of associating themselves with the virtue, determination and strength of Hercules. Contemporary visitors to Castello would have been quick to understand the place of the fountain in the garden's iconography. The mythical hero on the fountain represented Cosimo, and Tribolo focused the allusion by decorating the first of the two shallow bowls on the fountain's shaft with capricorns, the fish-tailed goats that the Medici had used as their *impresa*, or emblem, ever since Lorenzo the Magnificent had adopted it in the fifteenth century. The fountain could also be read as a celebration of the very first triumph of Cosimo's political career, the Battle of Montemurlo, where Cosimo defeated all the disaffected

Florentines who threatened to depose him less than a year after he took his place as head of the republic.

The circular labyrinth at the centre of the garden was made from cypress interplanted with laurel, myrtle and roses, and surrounded by box hedges. Vasari describes the trees in the labyrinth as, 'so even and grown with such beautiful order that they have the appearance of a painting done with a brush'. This complex structure was planted at the intersection of numerous straight paths, stopping the view up the central axis. The second fountain – a slender shaft and a single bowl supporting a bronze figure of the goddess Venus – was concealed at its heart. Tribolo chose to portray Venus wringing water from her hair, although the bronze was cast after his death by Giambologna. Venus was often used as a symbol of the city of Florence, but at Castello she took on additional meaning. The planet Venus is ruled by Capricorn, and this, of course, was Cosimo's emblem. On the basis of this association, Tribolo's fountain broadcast the message that Cosimo was absolute ruler of Florence.

During the summer Cosimo and his family sometimes passed the hottest part of the day at the centre of the labyrinth, where the air was cooled by the shade of the trees and the fountain's running water. Tribolo installed a web of bronze pipes beneath the paving slabs surrounding the fountain. These *giochi d'acqua*, or 'water tricks' could be activated at the turn of a key, drenching the unsuspecting visitor with fine jets of water. Similar mechanisms were installed all over the garden, adding another more frivolous dimension to the space. A letter in Florence's state archive draws attention to another use for the labyrinth. In 1544 Cosimo spent a happy afternoon with his son Francesco, aged three. They settled themselves on the edge of the labyrinth and watched the court dwarf snaring songbirds in the circular box hedge. Castello was also furnished with more formal fowling groves to the east of the main garden.

Tribolo's Orange Garden lay beyond the labyrinth. It was enclosed on one side by the new wall built to divide the two parts of the garden, and on the other by the retaining wall below Monte Mario. The garden's main axis ran through a doorway in the wall to its final destination, a grotto excavated from the hillside behind the retaining wall. This is the most unexpected and perhaps the most enchanting feature of the garden. While the iconography of Castello's two main fountains

ABOVE *Villa Castello and its garden as seen in the Giusto Utens lunette of 1599.*

RIGHT *Detail showing the labyrinth, the two fountains and pots of topiary decorating the steps in the foreground.*

focuses on the qualities and achievements of Cosimo, the grotto, with its sculpted menagerie, extends the political propaganda to the entire Medici dynasty, employing a marvellous sculpted menagerie to represent the most successful members of the family.

The creatures are arranged in three separate niches, each one decorated with an abundance of stalactites and elaborate shell, pebble and cut-stone mosaics depicting primitive masks and fleurs-de-lis. The central grotto is surmounted by a mosaic depicting the ducal crown, a triumphant reference added in 1569, after Cosimo became the first Grand Duke of Tuscany. Each niche houses a group of animals, probably designed by Giorgio Vasari and executed by Antonio di Gino Lorenzo. Many of the animals had a serious part to play in the iconographic programme, but there is something beguilingly light hearted about the strange troupe of creatures. They are carved from a variety of coloured stones that approximate their natural colours, and many of them are equipped with real horns, antlers or tusks. Domestic animals, such as oxen, sheep and goats, jostle for position with various

species of deer, a wolf, a bear and a boar, the animals that inhabited the woods and mountains of sixteenth-century Italy. Among these familiar creatures Vasari inserted more exotic animals – a giraffe, an elephant, a puma, a monkey, a lion, a dromedary and even a radiantly white unicorn. Some of these species had arrived quite recently in Europe, some were modelled from paintings or prints, and others may even have been based on verbal descriptions. The walls above the animals were originally decorated with bronze birds sculpted by Giambologna. There were owls and hawks, a swift, a thrush, a turkey, a dove, a pheasant, an eagle, a peacock, a cockerel and a thrush. Many of these are now safely housed in the loggia of the Bargello museum in Florence.

Water brought all the birds and animals to life, filling the grotto with sound and movement as it poured from mouths, shot from beaks, wings and claws, and flowed into the beautifully decorated marble basins below each niche. Water also trickled down the walls and sprayed up from the mosaic floor which was studded with powerful *giochi d'acqua*. The entrance to the grotto was fitted with a gate, and when the

giochi d'acqua were activated it automatically slammed shut, trapping Cosimo's guests and ensuring that they got a good soaking.

There was nothing casual about the choice of animals in the grotto menagerie. They all formed part of a complex and many-faceted iconographic programme that alluded to Florence, Tuscany, the different virtues and, more specifically, the qualities and achievements of various members of the Medici family. For example, it is possible that both the giraffe and the dromedary were an allusion to Lorenzo the Magnificent, who was one of the best loved members of the family, and also Cosimo's great-grandfather. Lorenzo received these creatures as diplomatic gifts from the Sultan of Egypt in 1487. The sculpted elephant with real ivory tusks in the central niche may represent Hanno, the elephant presented to Pope Leo X (Giovanni de' Medici)

in 1514 by Emanuel I, King of Portugal. Hanno had already served as the model for Giovanni da Udine's famous Elephant Fountain at Villa Madama in Rome (see page 27), and so the elephant could have triggered memories of both Leo X and Pope Clement VII (Giulio de' Medici) the patron of Villa Madama. The rhinoceros in the left-hand niche may have been a reference to an emblem used by the infamous Alessandro de' Medici, whose assassination in 1537 had brought Cosimo to power. In the foreground of the central niche a lion, a well-known symbol of Florence, and a goat, representing Cosimo's capricorn symbol, are juxtaposed, underlining the role of the city in the glorious history of the Medici.

The only imaginary creature in the grotto is the unicorn that dominates the central niche. Among its magical attributes the unicorn had the power to purify water. Clean water was still a luxury in the sixteenth century, and the presence of this mythical creature was an allusion to the abundance of clean water that flowed into the garden through the two new aqueducts that Cosimo had built. The water's

LEFT *View over Castello's main garden, stripped of fountains and of the labyrinth at its centre.*

ABOVE *Elaborate pebble mosaics decorate the ceiling of the grotto in Castello's Orange Garden.*

first use was in the garden, but then it supplied two public fountains used by the inhabitants of Castello. Tribolo made good use of this abundant water supply, installing *giochi d'acqua* all over the garden. One of Castello's great attractions was a treehouse built by Tribolo in an ivy-covered oak on the edge of the garden. A square dining room in the heart of the oak could only be reached by means of a ladder. Vasari describes numerous pipes that:

> mount upwards from the foot of the oak so well hidden by the ivy that nothing is seen of them, and the water can be turned on and off at pleasure by means of certain keys; nor is it possible to describe in full how many ways that water of the oak can be turned on, in order to drench anyone at pleasure with various instruments of copper, not to mention that with the same instruments one can cause the water to produce various sounds and whistlings.

On the hillside above the grotto Tribolo designed a small wood, or *bosco* that could only be reached by means of two staircases concealed inside the retaining wall. The *bosco's* main feature is a large fishpool. A rough, rocky island at the centre of the pool supports Ammannati's bronze figure that is generally interpreted either as Appenino, a personification of the Appenine mountains that are such an important feature of Tuscany's landscape, or as the month of January. Bearded and muscular, he clasps his arms over his naked torso, as though shivering beneath the stream of cold water that pours from the crown of his head.

LEFT *A mixture of domestic and exotic animals in the central niche of the grotto.*

ABOVE *The grotto at Castello, showing the real horns and antlers that adorn the animals' heads.*

Over the years Castello's garden has been greatly altered. It was conceived as a celebration of the Medici, and when the family died out in 1737 a slow process of destruction began. By the middle of the eighteenth century the Medici were extinct and Tuscany's new rulers, the House of Lorraine, had demolished the labyrinth, exposing the whole garden to the eye and killing the clever contrasts between light and shade, openness and enclosure. The complex grid of parterre beds was simplified and the Venus Fountain was removed and taken to the Medici villa at Petraia. Shortly afterwards the Fountain of Hercules and Antaeus was put in its place at the centre of the main garden. This sad chapter in Castello's history does not detract from the enormous success of Tribolo's original plan. His vision was so ambitious that it was never fully realized, but even in its unfinished state the garden achieved its primary aim, acting as a magnet to admiring visitors from Italy and abroad. Diplomats, ambassadors or historians, they all wrote vivid accounts of their experience at Castello, spreading the fame of the garden and its patron far and wide. However Tribolo's design was many layered, and beneath the formality of the political propaganda lay a comfortable family garden, a sanctuary furnished with countless enclosed and private spaces where Cosimo could take exercise in the fresh country air, or convalesce after periods of illness. With its

ingenious fountains and *giochi d'acqua*, complex labyrinth, treehouse, grotto and fowling groves, the garden also provided Cosimo, his children and guests with a variety of different amusements.

Tribolo's work at Castello was constantly interrupted by a multitude of other responsibilities. One day might find him designing a firework display, the set for a court masque, or the elaborate costumes and head-dresses for a play, and the next might see him in conference with Florence's commissioners of rivers and sewers, by whom he was employed as chief engineer. These demands were probably quite trivial in comparison to Cosimo's appetite for new gardens. In 1545 Tribolo embarked on plans for the Giardino dei Semplici (see Chapter 3), and in 1550, the year of his death, he took on the massive task of transforming the rough olive groves and vineyards behind the Pitti Palace into a garden landscape that was to be known as the Boboli.

The Palazzo Pitti was a fifteenth-century building, probably designed by Brunelleschi and abandoned by the Pitti family halfway through construction. In 1549 Cosimo's new wife, Eleanora of Toledo,

ABOVE *Stefano della Bella's seventeenth-century engraving of the treehouse at Pratolino.*

RIGHT *Bartolomeo Ammannati's statue of Appenino at the centre of the pool in Castello's upper garden.*

bought Palazzo Pitti, several acres of the rough hillside and an area of level ground between the palace and the Porta Romana. The soil was shallow, rocky and uneven. According to Vasari, it was Cosimo who wanted to: 'adorn [the palace] with gardens, groves, fountains, fishponds, and other suchlike things'. Tribolo set to work immediately on plans that were very much simpler than the complex and multi-layered design for the garden at Castello. The area immediately behind the palace was transformed into a *prato*, a level, grassy field, enclosed on all sides by trees planted in square blocks. Tribolo designed a colossal fountain adorned with the figures of Oceanus and the river gods to stand on the *prato* and mark the garden's main axis, which ran from the palace to the walls of the Forte Belvedere on top of the hill.

By May 1550 work had begun on draining the site and levelling the ground in preparation for planting the firs, laurels, cypresses and holm oaks that were to be arranged in strictly ordered stands of a single species. Once tree planting was underway Tribolo left Florence and travelled to the island of Elba to select stone for the basin of his colossal Oceanus Fountain. He chose a piece of granite six metres (20 foot) wide, and had to commission the construction of a special boat to transport it to the mainland. Tribolo fell ill with fever on the homeward journey

and died in Rome. It was not until 1576 that Giambologna finally realized Tribolo's plans, and the fountain was installed on the *prato* behind the palace.

After Tribolo's death work on the Boboli was divided between a number of different artists, and in time the garden became a showcase for many of Florence's greatest architects and sculptors, including Ammannati, Vasari, Baccio Bandinelli, Buontalenti and Stoldo Lorenzi. During his lifetime Cosimo saw the structure of Tribolo's original design realized under Ammannati, who also added new wings to either side of the Pitti Palace. These wings seemed to mirror the embrace of the U-shaped hillside behind the palace, creating an effective link between the building and the garden landscape. Under Cosimo the great open spaces of the garden began to find domestic use. In 1554 *ragnaie*, or bird snares, were installed among the groves of evergreen trees on the slope to the west of the palace. In 1556 Giorgio Vasari was called in to design a reservoir to the east side of the palace. The tank was concealed behind an elegant façade and stocked to provide a convenient supply of fresh fish for the kitchen. In the meantime Cosimo brought a steady stream of new plants into the garden: 1,000 asparagus plants in 1563, followed by quantities of saffron crocuses. He also planted

an orchard of dwarf fruit trees, an essential element in the patrician garden described by Agostino del Riccio in *Del giardino di un re* (A king's garden, *c.*1589). Del Riccio attributes many of his ideas to the Medici, and perhaps his orchard of tiny trees was inspired by the Boboli. In his description pots of flowering plants are sunk into the square compartments surrounding each tree. These could be removed when the fruit was ripe, allowing the ladies of the house to gather fruit 'without danger of dirtying their skirts'.

In 1569 Emperor Charles V crowned Cosimo as Cosimo I, Grand Duke of Tuscany, a moment that represented both the apogee of the family's political ambitions and the beginning of the inexorable decline that preceded their eventual extinction. Francesco succeeded his father as grand duke, and was in turn succeeded by his brother Ferdinand. They both made significant additions to the Boboli during the sixteenth century, as did Ferdinand II and Cosimo III in the seventeenth, developments that find their place in subsequent chapters of this book, serving to trace the history of the family's garden-making gene until their demise and its final extinction in 1737.

Prunus domestica, e Psittacus Alexandri

III | Botanical revolution
Botanical gardens and treatises 1536-1600

THE GARDENS OF THE SIXTEENTH CENTURY were made against the background of a revolution that transformed botany from an inexact and disparate collection of personal observations into a modern science. During the Middle Ages plants were valued principally for their medicinal properties. The three most important texts on plants were all classical. *Enquiry into plants*, a herbal written in about 300BC by the Greek botanist Theophrastus, was still in use, as was Pliny the Elder's *Naturalis historia* (1st century AD), an encyclopaedia of natural history. The ultimate authority on medicinal plants was *De materia medica*, written by the Greek physician Dioscorides in the 1st century AD. All over Europe the Latin translation of *De materia medica* was used as a source of information about the properties, cultivation, harvesting and storage of 600 different medicinal plants.

At first the development of botany was fuelled by progress in Italian medical schools, which were soon the best in Europe. By the early fourteenth century human dissection had become an essential part of the syllabus. Dissection gave students a greater understanding than ever before of anatomy and physiology. As a result they began to question ancient medical knowledge. Their critical appraisal of ancient texts extended from manuscripts about anatomy and physiology to pharmacology and from there, inevitably, to classical herbals of medicinal plants. The shortcomings of Dioscorides' *De materia medica* became all too obvious. Many of Italy's native plants were excluded from the text, the plant descriptions were often obscure and, over the centuries, the illustrations had become more and more stylized and

inaccurate. During the fifteenth and early sixteenth centuries several physicians wrote commentaries on Pliny, Theophrastus and, above all, Dioscorides. Some of them attempted to establish which native Italian plants corresponded to the plants named but often rather poorly described in the ancient texts. At first they focused on species that were traditionally thought to have medicinal properties, then they broadened their research to plants in general, identifying, naming and recording species that would have no place in a pharmacopoeia. By 1536, Antonio Musa Brasavola, a doctor in Ferrara and author of *Examen omnium simplicium medicamentorum*, was able to write:

> Not a hundredth part of the herbs existing in the whole world was described by Dioscorides, not a hundredth part by Theophrastus or by Pliny, but we add more every day, and the art of medicine advances.

The most important new herbal of the mid-sixteenth century was one volume in the *Commentarii in sex libros pedacii Dioscoridis*, first published in 1545 by Pietro Andrea Mattioli, a graduate from Padua's school of medicine and the physician to three sovereigns. Other books in the series were dedicated to marine creatures, land animals, reptiles, minerals and poisons. Although the title suggests that this is simply another commentary on the work of Dioscorides, Mattioli's book was in fact both a translation, a commentary and a detailed record of all the plants known to him and to some of the most important botanical scientists of his era. With each new edition, more information was added. Contributions were made by Luca Ghini, the first incumbent of Bologna's new chair of botany and founder of both the botanic garden in Pisa and the Giardino dei Semplici in Florence, Ulisse Aldovrandi, a professor at the University of Bologna, director of its botanic garden and antiquarian, doctor and prolific author, and the Swiss naturalist Conrad Gesner. The herbal gave the precise description, history, and indications of the medical uses and virtues of 1200 plants. Dioscorides had described only 600 plants, but Mattioli inserted new species imported from the Orient and the Americas. He also included the plants that were part of the popular medical tradition and pharmacopoeias of his own time, patiently recording every anecdote and unusual bit of information that he could uncover. The herbal came out in several editions, and with each revision the clarity and richness of the illustrations increased. The books were translated first from Latin into Italian, and then into French, German and Bohemian. They took their place on the shelves of the great humanist libraries assembled by popes and princes, and found their way into the meagre family libraries of the

LEFT AND RIGHT *Two fourteenth-century illustrations, one from the Trento herbal depicting a mandrake and the other a leek-laden woman from Aldebrando di Firenze's treatise on medicine.*

poor and semi-literate. By the end of the sixteenth century over 30,000 copies had been sold – an enviable figure in any century.

The success of Mattioli's herbal was due both to its excellence and to a new interest in plants that had already begun to spread far beyond Italy's medical schools and new botanic gardens. Strange and exotic plants and trees had begun to flow into the country, brought back by sailors, merchants, diplomats, missionaries and explorers. These new specimens caught the popular imagination, and affluent villa owners began to see how much foreign plants, with their odd fruits and exotic flowers, could contribute to their own gardens. Sailors were quick to respond to this new trend, seeing the potential for a new source of income, some of them learnt to collect and store specimens properly, using earth-filled trunks or a purpose-built compartment in the ship's hold.

Venice was Italy's chief trading port. For centuries her ships had travelled to the Eastern Mediterranean, the Near and Far East. Medicinal plants were one of the most valuable incoming cargoes. Imported in dried form, they could be fed directly into the market, where they fetched a price inferior only to that of gold, silver and spices. Venetian merchants often funded Portuguese voyages to the New World, and this proved to be a rich source of new medicinal plants. The influx of new plants had significant implications for the medical profession, where doctors struggled to keep abreast of an ever-expanding pharmacopoeia. This situation had prompted Francesco Bonafede, Professor of Medicine at the University of Padua, to suggest that a chair of botany should be established within the medical faculty to promote the study of botanical science. The Venetian Republic had responded to this suggestion by instituting a chair of botany at Padua in 1533, inviting Francesco Bonafede to be the first incumbent and awarding him the title of Professore Simplicium – professor of 'simples', or medicinal plants. The following year Luca Ghini, Professor of Medicine at Bologna since 1527, had been made first Lettore Simplicium and later Professore Simplicium. The medical faculties of several other universities had then followed suit.

As professor of medicine, Francesco Bonafede taught his students about the animals, minerals and plants that were deemed relevant to the subject. He was often unable to produce samples of the medicinal plants that formed part of the syllabus and this made it difficult for him to teach effectively. As soon as he became Professore Simplicium, he began to campaign for the foundation of a botanic garden where a

RIGHT *Behind its high walls, Venice was full of fertile and productive gardens. This detail from a seventeenth-century bird's-eye view of the city shows the gardens of the Redentore church.*

collection of medicinal plants could be cultivated. He also wanted to set up a *spezieria*, or 'herb store' containing samples of every known medicinal plant. The high value of drug plants made it almost inevitable that doctors should sometimes be defrauded by dealers. By teaching students to recognize plants in their dried form Bonafede hoped to put an end both to fraud and to its unhappy effect on patients.

Francesco Bonafede's long campaign finally bore fruit in June 1545 when the Venetian Republic sanctioned the foundation of an *orto botanico*, or botanic garden. In July a lease agreement was drawn up between the Republic and the University of Padua for an irregular patch of ground between the Basilica di Sant' Antonio and the convent and church of Santa Giustiniana. The young Daniele Barbaro (later to become Palladio's patron for Villa Barbaro in Maser, see Chapter 6) is traditionally said to have designed the garden with technical advice from the physician Pietro Noale. Andrea Moroni, who had already overseen the construction of Santa Giustiniana and the new university building, directed building work. The site was irregular, and by imposing a square or rectangular layout half the ground would have been lost. Barbaro cleverly surrounded the garden area with a circular wall and then arranged the site in quadrants divided by four axes that corresponded with the four points of the compass. The quadrants were labelled A, B, C and D. Within each quadrant the beds were composed of every imaginable geometric shape, and these beds were identified with numbers. A circular moat was then dug, both to provide water for irrigation, and to protect the garden from intruders. It is some indication of the value of medicinal plants that the beds were emptied almost at once in a series of nocturnal raids. As a result a higher and much more substantial wall was erected on the garden boundary. A list of rules was affixed to the wall by the main entrance. The first rule read, rather forbiddingly: 'Do not knock at the main gate before St Mark's Day [25 April] or before 10am.' This was followed by five more rules forbidding any kind of damage to the garden or the plants in it. Finally, anyone found disobeying these rules was threatened with fines, imprisonment and even exile.

Luigi Squalerno was appointed as the first director of the botanic garden. Squalerno was a member of a tight-knit group of plantsmen, physicians and botanists who exchanged seeds, plants, botanical illustrations and dried specimens. He was one of the first students to graduate under Luca Ghini in Bologna, where, inspired by Ghini's example, he had learnt the value of consistent and detailed observation of plants both in their native setting and in the small garden of simples that Ghini hade established in Bologna in 1528.

In 1591 Girolamo Porro published the first catalogue of the Orto Botanico, and this is now the oldest printed catalogue of plants in Europe. There were already 1,168 different plants and trees in the garden, including a European fan palm (*Chamaerops humilis*) given to the garden in 1585 by Prospero Alpini, author of *De plantis Aegypti*, together with other Egyptian plants. Today the palm is the oldest plant in the garden.

It is known as 'Goethe's palm' because Goethe saw it in 1786 and was inspired to write his essay on the evolution of plants.

The garden was rapidly established as an outdoor lecture theatre and laboratory. Medical students were now taught to identify plants at every stage of their development, and in dried form. The garden also acted as a memory theatre. Following the technique described by Quintilian (c.35–95) in *The education of an orator*, medical students trained themselves to remember the shape of each flowerbed within the quadrants, and the number used to identify it. They then memorized the appearance and name of each plant. Eventually a number could be used to trigger a mental image of an individual bed. They could then visualize the plants and recite their names as though declaiming the verses from an epic poem or a complex speech. Wherever they travelled after graduation, students from Padua's medical school carried a precise and very useful image of the Orto Botanico with them.

Soon after its foundation the botanic garden started to be used to trial new crop plants imported from the Americas. These plants attracted enormous interest, for reasons that were both practical and economic. During the sixteenth century the Venetian Republic learnt that it could no longer rely on overseas trade as a source of income. The Venetians had lost their monopoly of intercontinental trade when Spain discovered America and Portugal found a new route to the East around the Cape of Good Hope. By the mid-fifteenth century merchants trading in oriental goods had begun to drift away from the Rialto to Lisbon and its busy harbour. At the same time Venice itself had begun to suffer regular food shortages, and even famines. This combination of factors prompted the Venetian Senate to encourage the city's ancient merchant families to turn away from the sea and invest their money in agriculture on the terra firma. Agriculture was seen as a safer investment than sea trade and it had the added advantage of producing the food that Venice so desperately needed. Vast fortunes were invested in reclaiming the marshy land of the southern Veneto. Hundreds of miles of sea wall, canal and dyke were constructed, work that was paid for by individuals or religious orders and subsidized by the Republic. The insatiable hunger of Venice and the scale of agricultural investment drew great attention to new food crops that might produce high yields and lucrative returns. For example maize, known then as 'Indian corn', had already arrived in Europe via Spain, brought back by Columbus from his first exploration of Central America. It was introduced to Italy through the Veneto in the mid-sixteenth century. Here it undoubtedly did something to relieve the crisis, if only because the rural peasant population could be forced to make their bread from maize flour, freeing up the entire wheat harvest for Venice itself.

Which was founded first, the Orto Botanico of Padua or Pisa? The two gardens vie for the title of 'oldest botanic garden in the world', although the latest reseach seems to prove that Padua was founded in 1543, and Pisa in 1545. The archives of the Venetian Republic render up all the relevant material, but the foundation of Pisa's garden was

not so well documented. However, it is known that Luca Ghini was invited by Cosimo I de' Medici to leave Bologna for Pisa in 1544, and instructed to found a new botanic garden for the university medical school. Cosimo I was already an established garden patron, having commissioned Niccolò Tribolo to design the garden of Castello outside Florence (see Chapter 2). In a history of Tuscany published in 1781 by Riguccio Galluzzi, Cosimo I is said to have been the first person in Italy to have imported medicinal plants from the Americas and sought to acclimatize them in Italian soil.

Luca Ghini was an immensely likeable character and a charismatic teacher. Although trained as a physician, he worked hard to establish botany as an independent discipline rather than an adjunct to medicine.

ABOVE *The complex layout of the beds is clearly visible in this nineteenth-century view of Padua's Orto Botanico by A. Tosini. The circular wall acted as a flood defence as well as a barrier to intruders.*

He spearheaded the move away from classical texts towards the study of living plants, and trained a whole generation in descriptive botany. Ghini also established the concept of the herbarium, which rapidly developed into one of the basic tools of descriptive botany. It is not certain that he was the first to discover that plants could be preserved by drying between sheets of absorbent paper, but he certainly contributed 300 of his own specimens to the new herbarium in Pisa. Once they were mounted on board, the specimens could be stored almost indefinitely in a recognizable condition. They could also be shared or exchanged with other botanists, and Ghini sent some of his samples to Mattioli in 1551, so that they could be recorded in the *Commentarii*.

Ghini also contributed to the development of botanical illustration by commissioning accurate, illustrative records of live plants that could be displayed alongside the dried specimens in the herbarium. Ghini was acutely aware of the importance of scientifically accurate botanical illustration. Progress had been made in the early fifteenth century, when many manuscript herbals were carefully and accurately illustrated. However, the invention of the printing press in the mid-fifteenth century had proved very damaging to botanical illustration. Printers and publishers were aware of a sudden surge in the popularity of books about plants. Sensing an opportunity, they flooded the market with low quality herbals, many of them copied from inaccurate medieval manuscripts. Crude woodblock prints were used as illustrations, and in the worst cases the same block was used to illustrate several different plants. Ghini commissioned accurate illustrations and gave particular encouragement to Mattioli over the illustrations for the *Commentarii*. In the event these illustrations were unlike anything ever seen before. Each plant was recorded in the minutest detail, down to the finest leaf vein and hair.

Pisa's Orto Botanico was originally laid out on the right bank of the Arno, close to the Medici arsenal. In 1563 the arsenal was enlarged and the garden had to be moved to a site north-east of the city. This proved too far from the university, and in 1591 it was moved for the last time to its current location close to the Piazza dei Miracoli in the centre of Pisa. In 1549 Ulisse Aldovrandi wrote a catalogue of the plants in the garden. There were already 620 different entries.

Luca Ghini retired in 1554, and was replaced by one of his own students, Andrea Cesalpino (1524-1603). Cesalpino taught botany, medicine and philosophy at the University of Pisa for forty years. He made an enormous contribution to the understanding of the circulation of the blood and also created a new system of plant classification in the garden. Traditionally plants were classified according to the medieval Doctrine of Signatures. At the core of this system was the belief that God had placed plants on Earth for the good of mankind. The key to the medicinal use of a plant was hidden in the form – or signature – of the plant itself. For example the walnut, with its lobed wrinkled fruit, might be used to treat a disease of the brain. Cesalpino was among the first to classify plants by a new system based on the characteristics of their fruits and seeds, thus laying the foundation for a modern classification system. He also contributed 768 new specimens to the herbarium and organized them according to his classification system, thus transforming the collection into the first systematically organized herbarium in the world. In 1583 he wrote *De plantis*, a full statement of contemporary botanical theory and a description of 1,500 plants in fifteen volumes.

In 1596 Ferdinando I de' Medici (1549-1609) attached a natural history museum to Pisa's Orto Botanico, using part of the collection started by Lorenzo Il Magnifico in the Palazzo Medici in Via Cavour, now Palazzo Medici Riccardi. As was usual with collections of curiosities, the exhibits were displayed alongside works of art. In this case the paintings were portraits of the garden's earliest directors. There were hundreds of exhibits, some of them of plant origin, others animal, mineral or even man-made. Among the exhibits was a narwhal's tooth, exhibited under the title of 'unicorn's horn'. When it was recognized

during the first half of the seventeenth century that these 'horns' came from the narwhal they lost much of their value and prestige. There were also unusual animal skulls in the collection, a fossilized shell, a swordfish sword, rare minerals, several stuffed crocodiles suspended from the ceiling, a mummified bird swathed in cloth, the gigantic skin of an Indian snake, and other exhibits described by contemporary vistors as 'the bones of a giant', 'a piece of aloe wood six arms high and as thick as a man's leg', 'the tail of a sea snake with the mouth of a serpent', and 'a pair of Turkish boots'. Like the botanic garden itself, the museum had a practical purpose. It gave students the opportunity to observe objects at first hand.

LIMONIA MALA.

Cosimo I de' Medici also founded the Giardino dei Semplici in Florence, a garden of simples, or medicinal herbs. The garden was founded to allow Florentine students of medicine in Pisa to study and gain practical experience during the summer vacation. The square, walled site of the garden was between the Medici stables and San Marco, in the heart of the city. Cosimo I purchased the land in December 1545 and, working once again with Luca Ghini, he commissioned Niccolò Tribolo to design the garden. Records of the original layout survive in a description written by Leopoldo del Migliore in 1648. The centre of the garden was marked by an octagonal island and an elaborate fountain by Antonio Lorenzi, a sculptor from Settignano and a pupil of Tribolo. In his *Lives of the artists*, Giorgio Vasari describes the 'beautiful ornaments' that Lorenzi made for the fountain as 'very fine acquatic animals of white and variegated marble'.

An engraving of the botanic garden by Pier Antonio Micheli, a distinguished director during the eighteenth century, shows numerous ornamental pots on the octagonal wall surrounding the fountain. The garden is also described in some detail by Agostino del Riccio in *Del giardino di un re* (Of the garden of a king). Del Riccio uses the Giardino dei Semplici, which he calls 'the beautiful garden of the Grand Duke Ferdinand, close to the ducal stables', as a model for anyone wanting a garden that is filled with 'a great number of honourable plants'. Once again the site is divided into sections that are identified by letters of the alphabet. In this case there are eight sections, A-H, broken up into a great quantity of clearly numbered beds. Del Riccio is very clear about the purpose of the numbering system. 'All this is done', he says, 'so that, using the little noteboook that you have made into a plant index, you can find any plant you like in the garden.' This is certainly a less demanding method than the memory feats of the medical students. Del Riccio also mentions that each bed is devoted to a particular species. He points out that when the species has finished flowering, 'you will see nothing whatsoever of beauty in that bed', a circumstance that he deplores.

The Medici, who had already contributed so much to the development of Renaissance garden architecture, became avid plant collectors. They were drawn to foreign plants by the beauty of their forms and the sheer novelty of their flowers and fruits. Mulberries and potatoes were grown on Italian soil for the first time in Medici gardens, whether at Boboli, Castello or Pratolino. Francesco I de' Medici (1542-87) invited Jacopo Ligozzi to come to Florence from Verona in 1576, and appointed him

painter to the Medici court. Among his commissions was the task of recording plants in the Giardino dei Semplici. He did this with complete honesty, recording dead and damaged leaves and beautiful fruits and flowers with equal rigour.

The botanic gardens of Pisa, Padua and Florence set a precedent. Over the next twenty years the medical schools of universities in Bologna, Ferrara and Sassari all founded their own *orti botanici*. By this time it had become fashionable to collect exotic plants and the patrons of many villa and palace gardens felt the first stirrings of a passion for plant collecting that would explode into the full-blown mania in the seventeenth century.

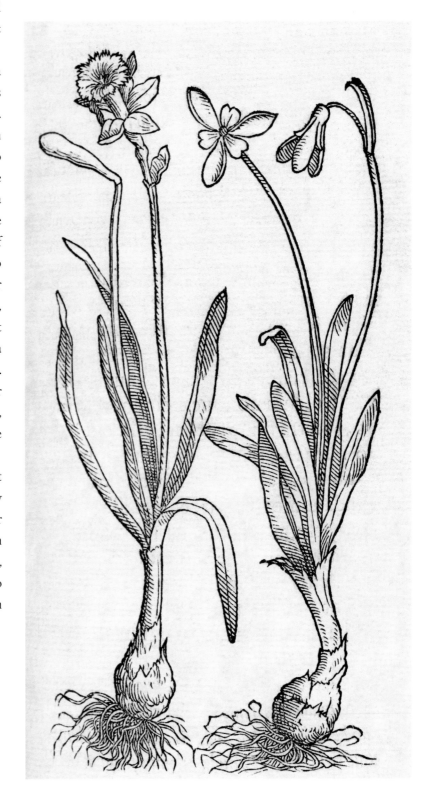

IV | Musical statues
High Renaissance 1560-1573

IMAGINE A LANDSCAPE CAUGHT BETWEEN FANTASY AND REALITY, a place where statues might easily move, fountains always spell out complex allegorical messages and the air is full strange noises and distant music. It may be the loveliest place you have ever seen, but experience can lunge from the sublime to the ridiculous in the time taken to turn a tap and release the full power of a hidden water jet. Suddenly your Venetian silks are drenched, the dye is running out of your shoes, your hair is flat and dripping and, worst of all, your host is looking on, helpless with laughter. This is the High Renaissance garden.

During the fifteenth and early sixteenth centuries the Italian garden had generally been a setting for sedentary activities, inviting quiet meditation, provoking philosophical discussion, poetry and music. By 1550, however, it had undergone a dramatic change, becoming a complex, theatrical combination of architecture, sculpture and hydraulic devices that made active protagonists – and sometimes victims – of its visitors.

The invention of the High Renaissance garden in the mid-sixteenth century coincided with the emergence of a new breed of mechanic, a man capable of studying classical treatises and rediscovering the techniques for building water-powered machinery that could lift heavy weights and move vast quantities of earth. It is no coincidence that garden architects became so ambitious in the middle of the sixteenth century, for now they had equipment that would allow them to impose architectural forms upon even the most rugged landscape.

Water, already a vital ingredient in the early-sixteenth-century Medici garden at Castello (see Chapter 2), now became more important than ever, and work on a new garden could not begin until the rights over a copious and reliable water source had been secured. It usually fell to the garden designer or his hydraulic engineer (*fontaniere*) to find a means of transporting water to the site. Many of these technicians would have referred to Frontinus's first-century treatise *De aquae ductibus*, which contained detailed instructions about making aqueducts, gently sloping pipes and underground channels capable of carrying water over great distances. Once on site the water was a precious resource, bringing life and colour to automata, fountains, *giochi d'acqua*, grottoes and the vast collections of plants that had become a vital element of the Renaissance garden. Water also contributed to the garden narrative, making its own addition to the allegorical message spelt out through the fountains, grottoes and water chains that it supplied.

The Renaissance garden achieved its apotheosis in Rome and the Lazio in the mid-sixteenth century, and its complex architectural forms became the blueprint for garden designers all over Europe. In Rome and the surrounding countryside garden patrons were generally popes and cardinals, princes of the church whose access to worldly wealth made them the most affluent inhabitants of the Italian peninsula. Among the most illustrious of the Vatican cardinals were Ippolito II d'Este, patron of Villa d'Este's garden in Tivoli (1560-75), and Gianfrancesco Gambara of Villa Lante in Bagnaia (1566-73). They made two of the finest and most extravagant gardens of their age.

Cardinal Ippolito II d'Este was the richest cardinal in Rome. Like the Medici, the d'Este were a family of garden makers. Ippolito's ancestors built a number of villas and gardens around Ferrara during the fifteenth and sixteenth centuries. His father, Alfonso I d'Este, continued the family tradition by transforming an island in the River Po in Ferrara into a beautiful garden landscape of orchards, colonnades, fountains and aviaries. In 1549 Ippolito returned to Rome after thirteen years spent in the French court of François I, and almost immediately he began to

show an interest in gardens. Villa Carafa on the Quirinal Hill in Rome became his suburban residence, and between 1550 and 1554 he employed Girolamo da Carpi to lay out an elaborate new garden there. In 1550 Pope Julius III was elected, and Ippolito, who had voted for him in conclave, was made governor of Tivoli and given an old and rather dilapidated monastery as his residence. Tivoli was a small hill town about thirty-two kilometres (20 miles) east of Rome. It was the ideal destination for a cardinal on *villeggiatura*, the habit of retreating from the heat of Rome during the summer, for it had an abundant water supply, a healthy climate and wonderful views. Tivoli's qualities had also been appreciated by the ancient Romans, whose ruined summer villas still littered the hillside. Ippolito must have enjoyed the idea that he was following in the footsteps of his classical ancestors. Like them he was in search of *otium*, that finely balanced combination of physical and

ABOVE *This trompe l'oeil version of Villa d'Este's garden, with the Fountain of the Dragons at its centre, decorates the Audience Hall*

inside the villa. Painted in April 1565 by Gerolamo Muziano and his pupils, it immortalizes the building in a state of partial restoration.

intellectual activity designed to produce a particularly enjoyable state of serenity combined with intellectual satisfaction.

The most significant classical ruin in Tivoli was the palatial villa and garden built by the Emperor Hadrian in the second century AD. It was not long before Ippolito commissioned Pirro Ligorio, his personal archaeologist, architect and artistic advisor, to begin surveying and excavating it. Ligorio made measured drawings of the site and wrote a series of reports on the digs, listing the mosaics, paintings, sculptures and marbles that he had excavated. Many of these discoveries made their way into Ippolito's personal collection. Although no written contract survives to confirm his appointment, Pirro Ligorio is generally thought to be the architect of Villa d'Este's garden. This belief is strengthened by numerous references made to Hadrian's Villa in the design of the new garden.

In 1555 Ippolito's political status altered dramatically. Julius III died and was replaced by Pope Pius IV. Almost at once Ippolito was stripped of all his professional titles, including the governorship of Tivoli, and banished to Ferrara as a punishment for alleged attempts to buy votes for himself in the papal conclave. It was not until the election of Pope Paul IV in 1559 that he was reinstated as Tivoli's governor. Work on constructing the garden and renovating the old monastic buildings began in earnest in 1560, and was almost finished on his death in 1572.

The site of the garden was a valley below the monastery. It was littered with large outcrops of rock and bounded on one side by the walls of the town. Ippolito created more space by ordering the demolition of entire streets of houses – a decision that can have done little for his popularity. Rocks were removed from the slope, the hillside was cut into terraces, and vast quantities of earth were brought in to create a level area at the bottom of the site. Alongside these gargantuan preparations, an enormous effort was made to secure 'an infinity' of water for the garden. In 1560 a new aqueduct was built to carry drinking water from the Rivallese spring to the town. Ippolito split building costs with the local community and gave up two thirds of the water to public fountains. The remaining supply was piped into the old monastery, which was rapidly being transformed into his palace, and from there it flowed into the garden. In 1563 the *fontanieri* complained that the water supply was still inadequate, and Ippolito commissioned the construction of an underground conduit to carry water from the River Aniene to the Oval Fountain in the eastern corner of the garden. Finally yet more water was brought from the Albule spring.

Although the design of Villa d'Este's garden is generally attributed to Pirro Ligorio, an Italian, the years that Ippolito spent in France had left their mark. His household included several Frenchmen employed as tailors, cooks, coachmen and musicians. This tendency was reflected in the team appointed to build the new garden. Antoine Muret, Ippolito's French humanist, was invited to contribute to the iconographic programme, and Luc Le Clerc, a French expert in hydraulic instruments, and his nephew and assistant Claude Venard were appointed to work alongside Curzio Maccarone, Rome's most distinguished *fontaniere*.

Ligorio's design consisted of a central axis that ran from the level area at the bottom of the garden and up the steep terraced slope towards Ippolito's villa. This simple layout was then complicated by several cross-axes and eight other vertical axes, creating a structure that compelled the visitor to engage with the garden, changing his role from that of a passive spectator to an active protagonist who constantly found himself at a crossroads where he was forced to choose between different paths or different kinds of entertainment.

Once the layout was established Ligorio furnished the garden with numerous fountains, grottoes, statues and cascades. There was nothing casual about these features, for they all took their place in his iconographic programme. Iconography, a visual language with a vocabulary constructed from architecture, statues and fountains, was an enormously important element of the High Renaissance garden. Statues and fountains were arranged to create a narrative that unfolded as the visitor progressed through the garden. Mind you, the narrative was only accessible to the kind of intellectual aristocrats or elevated clergy that might frequent the home of a cardinal such as Ippolito d'Este. A sound humanist education had equipped them to look beyond the visual images, to seek out the meaning behind Ligorio's statues and fountains.

Ligorio chose to explore three themes in the iconography of the garden. These were the relationship between art and nature, the beauty of the local area and the mythology of Hercules and the Garden of the Hesperides. The fluid and unstable relationship between art and nature was one of the most popular themes of Renaissance iconography, finding its way into paintings, frescoes, sculpture and architecture. The idea that art should imitate nature, and that natural beauty often rivalled the beauty of art had been inherited from antiquity. Ovid's description of Diana's grotto in the *Metamorphoses* is a perfect example of this tradition:

> … in its most secret nook there was a well-shaded grotto, wrought by no Artist's hand: But Nature by her own cunning had imitated Art; for she had shaped a native arch of the living rock and soft tufa.

The garden was a particularly appropriate setting in which to play with this familiar theme, giving nature a genuine opportunity to rival art (in this case, the garden architect). However art was equally inclined to imitate nature in the garden. In 1543 the humanist Claudio Tolomei remarked on this tendency in a letter describing a delightful evening spent in the garden of a villa in Rome:

> My second pleasure was the ingenious skill, newly rediscovered, to make fountains, in which mixing art with nature, one cannot judge if it is the work of the former or the latter; thus, one appears a natural artefact and another man-made nature …

The idea of a 'man-made' nature – or 'a third nature' as it came to be known – was an adjunct to the art-nature theme. It was a source of great amusement to garden visitors, who marvelled at the architect's ability to reproduce natural effects so accurately that it became impossible to decide whether art was imitating nature, or nature imitating her imitator, art.

Ligorio found much to celebrate in his second iconographic theme – the beauty of Tivoli and the Tiburtine area. After all the Emperor Hadrian himself had chosen Tivoli as the site of his magnificent palace and both Seneca and Vitruvius had praised the limpid waters of the Acque Albule, the local mineral spring. Ligorio made allusions in his own design to Hadrian's Villa, and created statues and fountains to celebrate the Aniene and Erculaneo rivers, and the Albule and Rivallese springs.

The final theme expounded by Ligorio was that of Hercules, and in particular his visit to the Garden of the Hesperides. Extraordinary though it may seem to the contemporary mind, d'Este genealogists had found a means of claiming Hercules, the mythical hero, as a family ancestor. The golden apples of the Hesperides appear as a constant motif on fountains and statues in the garden, and frequent reference is made to Hercules's heroism and his ability to choose good over evil. This theme glorified both Ippolito and the whole d'Este dynasty, both past and present.

Ligorio's programme was designed to be read from the bottom of the garden, its themes developing as visitors progress up the slope towards the villa. All but the old and infirm are told to leave their coaches in the narrow street beyond the boundary wall at the bottom of the site. They push open a gate in the wall and find themselves in the dappled shade of a wooden structure, part tunnel, part vine-clad pergola. The space is completely enclosed and they can see nothing beyond the solid wooden sides of the tunnel. They make their way through the shadows towards the pool of dazzling sunlight at the tunnel's far end, pausing for a moment under a wooden dome at the mid-point, and gazing down identical, vine-clad structures to left and right. As they approach the far end they begin to notice how noisy it is outside. There is a furious quacking and it sounds almost as if a gun battle is taking place somewhere far above their heads. At last they emerge into the dazzling sunlight, and immediately in front of them they see a steep flight of steps. Looking up they are amazed by the volume of water shooting into the air at the top of the steps. Through its veil they can just make out the distorted shape of Ippolito's villa, high above the garden. They climb the steps to the Fountain of the Dragons and stand entranced by the power of the water as it rises vertically into the air from the centre of the basin. The four heads of Ladon, the mythical dragon, seem to emerge from the depths, emitting a series of bizarre, gasping barks. There are other sounds too, the sharp rattle of continuous gunfire, and a strange booming reminiscent of distant cannons. Suddenly everything changes. The water loses none of its force, but the barking and cannon fire give way to a torrential downpour, a summer storm in a cloudless sky, its sound amplified by the curving stone walls that embrace the fountain basin. They have no idea how these effects are created. Is it some form of natural magic?

RIGHT *A comparison between this painting, made after an engraving by Étienne Dupérac in 1573, and the fresco on the previous page reveals the extent of the work carried out on the original* *monastic building. It also shows the layout of the garden, with the tunnel-like pergola that enclosed the path running from the entrance in the lower garden to the fish pools.*

Some of Ippolito's visitors are distracted as they leave the dense shade of the pergola. Glancing to left and right they notice four fish pools that form the garden's first cross-axis, and they are fascinated by the wonderful assortment of ducks milling about on the water. They go closer and gaze into the water. Among the familiar stew-pond species, they see other, far more exotic fish – strange colourful creatures that must have been brought back by merchants or sailors from the rivers and pools of distant lands. Now they can see that the pergola divides all of the level ground at the bottom of the garden into four equal compartments. Each compartment is planted as a garden of simples, the edges of the herb beds marked by clipped fruit trees. Wandering on, they find a maze planted in orange and myrtle. Some of them get lost in it, and it is at least an hour before a gardener hears their shouts and comes to rescue them. Later on, up at the villa, their host will be delighted to hear that his new maze is already so effective.

As the other guests wander about among the herb beds in the lower garden they hear strange far-away music coming from somewhere above their heads. Following the sound, they climb a flight of steps at the north-east end of the fish pools and find themselves in a little *piazza* shaded by plane trees. A huge statue of Diana of Ephesus looms over them, her chest adorned by numerous, mossy, water-spouting breasts. To either side of her two enormous herms support an extraordinarily ornate façade. The music is very loud now and it seems to be coming from somewhere behind Diana. This is Luc Le Clerc's

LEFT *Diana of Ephesus, a sixteenth-century copy of a classical statue in the Farnese collection. She was moved from her original position on the façade of the Organ Fountain in 1611.*

ABOVE *The centrepiece of the Fountain of the Dragons is Ladon, guardian of the golden apples in the Garden of the Hesperides.*

water organ and the visitors are entranced by its odd, splashy music. There were several classical precedents for a water organ that could be played by hand. Le Clerc could have referred to Vitruvius, who devoted a chapter of the *Ten books of architecture* to the subject; Hero of Alexander's *Pneumatica*, or the second-century works of Philo of Byzantium. However he outstripped them all by designing a fully-automated instrument. The water roared into the domed chamber behind Diana with such power that the air in the chamber was forced into a set of organ pipes, making them play. The visitors could also make out the sound of two trumpets playing in harmony with the music of the organ. This was Le Clerc's own invention. He made a toothed, water-powered wheel that struck the keyboard of the organ, making the trumpets sound. As soon as the music stopped a massive torrent of water poured out of the fountain, unexpected and startling. The water was released by the *fontaniere* who pulled on a rope to open the sluice gate of the great chamber in which all the water for the organ was stored.

By this time the party by the Fountain of the Dragons are making their way up the flights of curved steps that embrace the bowl. At the top they find themselves in the Alley of One Hundred Fountains – one

LEFT *A lion mask, encrusted with maidenhair ferns, in the Alley of a Hundred Fountains.*

RIGHT *The elaborate façade of the Organ Fountain in a photograph taken before its recent restoration. The d'Este eagle hovers above the family coat of arms.*

ALTRA VEDVTA PRINCIPALE IN PROFILO DEL VIALONE GRANDE DETTO DELLE FONTANELLE NEL GIARDINO ESTENSE IN TIVOLI

Gio.Francesco Venturini del.et sculp.

Io.Iacob.de Rubeis formis Romæ ad Temp.Pacis cum Priu.S.Pont.

10

of the garden's main cross-axes. They would like to go on climbing the vertical axis towards the villa and the glass of cool wine that they expect to be offered when they arrive. However the vertical axis has gone and they must choose between turning left or right. A three-tiered wall fountain runs from end to end of the alley. Moss and lush ferns adorn the stonework, the obelisks, d'Este fleurs-de-lys and eagles, and the stone boats on the top level of the fountain, and partially conceal the masks that spit water from the wall and into the trough below. Perhaps someone will realize that each tier represents a local river. By turning right, the party follows the three rivers downstream towards Rome. At the far end of the alley they find the Rometta Fountain, a model of the classical city. The buildings were carved to Ligorio's design by the Flemish artist Pierre de la Motte, and arranged in seven groups to represent the seven hills of Rome. It is a wonderful sight, and at first the children in the party are fascinated. They want to clamber into the stream, a miniature version of the Tiber that curves around the city. Sadly, their mother stops them, and then their tutor, inspired by the Rometta, invents an unpleasant little game. 'Can you see the Temple of Murcia?' he asks, 'or Trajan's Column, the Pantheon,

or the triumphal arch of Constantine?' It is not long before they run off in search of fresh entertainment.

Just below the Rometta the children find the Owl Fountain, its façade elaborately decorated with twining branches, the golden apples of the Hesperides and the d'Este fleur-de-lys and eagle symbols. A burnished bronze olive tree seems to be growing from a mount in the niche of the fountain's tall façade. As they get closer they can see that its branches are full of exquisitely painted bronze birds. There are linnets, goldfinches, nightingales, all of them singing in strange, gurgling tones. Suddenly, a huge bronze owl appears and all the other birds fall silent. As soon as the owl goes away they begin to sing again. Spellbound, the children are convinced that they have discovered a magical world, a place where statues can move and sing.

In 1589 Agostino del Riccio published *Del giardino di un re*, a treatise on gardens that included an account of the Owl Fountain at Villa d'Este. Del Riccio's description revolves around the experiences of a particular group of visitors. He makes it absolutely clear that they were not distinguished guests, describing them as little boys accompanied by their mothers and elder sisters. As they stand in front of the Owl

Fountain several powerful water jets begin to play in the courtyard that encloses it, soaking the ground for a considerable distance in either direction. They realize that they cannot leave the fountain without getting wet, but then the façade of the fountain itself begins to shower them with water as well. According to del Riccio they are quick to understand that it is a case of that old proverb 'drink or drown'. The really interesting part of this account is its conclusion. Some of the women start to cry, and others fly into a rage. However, 'the bearded women laughed because, as it says in the proverb, "you welcome bearded ladies with stones", and they know that you can't expect to enjoy an apple if you don't accept the wasp holes in its flesh or the bugs inside it.' This fascinating story with its bizarre conclusion draws our attention to the need for victims in the High Renaissance garden, lowly visitors whose suffering will entertain the garden owner and his more

esteemed guests. It also suggests – if somewhat fancifully – that the *giochi d'acqua* serve to deliver a moral message – 'no pleasure without pain'.

Pirro Ligorio and his *fontanieri* may have found inspiration for the Owl Fountain in Hero's *Pneumatica*. However it is equally possible that they had heard about contemporary metal tree automata from merchants, missionaries, diplomats or explorers who had seen them in the Turkish court at Constantinople, in Baghdad, or the Court of Tamerlane in Samarkand. François I fostered relations with the Turks, and Ippolito may have heard travellers' tales in the French court, and encouraged Ligorio to build a metal tree automaton for him at Villa d'Este. By 1588 Agostino Ramelli had published his book *Le diverse et artificiose macchine* (Various and ingenious machines), which includes two singing-bird devices. The book is a combination of classical expertise and contemporary practice, and so it is quite likely that he took the Owl Fountain as his model. In both of his examples birdsong is produced by tiny flutes inserted into the throats of metal birds. They are played, like the organ, by air that is forced through them by the weight of falling water. The birds' bodies are hollow. Their wings, beaks and tails are made separately and attached with very fine strips of

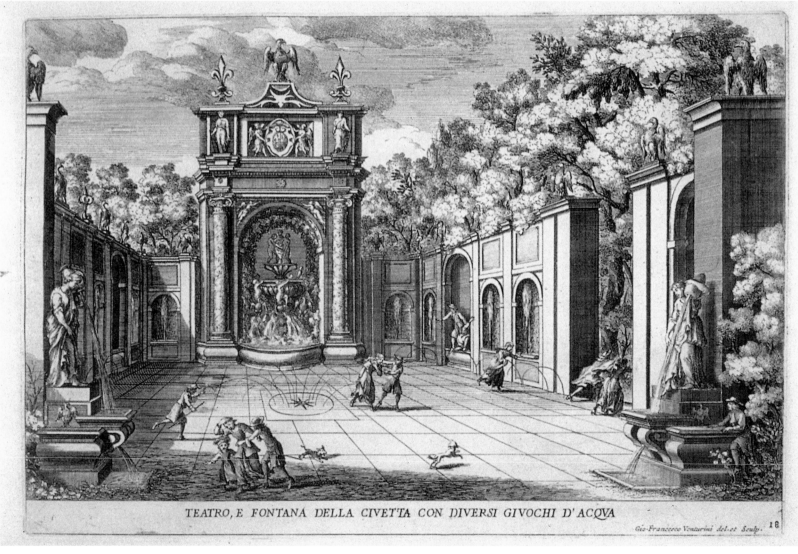

TEATRO, E FONTANA DELLA CIVETTA CON DIVERSI GIVOCHI D'ACQVA

Gio:Francesco Venturini del:et Sculp.

16.

leather. When air rushes through their bodies, all their parts move as though they were alive.

Some of the party may have turned left in the Alley of One Hundred Fountains and found themselves beside the largest and most important fountain in the garden. The Oval Fountain was built to receive the powerful waters of the River Aniene as they gush into the garden. Ligorio took inspiration for this fountain from the semicircular *triclinium* at Hadrian's Villa. Set at one end of a canal, the *triclinium's* curved side was concealed behind a veil of falling water. Ligorio's fountain consists of a large oval sheet of water backed by a curved arcade reminiscent of the *triclinium*. A cascade of water pours into the bowl from above, concealing the arcade and creating a curved, opaque curtain that hits the water's surface with tremendous force. River gods representing the Aniene and Erculaneo recline above the pool. Between them is a colossal statue of Albinea, the sibyl who inhabits the Albule spring. Water from the real River Aniene gushed from the aqueduct and ran down a small artificial mount above the sibyl's head before cascading into the fountain below.

Ligorio made the top of the artificial mount into a Parnassus. If they had recovered from their soaking by the Owl Fountain, the children in the party would have no trouble in recognizing the winged horse on top of the mount. They might even please their tutor by pointing out that he is striking the ground with his hoof, releasing the waters of the Hippocrene, source of all poetry and artistic inspiration. Pegasus dominates this part of the garden, and Ippolito's guests recognize the allusion to their host. Already a well-known patron of the arts, Ippolito has now inspired the creation of a new Parnassus in the little town of Tivoli.

As they finally make their way towards the villa, Ippolito's guests are filled with respect for their host. How are they to begin to express their admiration? Ligorio has used iconography to pour flattery and adulation upon every aspect of his patron's personality. The complex iconographic programme is itself a tribute to Ippolito's intellectual status. Then there are the countless allusions to Hercules, a constant reminder of the d'Este claim to descent from that most popular of all classical heroes. Ippolito is also cast as creator of a new Parnassus, or Garden of the Hesperides – or possibly both. The pure physical splendour of the garden is also immensely impressive, and it conveys a very simple message. Even the children in the party will realize that their host is extraordinarily wealthy. His wealth has bought a team of experts – scientists capable of devising fountains and other hydraulic and pneumatic devices that have no equal in the contemporary or the classical world. Those who know him well will understand that much of his income is derived from the lucrative French benefices showered upon him by his dear friends, the kings of France. At last they reach the villa on the uppermost terrace. Are they nervous? Just a bit.

Even in the context of sixteenth-century Rome, some people would see the Villa d'Este and its garden as examples of conspicuous and inappropriate consumption by a cardinal of the Roman Catholic Church. Cases of this kind did not always pass unnoticed at the Vatican, especially during the Counter Reformation. In 1578 Pope Gregory XIII visited Cardinal Gianfrancesco Gambara at Villa Lante in Bagnaia. The villa was just a little *casino*, a relatively modest affair, but the Pope was so struck by its garden that he promptly cancelled the special 'poor cardinals' allowance that Gambara had the audacity to claim from the Vatican each year. Cardinal Carlo Borromeo, Archbishop of Milan and an active member of the Council of Trent, also paid Gambara a visit and was equally shocked by his profligate spending. He wrote to him afterwards accusing him of 'squandering money' on dwelling places for birds, fish and beasts in his garden, when he should have been building 'convents for nuns', or caring for 'poor, refugee Catholics'.

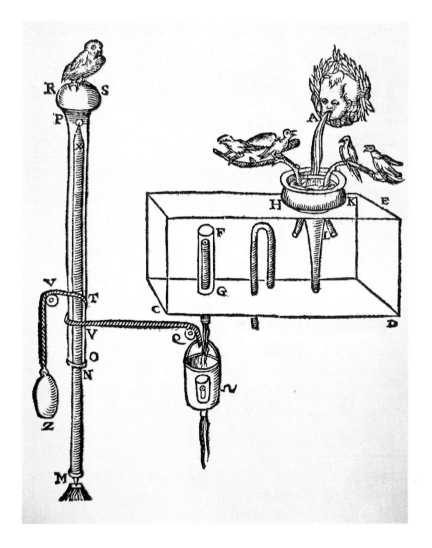

LEFT *Venturini's engraving of the Rometta Fountain shows its original structure very clearly. The fountain basin, with its boat, represents the Tiber running past a miniature version of the ancient city.*

BELOW LEFT *Giochi d'acqua have maximum impact in the enclosed space of the Owl Fountain. The birds sing in the niche behind the three figures at the centre of the fountain.*

RIGHT *A design for a singing-bird fountain in Hero of Alexandria's* Pneumatica, *which may have inspired the Owl Fountain at Villa d'Este.*

Cardinal Gambara, who was a close acquaintance of Ippolito d'Este, received the bishopric of Viterbo in 1566, and with it the right to escape Rome in the hottest months of the year and take up residence in the castle of Bagnaia. A small town just outside Viterbo, Bagnaia was once a thriving classical settlement, famous for its mineral springs and the impressive bath complex that they served. Ever since the beginning of the sixteenth century the bishops of Viterbo had gradually added to the attractions of Bagnaia. In 1514 Cardinal Riario enclosed an area of woodland outside the town to make a *barco*, or hunting park, and then furnished it with a modest hunting lodge and introduced a good selection of game. In 1549 Cardinal Ridolfi commissioned Tommaso Ghinucci from Siena, the training ground for Italy's finest hydraulic engineers, to build an aqueduct that would carry pure water to the town, restoring, to some degree, its classical status.

Almost as soon as he received the bishopric, Gambara wrote a letter to his illustrious cousin, Cardinal Alessandro Farnese. Cardinal Farnese was Ippolito d'Este's greatest rival, both as a patron of the arts and as a contender for the papacy. Like Ippolito he was engaged in a gargantuan building project, transforming a gaunt castle into a luxurious palace and creating a spectacular garden. Giacomo Barozzi da Vignola was the Farnese architect, and in his letter Gambara asked Cardinal Farnese if he could 'borrow' Vignola for Villa Lante. This letter survives, and

so does a letter informing Gambara that Vignola has set off for Bagnaia. There is no archival evidence to prove that Vignola actually designed the garden for Villa Lante, but this is generally believed to be the case.

When Pirro Ligorio set about the design for Villa d'Este he had a clean slate, a rough, uncultivated hillside with somewhat inflexible boundaries – a problem that Ippolito solved by demolishing part of Tivoli to make more space for his garden. Vignola's commission was quite different. Gambara had already contracted Tommaso Ghinucci to return to Bagnaia, construct a wall to enclose part of the hunting park, and then build the first of two matching casinos inside it. Again there is no archival proof, but it seems safe to assume that Ghinucci stayed on to build the fountains for Villa Lante's park and garden.

Although there was a wall between the hunting park and the space allotted to the garden, the garden architect treated park and garden as two elements of the same iconographic programme. The iconography was built around two parallel themes: the relationship between art and nature, and man's ascent from the primitive existence of the Golden Age

ABOVE AND RIGHT *This fresco in the casino at Villa Lante shows the park and garden. The semicircular Pegasus Fountain is visible at the entrance to the park, but the Grotto of the Deluge and the Temples are lost among the trees at the top of the garden.*

to civilization. These were not unusual themes in the garden, but they were particularly well suited to the site. So well suited, in fact, that one might describe the design as a 'site-specific' layout, suggested by the shape of the existing landscape. The spacious informal park was the perfect visual metaphor for the Golden Age, while the small enclosed garden near the *casino* invited intense cultivation, becoming a vivid expression of human civilization.

The themes of art, nature and human civilization into a visual narrative of statues and fountains that would flatter Gambara, drawing particular attention to his role as a generous and imaginative patron of the arts. The programme is built upon images that would be accessible to Gambara and his aristocratic and classically educated circle. When visitors arrived at Villa Lante and saw a magnificent statue of Pegasus surrounded by the Muses they would immediately understand the designer's intention. Pegasus marked the boundary of Gambara's property; he stood on the threshold of a second Parnassus, the source of inspiration, poetry and music, the site of beautiful woods, grottoes and flowery meadows, and the dwelling place of the Muses. Pegasus also introduced the idea of the Golden Age, the theme that would be explored inside the park.

The park was the first chapter in the narrative and it was furnished with a series of fountains depicting the innocent rustic pleasures of life during the Golden Age. One fountain was decorated with acorns, one with ducks, and another with bacchic figures revelling in rivers of wine. The Unicorn Fountain strikes an odd note in this classical setting, but these magical, medieval beasts often featured in the classical iconography of the Renaissance garden, symbolizing the purity of the water. Over the years the fountains in the park have been virtually destroyed, but they were recorded at the end of the sixteenth century in a series of drawings made by Giovanni Guerra for Cardinal Pietro Aldobrandini and they were also described in the inventory made on Cardinal Gambara's death in 1587. The inventory also includes the wonderful selection of trees growing in orchards, groves, hedges, avenues and thickets. There were figs, pomegranates, plums, peaches, medlars, olives and quinces – an abundance of fruit that captured the spirit of the Golden Age when, in Ovid's description, 'earth unbroken by plough or by hoe piled the table high'. The fruit trees were often interplanted with vines and roses, and stands or avenues of larger trees such as elms, oaks, chestnuts, cypresses and holm oaks. The trees divided the park into numerous different areas, and created a carefully structured setting for each fountain. Many of the fountains were also enclosed by wooden, vine-covered arbours, trellises or hedges.

As they turned back towards the villa, Gambara's visitors would pass between two simple bowl fountains topped by dragons with shining copper wings. By flanking the path the dragons created a gateway between the park and Gambara's personal Garden of the Hesperides, a threshold guarded by the cardinal's own version of the mythical dragon, Ladon.

It did not much matter what route a visitor took around the park because the fountains all contributed to the image of carefree innocence during the Golden Age. In the highly constructed landscape of the garden, however, where happily most of the fountains and statues survive, the iconography takes on a narrative form and it becomes essential to view the images in the correct order. Originally visitors to the park entered the garden through a gate near the aviary on the garden's highest terrace. Today this entrance is closed and visitors must come in through a door at the bottom of the garden. This reverses their reading of the iconography, forcing them to encounter the final chapter first and spoiling the rest of the story.

The park, with its orchards and groves, was an informal, light-hearted landscape. Birds sang in the trees and the fountains made their own gentle sounds. As visitors left the park and entered the garden they would notice an instant and dramatic change in atmosphere. They were on the highest terrace, an area dedicated to nature, and yet the influence of art could already be felt, intensifying their experience and sharpening their senses. They had been pleased by gentle birdsong in the park, but now they found themselves engulfed by the music of a myriad of different songbirds housed in a spacious aviary. The birds darted about among shrubs especially chosen for their nutritious berries and graceful pillars designed to support the brass mesh that confined them. As they moved away from the aviary and into the densely-furnished enclosure of the garden, the birdsong diminished and they were surrounded by the sound of running water. At the centre of the boundary wall, the division between park and garden, they found a beautiful natural spring seeping from rough fern-covered rocks into a dark pool. Drawing closer, they might realize that the main body of water issued from the mouth of a grotesque stone face concealed among the ferns. Art or nature? The old sparring partners were in the ring again, competing and colluding to produce a 'third nature', a fusion of natural and manufactured beauty designed to delight and amuse a Renaissance audience. The rocky cliff face was entirely man-made and adorned with tufa, the volcanic rock associated with untouched nature in the Renaissance mind, an impression reinforced by naturalized moss and ferns clinging to every crevice.

The Grotto of the Deluge also introduces two other strands of iconography into the garden. In Ovid's version of world history, the Golden Age gave way to a period of ever-increasing corruption and degradation, followed by a catastrophic flood that reduced the earth to 'a single sea without a shore', and virtually eradicated mankind. The grotto, with the simple wall fountain at its centre, represents the notion of form beginning to emerge from the chaos of the post-diluvian world. It also serves as a division between the end of primitive life and the beginning of the slow process of civilization.

Two buildings described as temples dedicated to the muses stand on either side of the grotto. The walls that flank the grotto are faced in rough volcanic stone, reinforcing the impression that nature is in control of this area of the garden. Cardinal Gambara has already begun to be written into the iconography of the garden. The *gambero*, or crayfish, that was his heraldic device appears high up on the façade of each temple.

In its original condition the garden's first fountain served as a wonderful symbol to complete the idea of form finally emerging from chaos. A relatively simple structure in this context, the Fountain of the Dolphins was originally crowned by a magnificent branch of natural coral that was protected from the elements by a wooden roof.

While wet, coral is soft and flexible, a marvellous symbol for the amorphous state of the waterlogged world. Allowed to dry out, as it was in the garden, it takes on a solid and permanent form, the perfect expression of a new sharp-edged world emerging from the saturated wreck of the past.

Form has been established, and now the audience watch as the designer orchestrates the slow but irreversible domination of art over nature, an idea that neatly mirrors the theme of mankind's gradual civilization. He builds up the layers of symbolism, combining planting, fountains, statuary and water to focus attention upon his themes.

On the 'natural' uppermost terraces of the garden there were relatively informal plantings of holm oak, arbutus and plane trees. These gave way to a gradually more formal arrangement lower down

LEFT AND BELOW *Villa Lante's water chain, with the cardinal's crayfish emblem at its head, forms the central axis of Villa Lante's garden. It soon became a blueprint for later water chain designs, but few could compete with its beauty or the clever fusion of form and meaning.*

the garden, culminating in the square parterres, bowl fountains and clipped fruit trees that originally filled the area in front of the two casinos. Again the increasing formality of the planting served a dual purpose, triggering thoughts of the literal domination of horticultural art over nature and the refining effects of civilization upon man.

Water, introduced into the garden as a destructive and chaotic force, undergoes a transformation as Vignola's narrative unfolds, re-emerging from the Fountain of the Dolphins in the wonderful water chain. The links in the chain are formed from carved shells, each one a slightly different shape. This tiny detail subtly alters the sound that the water makes as it descends. Enclosed by linked volutes on each side, the water comes to represent nature itself, embraced, controlled and channelled by art. Vignola strengthens the allusion and makes it more specific by placing a crayfish at top and bottom, turning the water chain into a flattering metaphor for the cardinal's role as patron of the arts. The glittering, transparent, fast-flowing stream of clear water represents the creative genius of civilized man, a force that we can see physically shaped and channelled by the elongated body of the crayfish.

The flattery continues with the water from the chain falling between the giant pincers of the crayfish and into the Fountain of the River Gods. The two recumbent gods represent the rivers Tiber and Arno that water the cardinal's territories. The abundant water supply brings fertility to the land, suggested by the gods' own cornucopiae and the statues of Flora and Pomona to either side of them. Fertility and abundance become a metaphor for Gambara's own generosity as landowner and governor.

Below the fountain is a gigantic stone table with a channel of water running down its centre. Once again the symbolism is multivalent. The outsize table reinforces the image of fertility and abundance, simultaneously triggering thoughts of a polished marble basin that Pliny the Younger had in his classical garden and used during dinner parties to amuse his guests by serving *antipasti* in little boats on the water (see Chapter 1).

The windows of Gambara's *casino* overlooked the lowest level of the garden, a space entirely filled by square parterres adorned with neatly clipped fruit trees and simple fountains. This disciplined landscape represented both the final domination of nature by art, and the completion of mankind's progress towards civilization. At the centre of the garden Vignola placed the last and perhaps the most pleasing of all the garden fountains. It has a surprisingly large square basin surrounded by a balustrade. In the centre of the basin there is a circular island linked to the 'mainland' by stone bridges that divide the basin into four pools. Each pool contains a stone boat that was originally sailed by a crew of three minute stone figures grasping harquebusiers and blowing trumpets. Water still shoots from the trumpets of the remaining figures, creating a sparkling arch over each pool. When Pope Gregory XIII paid his fateful visit in 1578, four dragons' heads were arranged in the pool, a reference to the dragons in his coat of arms, and made to shoot first fire and then water.

The inspiration for the island fountain probably came from two classical sources. The first was the Marine Theatre at Hadrian's Villa in Tivoli, which had so recently been excavated by Pirro Ligorio. The theatre consisted of a circular canal surrounding a tiny garden house on an island. The emperor could cut himself off from the 'mainland' by removing the wooden bridges across the pool. Vignola's fountain is also reminiscent of Varro's island aviary, which was discovered by Pirro Ligorio during another excavation in Tivoli. The logic of Vignola's layout, with its square fountain reflecting square parterres, was lost when the beds were replaced by a swirling *broderie* design in the seventeenth century. Happily this is the most significant change in a garden that has generally survived the effects of time and multiple ownership very well.

LEFT *The water from the water chain tumbles into the pool of the Fountain of the River Gods. The huge crayfish claws at the base of the chain are just visible above the heads of the reclining gods.*

The gardens of Villa Lante and Villa d'Este were perfect expressions of the *status quo*, the accepted political and cultural order of things. They also seem to reflect the wider certainties of the Renaissance, an eager confidence in humanity, belief in man's elevated position in the cosmic hierarchy, and a wholesale acceptance of classical ideals.

However at the time that the Villas Lante and d'Este were being built other more subversive and eccentric gardens were taking shape. Adhering to no particular model, these were the expressions of Mannerism in garden architecture, a parallel rather than a subsequent chapter in the history of garden design.

LEFT *The semicircular Pegasus Fountain at the entrance to the park. The nine muses look on as Pegasus strikes the ground to release the inspiring waters of Hippocrene.*

ABOVE *Civilization has finally conquered the forces of nature in the lower garden, although the original box compartments were replaced in the eighteenth century by less disciplined parterres de broderie.*

RIGHT *The stone table built on a scale for entertaining the river gods that occupy the fountain behind it. For many years a monstrous plastic crayfish inhabited the water channel.*

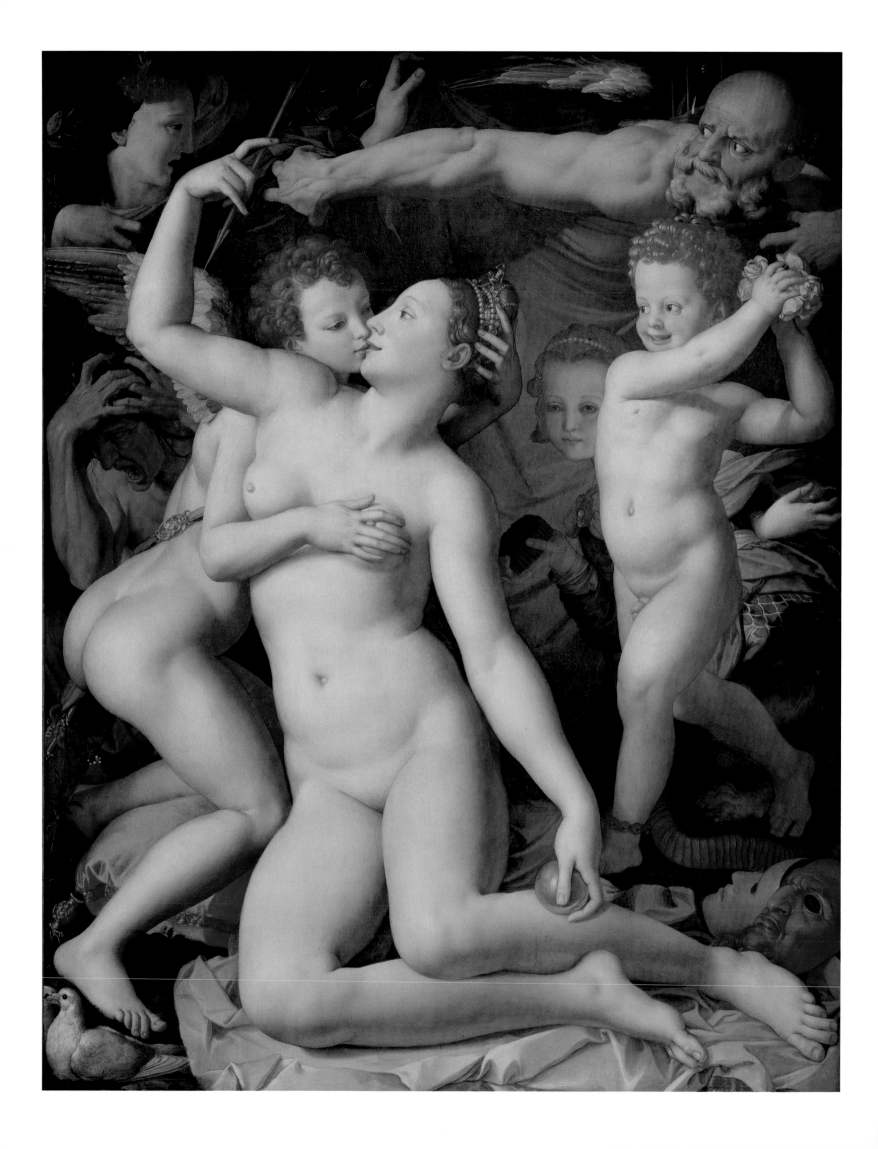

V | Esoteric jokes
Mannerism 1550-1580

DEFINE THE MANNERIST GARDEN… No easy task, for whether it appears in painting, architecture, sculpture or even literature, mannerism defies neat, hard-edged definitions. Never a movement in its own right, it was a bizarre, rebellious strand of Renaissance style that produced some of the most fascinating and capricious gardens of the sixteenth century.

Mannerist symptoms were first manifest in the paintings of a small group of artists working in Rome during the 1520s. They produced canvases that stood out from the mainstream of Renaissance art because they seemed to flout all the rules set down by classical artists and architects and slavishly observed by other Renaissance practitioners. The Italian word *maniera* means 'style' and mannerist paintings were intensely stylish, polished and complex, their composition bizarre and their subject matter often fantastic. As mannerism developed, its boldest and most blatant manifestations were in the architecture of buildings and gardens. Architects traditionally worked within the rigid rules set down by Vitruvius in his first-century treatise *The ten books of architecture*. When an architect defied these rules the effects were shockingly obvious.

Mannerism found immediate support among bored and affluent courtiers who welcomed the style for its refreshing drama and variety. Their enthusiastic patronage fuelled mannerism's development and kept it alive until about 1600. The earliest mannerist garden still extant is Villa della Torre in Fumane, about twenty kilometres (12 miles) from Verona. The partial destruction of the della Torre archive means that there is no confirmed date for the inception of construction work, although both villa and garden are thought to have been complete by

1559. The villa is built around a witty mannerist version of a Vitruvian peristyle garden. The peristyle was originally found in the houses of the ancient Greeks, who began to use it to link the house to the garden in the fourth century BC. The Romans introduced this idea from about the third century AD, when their houses began to be built around an internal garden surrounded by a peristyle. Without its peristyle, the courtyard would simply be an 'atrium' or hallway, but the peristyle's colonnade transformed the atrium into an open air room, creating an architectural link between the interior and exterior spaces of the house. Used as an outdoor drawing room the peristyle could absorb a crowd. Diodorus Siculus, a Greek historian writing in the first century BC, described it as 'a means of avoiding muddle and confusion when there are lots of visitors'. The peristyle garden was often decorated with statues, fountains, pots of plants and frescoes. At Villa della Torre the garden extends beyond the confines of the peristyle. A terrace in front of the building contains two fish pools spanned by a classical, triple-arched bridge, and a grotto occupies the retaining wall beneath the terrace. A small chapel in the grounds is attributed to Michele Sanmicheli, Verona's leading mannerist architect.

Villa della Torre was built for Giulio della Torre (1480-1563), an important figure in the political and cultural life of Verona. He was professor of law at Padua, a renowned antiquarian, a designer, the author of treatises on a variety of subjects and an accomplished humanist scholar. It is sometimes suggested that this erudite and capable man was his own architect. However the villa and garden are traditionally attributed to Giulio Romano, Raphael's favourite pupil, and his chief assistant on the revolutionary gardens of Villa Madama in Rome (see Chapter 2). When Giulio Romano left Rome in 1523 and took up residence in the court at Mantua he introduced mannerism to the Po Valley. It spread just over the regional border into the Veneto, but never really took hold in Venice itself.

LEFT *Agnolo Bronzino's erotic* Allegory *is a wonderful example of Mannerism in painting. Bronzino reacted against the certainties of the* High Renaissance. *The complexity of the painting, the bizarre subject matter and the contorted poses of the figures are all typical of the mannerist style.*

Giulio della Torre acquired the villa in Fumane on his marriage to Anna Maffei. The original structure consisted of a single block with a string of modest rooms on the ground floor and a series of granaries and low-ceilinged bedrooms above. Della Torre had this simple structure transformed into a mannerist version of the classical Roman town house built around an open peristyle. This transformation was achieved by constructing an identical building close to the first, and then linking the two buildings together with the peristyle.

The successful mannerist architect had to be fluent in Vitruvius's architectural vocabulary. Only if he mastered the rules could he break them successfully, creating clever, distorted, irreverent structures like the peristyle at Villa della Torre. His success was dependent upon a pre-selected audience composed of people almost as familiar as he was with Vitruvius and the accepted idiom of architectural design. They would recognize transgression when they saw it, and understand his witty distortion of classical forms. We are not that audience. We are ill equipped to appreciate Villa della Torre today and to enter into either the humour or the outrage that it was designed to provoke. Given our shortcomings, it may be most effective to describe the peristyle garden as it might have appeared to a young architect from Verona, invited for the first time to a summer party at the villa. He is an entirely fictional character, and yet he is better equipped than we are to appreciate what he sees.

He left Verona late in the afternoon, and dusk had already fallen when he reached the gates of the villa in Fumane. A light breeze stirred

ABOVE *Steps lead to the upper terrace and the family chapel that was designed by Michele Sanmicheli and dedicated to the Madonna of the Snow.*

RIGHT *The entrance to Giulio Romano's peristyle, which was rescued from dereliction when it was bought by the father of the current owners during the 1950s.*

the heavy summer air. He gave his horse to a groom and walked through the tall gates into the upper garden. Opposite him the doors of the chapel stood open. The interior was dimly illuminated by candles on the altar. He glanced inside at the pale perfection of the dome and the quirky octagonal floor. Then he made his way along the terrace and stopped at the top of a flight of steps above the entrance to the peristyle. He had heard so much about this building, and yet he hardly knew what to expect. Everyone had something to say. One of his young friends, a fellow architect, talked of little else. He told everyone that they must go and look at it. He said it would change their view of architecture, and probably of life as well. Then there were the other people, the ones who described it as a travesty of true architecture, an outrageous contradiction of all the classical rules of decorum. One old architect even claimed that it was blasphemous. He gazed down at the handsome entrance. The space beyond it was lit by the flickering glow of torchlight. He could hear the swell of voices and laughter overlaid with light-hearted music. He lingered a moment longer in the gathering dusk. The brightly lit space below reminded him of something that Leon Battista Alberti wrote in his treatise on architecture. He knew the book almost

by heart and yet, as he looked at the courtyard pulsing with life and movement, he felt that he understood for the first time what Alberti meant when he described the atrium as the 'heart' of a villa.

Now he shook the dust from his clothes and made his way into the peristyle. He paused just inside the entrance to examine the fine classical figures in the niches to each side of him. Water poured from them into handsome red marble basins supported by slender pedestals. He moved on and at once he was enveloped in golden light thrown off by flaming torches in sconces against the ochre-coloured walls. The space was crowded but he noticed, almost without meaning to, that it was an exact reproduction of Vitruvius's peristyle. He could even place the quotation: Book VI, III of *The ten books of architecture*. He recited the text to himself, checking each measurement by eye as he went. 'The columns are to be as high as the width of the portico', yes. 'The space between the columns must not be less than three nor more than four diameters of the column', correct. So why did he feel so uneasy? When he looked more carefully, he saw it at once. The columns of the perfect Vitruvian peristyle were composed from lumps of coarse rusticated stone. Some of them were inset with ugly masks that spat water from their open mouths. It was shockingly unorthodox, and so liberating that he laughed out loud. Now he noticed that some of the columns were made up from a different number of blocks, making the whole building appear unstable. The capitals on the columns had never been finished, and neither had the architraves over the doors into the villa, or the frieze. And yet other details of the building were perfectly complete. There was even a rail between the columns hung with red velvet curtains. He remembered a description by Pliny the Younger of a similar arrangement in his own garden, and presumed that the curtains would be drawn on hot days to shade the colonnade.

Gazing around him at the strange, crude building, he thought that he had never seen anything as beautiful. It was so full of contradictions that it reminded him of an epigram by Celio Calcagnini that he had read and committed to memory a few days before:

Sunt quaedam formosa adeo, deformia si sint;
Et tunc cum multum displicuere, placent.
(There are certain things that are beautiful
Just because they are deformed,
And thus please by giving great displeasure.)

The building was deformed; it seemed to be caught in a strange, amorphous condition, somewhere between crude rustic simplicity and classical perfection. The tension between these two extremes was almost intolerable. He thought of all the different kinds of metamorphosis dreamt up by Ovid, and realized that even the great poet had failed to invent anything as exciting, ridiculous and fantastic as this. The peristyle was indeed the heart, not of a cold, stone structure, but of an organic being that appeared to be changing before his eyes.

If the young architect had made his way through one of the unfinished doorways into the villa, he would have found much to please him. The themes of the peristyle were developed in the lavish furnishings of rooms hung with tapestries depicting Ovid's *Metamorphoses*, magnificent fireplaces by Bartolomeo Ridolfi were made to represent a series of grotesque faces with a hearth in each open mouth. An earlier commission included similar fireplaces on the ground floor of Palladio's Villa Thiene in Vicenza. Perhaps it would be too dark for him to explore the rest of the garden properly that evening, but he might make his way by torchlight across the bridge spanning the fish pools and go down the handsome staircase to the lower garden. If he reached the grotto set into the retaining wall he would find it illuminated by fires burning in alcoves in the walls. He might make his way into the overheated interior to examine the snarling mask enclosing the wall fountain, and the octagonal walls inset with river stones, and gleaming freshwater shells. Enchanted by all he saw, he would notice that the octagonal grotto echoed the shape of the study in the new wing of

the villa and the floor of Michele Sanmicheli's chapel on the upper terrace. He might also admire the complex hydraulic arrangements designed by Cristoforo Sorte to bring water first to the fountains in the peristyle, then to the fishpools and finally to the grotto fountain. The heat would soon become intolerable and he would rush out into the cool summer night.

The lower garden was divided by a single path that continued the line of the bridge across the pools on the upper terrace. The path would draw him away from the heat of the grotto and the noise of voices and laughter in the peristyle. When he reached the fountain at the centre of the garden he might stop and look back. Only then would he realize that the outside of the grotto was a hell's mouth, as well, its wicked eyes illuminated by the dancing light of the fires inside. Above the grotto he would see the peristyle framed by the elegant Vitruvian portal. And now he would understand the purpose of the villa, the message that the architect had built into every feature of the place. The peristyle, glowing with light and echoing with cultivated conversation, was a metaphor for man's civilization. Seen from this perspective, he would realize that civilization was only a veneer, it barely concealed the primitive forces represented by the flaming, distorted face of the grotto just below the pleasant surface of the visible world. A cool, unsettling breeze might rustle through the leaves of the vines on the pergola. Hurrying back towards the peristyle, he would avert his gaze from the grotto as he passed.

Villa della Torre demonstrates a single aspect of mannerist style – the deliberate distortion of an established architectural vocabulary. The Sacro Bosco, a peculiar, wooded park decorated with bizarre buildings, gigantic statues and fountains, is a much larger and more elaborate expression of the eccentricities and complexities of mannerism.

The Sacro Bosco – or 'Sacred Wood' is outside the village of Bomarzo in Lazio. It was built for – and probably by – Pier Francesco 'Vicino' Orsini (1523-84). If one had to create a human personality in the mannerist style, the result might very well resemble Vicino Orsini. A soldier in Pope Paul III's army, he served in Germany and north-east France, where he was held prisoner for two years. He was married to Giulia Farnese, the Pope's great-niece, and was the close friend of some of the Vatican's most eminent cardinals. Although Orsini began work on the Sacro Bosco in 1552, it was only when he retired from the army in 1567 that he could devote himself to the park. He continued work on it until his death in 1584. This superficial biography evokes a conventional image, but his voice tells a different story. Witty, irreverent, and often mocking, it can be heard through his letters and

LEFT *Although the villa was used largely during the summer, the grotesque faces of Bartolommeo Ridolfi's fireplaces are overlaid with a patina of ancient soot.*

RIGHT *Bomarzo's leaning house was deliberately designed to look like a casualty of chronic subsidence. Inside, the floors slope at an unnervingly steep angle.*

through the numerous inscriptions that he made on monuments in the park. A letter of 1563 to his dear friend Cardinal Alessandro Farnese is written in a characteristically facetious tone:

If you ask what I am doing, turn the page.

Item: looking after my offspring, both he and she, both great and small.

Item: the harvest which, since I have no hope of selling the grain, is unpleasant.

Item: I look after my whores of whom, thank God, being now forty, I keep more than one for my own purpose.

Item: granting a delay to many debtors until they come again, which seems to me no small thing.

Item: putting the fountains in my grove in order, it is a burden to be about them every day.

Item: apologising somewhat to the Cardinal of Trent who I am sure will complain of me.

Item, item, item: but none of them matters except serving your lordship, whose hand I kiss.

The same light-hearted tone characterizes the inscriptions in the garden, many of which address the visitor directly. For example, the words on a plinth supporting the statue of a sphinx read:

TV CH'ENTRI QVA MENTE PARTE A PARTE

E DIMMI POI SE TANTE MERAVIGLIE

SIEN FATTE PER INGANNO O PVR ARTE

(You who enter here, study every detail and then tell me if all these marvels are made for deceit or for art.)

This inscription distorts the question more commonly asked in the Renaissance garden: 'Is it art or is it nature?' The words might be read as an implication that nature has been entirely excluded from the Sacro Bosco, where all is manufactured deceit. This is deceitful in itself,

LEFT *Pegasus, symbol of art, poetry and beauty. His Mount Parnassus originally teemed with water but today, like many of Bomarzo's fountains, it is dry.*

ABOVE *Many of Bomarzo's statues are made on the same, gigantic scale as this recumbent river god and many, like him, are clothed in moss.*

as no other mid-sixteenth-century garden – or park – gives nature the free hand that she enjoys in the Sacro Bosco.

The assumption that Vicino Orsini is the author of the garden inscriptions derives from the lack of any archival evidence to the contrary. It is sometimes suggested that Pirro Ligorio was the architect of the Sacro Bosco, and yet the perverse distortion of the garden idiom seems to undermine this attribution. Ligorio was immersed in the enormous job of designing and constructing Ippolito d'Este's garden in Tivoli. Surely it is inconceivable that he could work in the earnest and traditional idiom of Villa d'Este's garden, while simultaneously associating himself with Orsini's irreverent, mould-breaking project in Bomarzo?

Informality set the Sacro Bosco apart from other gardens of the period. Garden making was a fashionable activity in Lazio. Pirro Ligorio's patron, Ippolito d'Este was doing it, and so were Vicino

Orsini's friends the cardinals Farnese and Madruzzo. From beginning to end, however, Vicino Orsini's attitude to the making, and indeed the whole purpose of a garden was the antithesis of theirs. A traditional garden was built on land that had been cleared of native vegetation, stones or boulders. The cleared land was made as level as possible, sometimes using large quantities of imported soil. A sloping site would be cut into a series of regular terraces, and then the entire garden was divided by a grid of geometric axes that would eventually be decorated with fountains and statues. A palazzo, a villa or an especially dramatic fountain formed the focal point of the layout, bringing the garden narrative to a climax and a conclusion. The landscape of the Sacro Bosco was neither prepared nor laid out in a traditional manner. Lumps of volcanic rock littered the narrow valley, but instead of being tidied away, they became the raw material for statues, and were often carved where they lay. No grid of intersecting axes was imposed on the site.

The statues and buildings were arranged in groups linked by narrow winding paths that followed the contours of the hillside. Each group of statues was of equal significance, and so the garden lacked a focal point and the design never reached a climax, remaining forever open and unresolved.

The choice of statues in the Sacro Bosco was also unique. Orsini's words in the inscription over a covered bench read:

VOI CHE PEL MONDO GITE ERRANDO
VAGHI DI VEDER MERAVIGLIE ALTE ET
STUPENDE, VENITE QVA, DOVE SON
FACCIE HORRENDE, ELEFANTI, LEONI,
ORSI, ORCHI ET DRAGHI.
(You, who have travelled the world in search of great and stupendous marvels, come here, where there are horrendous faces, elephants, lions, ogres and dragons.)

All the statues in the wood are startling, vigorous and unexpected; the elephant lifts a Roman soldier in its trunk, and the two lions fight a dragon. Similarly 'great and stupendous marvels' were the symptoms of mannerism in any medium. They characterized the *intermezzo*, a quintessentially mannerist and highly fashionable form of entertainment that was traditionally staged during scene changes between the acts of a play. The plot of an *intermezzo* was usually thin, but the audience was captivated by *meraviglie* delivered by ingenious special effects and spectacular scenery. They enjoyed the bizarre, magical landscape and the expectant atmosphere that made anything seem possible. This was the atmosphere of the Sacro Bosco. The statues and buildings were arranged in the rough wooded landscape to form a series of strange and fantastic scenes, like an *intermezzo* conceived on a vast scale.

The startling nature of the statues in the Sacro Bosco is due both to their size – very large – and their subject matter. The choice of figures

LEFT AND RIGHT *The gaping Hell's Mouth and this monstrous woman are undoubtedly among the 'stupendous marvels' and 'horrendous faces' described in Orsini's inscription. A stone dining table is just visible inside the mouth. It appears to have been deliberately placed to resemble an enormous tonsil.*

in a garden was generally governed by the principles of *decoro*, a word that corresponds more closely to our idea of 'appropriateness' than 'decorum'. The concept of *decoro* was borrowed by visual artists from treatises on the classical art of rhetoric. In their original context the rules of *decoro* related to the style of a speech and the language and gestures used by an orator. If these were carefully considered and appropriate to both audience and subject matter, the orator was better able to convince the audience of the validity of his argument. Applied to the visual arts *decoro* defined the images that were appropriate in different settings. A formal architectural space might be used for political or even religious events. Under the rules of *decoro* the frescoes, paintings or statues used to decorate such a space should be inspired by the events of classical history or the Bible. The garden was always perceived as an informal space, and for this reason the statues

prescribed by *decoro* depicted the lighter-hearted gods, goddesses, nymphs and satyrs of classical mythology and pastoral poetry. These figures served as the building blocks of the garden iconographer's narrative, and they were repeated again and again in sixteenth-century gardens all over Italy. Restriction and repetition helped the iconographer by making it easier for his audience to read and interpret the garden narrative.

It comes as no surprise to discover that the rules of *decoro* count for nothing in the Sacro Bosco, where the familiar cast of classical figures is replaced by a combination of strange distorted buildings, long inscriptions, giants, ogres and fantastic animals. These images were drawn from a variety of sources that included classical mythology, and combined with images from the villa of the real Roman emperor Hadrian, under excavation in Tivoli, and from Etruscan sites that had been discovered near Bomarzo. The garden also drew inspiration from literary sources, but instead of the traditional classical texts it uses Ariosto's mannerist romance epic *Orlando furioso*, and the fourteenth-century poetry of Francesco Petrarch and Dante Alighieri.

Ariosto's story of Orlando's madness is told in the manner of a medieval chivalric romance, a style that had been revived in the Italian courts and enjoyed a great vogue among the aristocracy. The narrative unfolds against a vast landscape that encompasses numerous different countries and acknowledges no boundaries between magic and reality. The action is fast-moving, dramatic, highly entertaining and infinitely surprising. This is the style of Vicino Orsini's rugged little wood. Its atmosphere is quite distinct from that of the traditional Renaissance garden, where classical statuary was designed to evoke the serenity and gravitas of the Golden Age.

Orlando furioso attracted a huge readership and Vicino Orsini's visitors would have been quick to recognize the figure of Orlando on the hillside when they entered the garden. The scene depicted is one that encompasses horror and humour in equal measure, veering between the two in a way typical of Ariosto and of mannerism itself. The massive statue depicts Orlando, maddened by unrequited love. He has spent the preceding cantos wandering through France, an isolated figure, violent and naked, killing anything that crosses his path. Now he has reached 'the mountains that divide France from Spain', and on a narrow path he encounters two young woodcutters driving a donkey. When they ask him to clear the path, Orlando gives the donkey a sharp kick in the chest, sending it into orbit, 'so that to an observer he looked like a little brown bird on the wing'. The emotional seesaw is already tipping, and this comic image is rapidly followed by something much less

LEFT *With chilling calmness, Orlando tears the woodcutter apart. This statue dominates the lower garden, creating a complex mood that is typically mannerist. It reminded visitors both of Orlando's* *pitiful condition and of the comic vision of the donkey kicked into orbit. Like many of the statues in the wood, it was carved where it stood, from an outcrop of volcanic rock.*

pleasant. The two young men wisely attempt escape, but Orlando grabs one of them by the ankle, and then tears him in half, 'the way one may see a man tear a heron or chicken apart to feed its warm entrails to a falcon or goshawk'. It is this ghoulish scene that the statue depicts. However in the imagination of a sixteenth-century spectator, the sight of Orlando tearing the woodman apart would also trigger a comic memory of the flying donkey.

One of Vicino Orsini's inscriptions declares that the Sacro Bosco:

… SOL SE STESSO E NULL ALTRA SOMIGLIA
(… resembles only itself, and nothing else.)

The Sacro Bosco was unique in every respect, but the same might be said of every mannerist garden of the period. Any attempt to pin mannerism down with neat generalizations is quickly thwarted by the powerful influence of individual architects and patrons. The essence of mannerism was the freedom that it allowed for unfettered individual expression at a time when creativity was generally circumscribed by rules.

The design and layout of the mannerist landscape may take an infinite variety of forms, but gardens falling within the loose boundaries of mannerist style share other more abstract qualities. They are all characterized by complexity, wit and a sense of movement, metamorphosis and instability. This creates an atmosphere that is changeable and insecure. The garden also generates tension and expectation, because there are *meraviglie*, shocks and surprises around every corner.

Water was often a vital tool in the creation of a mannerist environment. At the simplest level it enabled the growth of plants, the natural metamorphosis upon which the garden was founded. It also brought movement to the garden, fuelling a more abstract sense of instability. Surprise was an important element of any mannerist work. In the garden it was easily provoked with *giochi d'acqua,* water jets concealed between paving slabs, in benches, staircases and statues. Visitors never knew when they might be in for a good soaking.

Water also played a vital role in the creation of the *meraviglie* that were such a vital element of mannerist garden style. Water-powered figures, or automata, were the true marvels of the mid-sixteenth-century garden. They encapsulated movement, metamorphosis, mystery, illusion, complexity, all the characteristics that defined the mannerist style. One of the most talented designers of these complex moving figures was Bernardo Buontalenti (1536-1608), the Medici family's man-of-all-work, pyrotechnic, mechanic, engineer, designer of *intermezzi,* stage sets, grottoes and automata for both garden and stage. In 1569 Buontalenti embarked upon the creation of Pratolino, north of Florence, one of the most ambitious mannerist landscapes ever made. His patron was the Grand Duke Francesco I de' Medici, an experimental scientist in his own right.

Pratolino survived for more than two centuries before both villa and park were destroyed in 1821. Sixteenth- and seventeenth-century accounts dwell on the grottoes that Buontalenti created beneath the villa, and in particular upon the extraordinary cast of automata that inhabited them and the gardens outside. The English traveller Richard Lassels visited Florence in the mid-seventeenth century and he included a vivid account of Pratolino in his *Voyage or a Compleat Journey through Italy,* published in 1670. Mannerism fell out of favour in about 1600, but the automata still created a potent and startling impression upon this garden visitor:

> Here we saw in the Garden excellent *Grots, Fountains, Waterworks, Shady-walkes, Groves* and the like, all on the side of a Hill. Here you have the *Grotte of Cupid* with the wetting-stooles, upon which, sitting down, a great Spout of water comes full in your face. *The Fountain of the Tritons* overtakes you too, and washeth you soundly. Then being led about this garden, where there are a store of Fountains under the Laurel Trees, we were carried back to the *Grottes* that are under the *Stairs* [of the villa] and saw there the several *Giuochi d'Aqua*: as that of Pan striking up a melodious tune upon his Mouth-Organ at the sight of his Mistress, appearing over against him: that where the *Angel* carries a Trumpet to his mouth and soundeth it, and where a *Countrey Clown* offers a dish of Water to a *Serpent*, who drinks of it, and lifteth up his head when he has drunk: that of the Mill which seems to break and grind Olives: the *Paper Mill,* the *Man with the Grinding Stone,* the *Sarazens* head gaping and spewing out Water: the *Grotte of Galatea* who comes out of a *Dore* in a *Sea Chariot* with two *Nymphs* and saileth awhile upon the Water… and all this is done by water, which sets these little inventions awork and makes them move as if it were of themselves. …

Part of the delight that sixteenth-century visitors derived from Buontalenti's automata resulted from the wilful juxtaposition of heroic classical figures with the models of ordinary people, albeit automata, apparently carrying out ordinary tasks. In the mind of a sixteenth-century observer, however, these moving figures represented much more than simple amusement. In 1589 Bernardino Baldi translated *Pneumatica,* a first-century treatise by the Greek mathematician Hero of Alexandria. The treatise contained detailed descriptions of an enormous variety of water-powered mechanisms. In his introduction Baldi describes the science of self-moving machinery as being 'nobler than mathematics …' because it 'penetrates the spirit of the universe more deeply in that it reveals the most secret and hidden mysteries of philosophy'. This mysterious, almost miraculous quality made the automaton the ideal ornament for a mannerist garden.

Water was the principal ingredient in the Grotta Grande (1582), the complex grotto that Bernardo Buontalenti designed in the Boboli Gardens in Florence. Working once again for Francesco de' Medici, Buontalenti built the grotto around the illusion of water as agent of metamorphosis. In the first chamber of the grotto the walls are partially covered by sculptures in semi-relief against the fresco of a beautiful

mountainous landscape by Bernardino Poccetti. The sculptures are of pastoral figures – shepherds with their sheep and goats, a river god, sleeping nymphs and a woman balancing a pitcher of water on her head. Their faces, arms and legs are formed from chips of flesh-pink marble, but their bodies are encrusted with *spugna*, a volcanic porous rock, and with stalactites. The weight of the domed ceiling appears to be supported by Michelangelo's *Slaves*. Executed in the *non-finito* style, the muscular, male figures appear to be wrestling themselves free from the slabs of rock that still enclose them. Humans, animals and gods were all made to be bathed in water that seeped continuously from narrow pipes set into the walls. The water encouraged moss and ferns to flourish and clothed the statues in a second skin of moving water. Buontalenti used this effect to create the illusion that all of the grotto figures were caught in a continuous state of metamorphosis. This was the perfect conceit for the grotto of a patron enthralled, as Francesco was, by alchemy and the metamorphosis of materials.

ABOVE *Michelangelo's Slaves flank the door of the first chamber in Buontalenti's Grotta Grande. The damage done by water seeping out of the walls for hundreds of years has recently been repaired in a magnificent restoration.*

RIGHT *Utens' lunette of Pratolino shows the paths punctuated by innumerable fountains, pools and water chains. Francesco also commissioned a gossamer arcade of water that it was possible to ride under without getting wet.*

Buontalenti's inspiration for the Grotta Grande was Ovid's tale of Pyrrha and Deucalion, the only humans to be spared by the flood that Jove provoked when he could no longer bear to witness the corruption and decadence of mankind. The two survivors re-seed the human race by throwing stones over their shoulders on to the earth. The moment that Buontalenti depicts is described by Ovid in these words:

Those stones (who would believe did ancient lore
Not testify the truth?) gave up their hardness;
Their rigidness grew slowly soft and, softened,
Assumed a shape, and as they grew and felt
A gentler nature's touch, a semblance seemed
To appear, still indistinct, of human form,
Like the first rough-hewn marble of a statue,
Scarce modelled, or old uncouth images.

The extraordinary dramatic tension of this scene was heightened, just as it would be on stage, by careful lighting. Buontalenti designed a large crystal tank to fill the oculus of the dome over the chamber. This he filled with water and fish. Sunlight could only penetrate the chamber through the crystal tank, filling the room with water light and the flickering shadows of fish.

At the end of the sixteenth century the intriguing, idiosyncratic world of the mannerist garden gave way without a murmur to the grand certainties of the baroque landscape.

VI | Formal splendour
Baroque 1598-1786

BY THE END OF THE SIXTEENTH CENTURY the capricious, provocative gardens inspired by mannerism had given way to the bold certainties of the baroque – a visual expression of confidence and power. A single axis pinned the baroque garden to the wider landscape, the architecture was muscular and abundant statues were gathered into powerful groups. These ingredients combined to create spectacular rather than contemplative gardens with an atmosphere that was generous, theatrical and energetic. Almost invariably the baroque layout included a *giardino segreto*, a 'secret' or private space within the grand, open landscape. It was generally situated close to the villa and used for the cultivation and enjoyment of a collection of rare or exotic flowering plants.

The baroque originated in Rome, but the hub of early baroque landscape design was Frascati, a small town set on the edge of the Alban Hills, south-east of the city. It had been a resort ever since the ancient Romans began to migrate to the area each summer, escaping the worst of the city heat. Cato, Cicero and Lucullus all built villas near Frascati, and this gave the little town an atmosphere that was greatly appreciated by humanist popes and cardinals in the sixteenth century. Several of them built summer villas at the foot of the hills above the town. In 1598 Pope Clement VIII gave his nephew, Cardinal Pietro Aldobrandini, a sixteenth-century villa in a supremely fashionable location just above Frascati. The villa was a reward for Aldobrandini's skilful negotiations with France which resulted in the peace treaty of 1595, and his part in annexing Ferrara to the Papal States.

Clement VIII had always loved Frascati and he was in the habit of spending at least three weeks there every year. His enthusiasm combined with that of his nephew to fuel the town's development into a supremely fashionable resort. By the early seventeenth century the inhabitants of the Vatican would descend *en masse* each summer. Whether villa owners, tenants or guests, these summer visitors were all taking part in an annual migration known as *villeggiatura*, a tradition established by the ancient Romans and revived during the Renaissance. Leaving the anxieties of work (defined in Latin as *negotium*) in Rome, far away across the plain, they devoted themselves to *otium*, the classical term to describe a carefree existence characterized by gentle physical and intellectual activity (see Chapter 1). In Frascati this translated into a good deal of hunting in the woods on the Alban Hills, any number of parties, and many hours spent strolling, talking and reading in the gardens of new villas that sprang up on the edge of the town.

The villa given to Cardinal Aldobrandini by his uncle was three storeys high, but it was described in a contemporary account as 'comfortable for one private person'. This was clearly inadequate accommodation for a cardinal, particularly one obliged to entertain the Pope and his enormous retinue. In 1598 Aldobrandini commissioned the Roman architect Giacomo della Porta (1537-1602) to transform the building into a palace surrounded by the first baroque garden ever made. The new house was tall and narrow with rooms that spanned the width of the building. It was a box of light, a precious casket designed to contain the cardinal's treasures, the 'excellent Marbles and rare Pictures' described by the English author and diarist John Evelyn.

Cardinal Aldobrandini was especially interested in della Porta's plans for the garden. He sent the artist Giovanni Guerra to visit all of the most impressive sixteenth-century gardens in Lazio and Tuscany, and to return with detailed drawings. These drawings became his benchmark, the achievement that he was determined to surpass. It is clear from the cardinal's correspondence that he was particularly excited by Guerra's drawings of the gardens at Villa Lante, Cardinal Gambara's mid-sixteenth-century *casino* in Bagnaia (see Chapter 4), although della Porta's final layout also contained allusions to other local gardens. A grotesque face, or 'hell's mouth' carved into the rock face behind the villa is reminiscent of Bomarzo (see Chapter 5), and the water-enshrouded sphere held by Hercules in the water theatre is similar to the veiled Oval Fountain at the bottom of the garden at Villa d'Este (see Chapter 4). These gardens depended upon copious quantities of water for their effect and Cardinal Aldobrandini soon realized that the existing water supply was inadequate. The situation had been getting worse in Frascati for years. Several new villas and gardens had been built during the sixteenth century, but very few of their patrons made the effort to secure adequate supplies of water for their large households and elaborate gardens. By the end of the sixteenth century there was fierce competition for the dwindling supply. In 1582 Cardinal Guido Ferreri took the audacious decision to divert the water from a neighbouring villa to the fountains in his own garden. In the fierce heat of August, Paolo Sforza, the owner of the villa, despatched an armed gang to vandalize the fountains of Villa Ferreri. Pietro Aldobrandini had no desire to be involved in these undignified skirmishes. He commissioned the construction of a new aqueduct to span the eight kilometres (five miles) between the Molara spring on Monte Algido and the hillside above the site of the new garden. Pope Clement VIII is said to have contributed 50,000 scudi to the costs, muttering darkly, 'the villa is not worth as much as the water'.

By 1603 Giacomo della Porta was already dead, but Villa Aldobrandini was complete. Della Porta's ambitious plan for the garden took another twenty years to realize, but this did not stop Cardinal Aldobrandini inviting Pope Clement VIII to stay. He probably held a party to celebrate the Pope's presence, and the *salotto* of the new villa would soon have been crowded with cardinals in holiday mood. Looking through the north-facing windows they might see an ink-blue twilight engulfing the plain that lies between Frascati and the sea, expunging Rome and its cargo of responsibility from their sight. The windows on the opposite side of the room overlook the garden. Perhaps Aldobrandini would invite a few friends to slip out of the room and make their way upstairs. A steep climb would bring them into the eyrie of a loggia perched on the central block of the rear façade, a full storey above the wings of the villa to either side. Although the loggia was added to the building by Carlo Maderno (1556-1629), the architect engaged after della Porta's death, it gave an ideal view of della Porta's water staircase cutting a swathe through the wooded hillside. This was the controlled viewpoint, the point at which all the lines and levels of della Porta's grand perspective appeared to converge. The cardinals

RIGHT *Joan Bleau's view of Villa Aldobrandini (1663) shows the full extent of the water staircase. At its highest point, the stonework and fountains are quite rustic. The design becomes progressively more formal closer to the villa.*

gathered in the loggia might watch the water catching the last of the evening sunlight to form a torrent of liquid gold. By using mathematical perspective, della Porta created the illusion that the water was falling vertically between the two Pillars of Hercules that flank the base of the staircase. Seen from inside the loggia, the garden appeared as a seamless extension of the villa.

Mathematical perspective was an important tool in the baroque landscape. It allowed the architect to manipulate space, altering the apparent dimensions of the garden and the gradient of the central axis so that it appeared much steeper and more dramatic than it really was. In 1786 Ottavio Diodati was employed to renovate the baroque garden of Villa Garzoni in Collodi, Tuscany. Diodati's aim was to increase the

impact of the garden without changing its overall structure. To this end he designed a spectacular cascade on the hillside immediately above the site. He cunningly widened the watercourse towards its summit. Seen from the lower garden the top of the cascade appears very much closer than it really is, creating the spectacular illusion of water descending a particularly steep and dramatic fall.

Della Porta and Diodati were both commissioned to work on relatively narrow and enclosed sites. By using artificial perspective they were able to manipulate their spectators' perception in order to create maximum impact in a restricted space. The architects of baroque gardens set in more open landscapes had no need of visual illusion to create spectacular effects. In 1676 the Roman architect Carlo Fontana (1634-1714), a pupil of Bernini and the architect of several significant buildings in Rome, was commissioned by Cardinal Flavio Chigi to transform a rough Tuscan farmhouse near Siena into an elegant villa and garden. Cetinale stands in an area called the Montagnola, west of

LEFT AND ABOVE *Seen from the water staircase, the third floor loggia is framed by the Pillars of Hercules.*

When viewed from the loggia, the water on the staircase would appear to fall in a vertical torrent.

LEFT AND RIGHT *Fame blows her own trumpet on the summit of Villa Garzoni's water staircase, where Diodati cleverly altered the perspective to increase the drama of the view. Shallow steps flank the staircase, and paths lead off into the woods on either side.*

LEFT *A hermit's-eye view of Cetinale, taken from the* romitorio. *Two hundred steep steps pull the* romitorio *into Fontana's powerful, axial design. Mazzuoli's statue of Hercules is just visible beyond the villa, marking the end of the five-kilometre axis. From the windows of the first-floor* salotto, *Flavio Chigi could see both Hercules and the Romitorio.*

RIGHT *One of Giuseppe Mazzuoli's statues, charmingly framed by a pale, climbing rose that grows against the garden wall.*

BELOW *This Latin inscription on the wall of* Villa Cetinale *seems to capture something of its patron's personality: 'Whoever you are who approach, that which may seem horrible to you is pleasing to me. If you like it, stay; if it bores you, go away. It's all the same to me.'*

Siena, where the Chigi family owned a large area of agricultural land and wild, wooded hills. In this setting Fontana had no need of false perspective to create an impact. By using a single axis of extraordinary length he was able to draw the drama of the hilly, muscular landscape into the garden. The farmhouse was extended with two lateral wings and transformed into a modern villa in the Roman style. It became the mid-point of a north-south axis. From the windows of the *salotto* on the first floor the view stretches to the far end of the axis in both directions. To the south the windows overlook the *giardino segreto*, the small, enclosed garden behind the villa that was replanted in the early twentieth century by the Count Chigi Zondadari and his English wife. Beyond the boundary wall of the *giardino segreto* the axis plunges down into a valley. Here the view is eventually stopped by a colossal statue of Hercules executed by Giuseppe Mazzuoli, another of Bernini's pupils. The northern axis opens on to the main garden and the original entrance from the road. There is a cypress avenue flanking the axis today, but it was not marked on Fontana's original plans. Beyond the avenue two tall brick piers enclose the axis, focusing the view of the densely wooded hillside beyond and the point at which the axis begins its sudden and dramatic climb. Two hundred stone steps link the lower garden to the *romitorio* or hermitage that stops the view at the top of the hill. Its façade is decorated with a huge double cross and busts of Christ and the evangelists. The grand scale of the decoration ensures that it can be seen from the villa and garden below.

There was no garden at Cetinale before Carlo Fontana imposed the single axis of his baroque layout upon the small fields and orchards of the agricultural landscape. In some ways the task of an architect commissioned to rework an existing landscape in the baroque manner was more complex than Fontana's transformation of a 'green field' site. There has been a garden on the site of Villa Barbarigo at Valsanzibio in the Veneto since the fifteenth century. By the mid-sixteenth century it had evolved into a series of garden rooms, orchards, fowling groves and freshwater pools stocked with 'foreign' fish. According to Cardinal Alessandro Piccolomini, a celebrated professor of philosophy at the University of Padua from 1540, nature had endowed the place with every

charm, including pure air, sweet water and delicious fruit. By the end of the sixteenth century the garden and a small hunting lodge already belonged to the powerful Venetian Barbarigo family. Between 1665 and 1669 Antonio Barbarigo, ambassador for the Venetian Republic, senator and finally Procurator of St Marks, commissioned an unnamed architect to make a villa out of the hunting lodge and a baroque landscape in place of the Renaissance garden.

Villa Barbarigo and its garden lie in the curved embrace of the Eugenean hills, a site not unlike that of Villa Cetinale. The architect drove a north-south axis down the precipitous slope opposite the villa, across the level ground and up Monte degli Staffoli, the steep hill behind the villa. The axis was sharply defined at each end by avenues of cypress that scaled the hills. On Monte degli Staffoli the line was further accentuated by a stepped cascade. On the level ground of the garden itself, hedges were planted to flank the axis. These hedges had a dual function. They focused the view, drawing the eye along the axis to the villa, and they concealed the garden rooms to either side. Behind these living screens the architect hid amusing surprises – a large

maze with a mount at its centre and a rabbit island surrounded by a circular moat.

Unlike the gardens of Villa Aldobrandini or Cetinale, Barbarigo has a second, east-west axis intersecting the first. This axis was a part of the original garden and it was marked by the two fifteenth-century rectangular fish pools. From these simple ingredients the architect created a spectacular view of ascending pools decorated with statues. The stonework and sculpture in the garden is all attributed to two men contracted in 1665 under the names Pio and Domenico Tagliapietra – the surname simply means 'stonecutter'. As so often in the baroque garden, the statues are gathered into imposing groups, a technique that greatly increased their impact. A third pool was dug at the top of the axis, and the point at which the two axes crossed was marked with a fountain.

ABOVE AND RIGHT *There is nothing to stop the view of Villa Barbarigo along the garden's main north-south axis.*

The second axis, which runs from east to west, is punctuated by a series of fountains and pools inhabited by swans.

GARENNA O LVOGO DI CONIGLI CON VCCELLIERA PER VCCELLI MINVTI NEL GIARDINO DELL ECCELLENTISSIMA CASA BARBARIGO POSTO IN VAL SAN ZIBIO TRA COLLI EVGANEI

The *pièce de résistance* at Barbarigo is a graceful watergate that stops the eastern end of the second axis. Although it is very elaborate, the style of decoration on the watergate is lighter than the ponderous river gods who cluster around the pools. The wrought iron gates look out over a pool that was once surrounded by undrained marshland. Diana, goddess of hunting, stands above the broken pediment of an arch on top of the gate, her dogs close at hand. The façade below is decorated with bas-reliefs of game that has already been slaughtered and neatly hung. Deer, wild boar, hares, a bear and a fox are all accurately portrayed alongside weapons associated with the chase.

The effect of the statues at Barbarigo is reinforced by numerous inscriptions. Although many of the original inscriptions have been damaged or lost, they were all collected and transcribed by J. Salomonio in his *Inscriptiones patavinae prophanae* of 1696. Despite quite radical differences between the design of Renaissance and baroque gardens, the inscriptions give voice to a purpose and spirit that had remained almost unchanged since the earliest humanist gardens were created in Tuscany in the mid-fifteenth century. They convey the image of the garden as a sanctuary where 'activity gives way to extreme idleness and peace', a message that is reinforced by another inscription reading, 'this is no place for tears, but the seat of laughter.' On the steps between the main north-south axis and the *giardino segreto* in front of the villa the longest inscription in the garden reads:

> Here the sun's rays shine more brightly
> Venus rises more lovely from the sea
> The phases of the moon are clearer
> Jupiter plays with carefree smile
> And Mercury sets aside all clever deceits.

With these words ringing in their ears, seventeenth-century visitors would have entered the *giardino segreto*, a sunny south-facing terrace in front of the villa. Here they would find themselves surrounded by small, geometrically arranged beds filled with one of the finest and most extensive plant collections in Italy. The family was well placed to collect

ABOVE *The rabbit island at Villa Barbarigo. When the drawbridge is up, the rabbits' only potential predators are hawks but they are deterred by the decoy, brass hawk that hovers above the aviary.*

RIGHT *Steps inside the Watergate lead to a terrace on the roof. From this viewpoint it is possible to appreciate the garden's setting in the embrace of the Euganean hills.*

rare and exotic plants. They lived very close to Padua's magnificent botanic garden, by then already established for over a century, and they were in constant contact with international trade through Venice. The *giardino segreto* at Barbarigo is referred to by Paolo Bartolomeo Clarici in *Istoria e cultura delle piante* (1726). He was particularly impressed by the stocks, which were a double variety and surprisingly large. However, according to Clarici, this was just one of 'the many rarities of this delightful garden'.

Although the single axis was an essential feature of the Italian baroque garden, there are a number of gardens in the Veneto that appear to adopt this style while belonging to a quite different and somewhat older tradition. By the beginning of the sixteenth century many circumstances had combined to undermine trade between the Venetian Republic and the Middle and Far East. Trade had always been Venice's main source of income but now several merchant families felt compelled to turn their backs on the sea and seek a safer investment in agricultural land on the terra firma. This new pattern of investment

emerged at the beginning of the sixteenth century and by 1600, 250 new farmhouse villas had been built. The gardens of these early villas tended to be set out around a single axis that reached far beyond the garden boundary and into the fields and orchards that surrounded it. The garden to either side of this axis generally consisted of parterre beds and other low-lying features, as nothing could be allowed to impede the landowner's view over his fields and the peasants working in them.

This practical layout was originally used in 1560 by Palladio at the Villa Barbaro in Maser, and continued to serve as the blueprint for gardens laid out in front of Venetian farmhouse villas for over a

ABOVE *Nothing remains of the garden that once occupied the space to either side of the central axis in front of Villa Barbaro.*

RIGHT *Little has changed at Villa Allegri Arvedi, although the illustration in Volkamer depicts a curious mixture between the square compartments of the original layout and the broderie parterres that replaced them.*

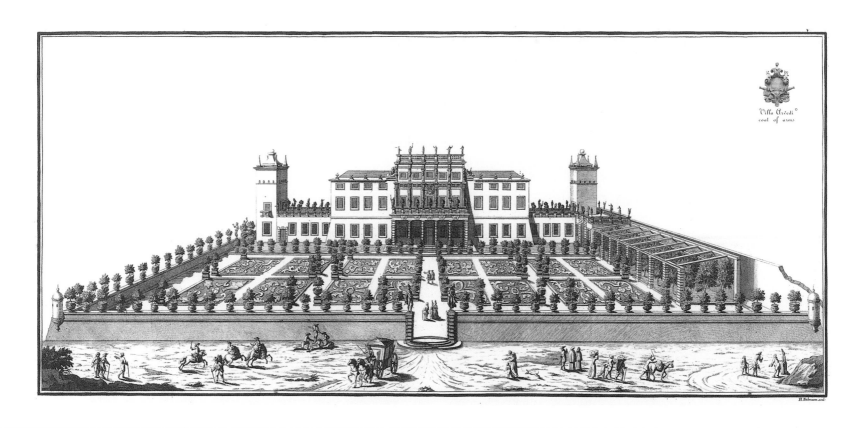

hundred years. The garden of Villa Allegri Arvedi in Cuzzano, near Verona, adheres to this local Venetan tradition. It was designed in 1653 for Giovanni Battista Allegri by Giovanni Battista Bianchi. Although it is built to a grand baroque design, the villa sits among barns, stables and granaries. Like Villa Barbaro, it is flanked by two dovecots. Bianchi continued to follow the Palladian blueprint in the garden, which lies immediately below the house. A single axis runs from the villa, through the gardens, across the public road and into the fields beyond. In the garden the space to either side of the main axis is filled by elaborate *broderie* parterres punctuated with topiary cones. The idea of planting

these intricate arabesques in box came from France, and it was not generally adopted in Italy until the eighteenth century. On a fresco inside the villa, the garden is shown with typically geometric parterre beds, and this was probably the original design. Beyond the garden boundary the axis runs through open fields. It is flanked by blocks and cones of topiary and sturdy persimmon trees.

The garden of Villa Allegri Arvedi contains none of the grandiose baroque architecture and decoration common to other seventeenth-century gardens, where a spectacular impression was heightened by the use of explicitly theatrical forms. A link had already been established

between garden and theatre in the sixteenth century, when the garden was often a setting for drama or music. A loggia or a graceful flight of steps might serve as an impromptu stage, and grottoes, nymphaea and fountains created an appropriately theatrical backdrop. During the seventeenth century the spectacular theatrical element of the Italian garden became more pronounced, and the link between garden and theatre more emphatic. The garden was the inspiration for innumerable seventeenth- and eighteenth-century stage sets, notably those designed by Filippo Juvarra (see Chapter 9), and visitors may often have felt

that they had unwittingly joined the cast of a performance with an unknown plot.

The theatrical atmosphere of the baroque garden corresponded to a more general fashion for spectacle and pageantry linked to the cult of *magnificenza* – magnificence – in the courts of the kings, princes, dukes, popes and cardinals who ruled Italy. Although green theatres were almost unknown in the seventeenth century, a few gardens contained structures expressly designed for theatrical use. An amphitheatre was built in the Boboli Gardens between 1631 and 1634 by Giulio Parigi, commissioned by Grand Duke Ferdinand II de' Medici. The theatre was built on the *prato*, a level area in the Boboli gardens, immediately behind the Pitti Palace, and in 1637 it became the venue for a *festa a cavallo*, an extraordinarily complex equestrian performance in honour of Ferdinand II de' Medici's marriage to Vittoria della Rovere (see Chapter 8). The amphitheatre was part of a larger project that had been initiated under Cosimo II de' Medici, Ferdinand II's father, in 1618. Giulio Parigi had been commissioned to extend the Pitti Palace, and a powerful new axis had been driven east-west across the garden. Cosimo also extended the formal part of the Boboli gardens on a great tongue of new land reaching westwards to the Porta Romana. The most flamboyant feature of this new baroque garden was the Isolotto, an island decorated with a fountain and pots of lemons, and surrounded by a balustrade and a narrow oval moat. The fountain and moat were originally peopled by hordes of *putti* and *amorini*, all of them intent on shooting arrows or breaking into hearts with the aid of keys, or even hammers. This ornate baroque confection was linked to the shore by two gated bridges, the gate posts are surmounted by the capricorns that were Cosimo II's personal symbol.

The first phase of the baroque reworking of the Boboli gardens was interrupted by Cosimo II's premature death in 1621, and was only resumed by Ferdinand II in the 1630s. Objectively it was a most inauspicious moment. Plague engulfed most of the Italian peninsula, and in Florence the epidemic was combined with a dramatic economic depression that left thousands of workers in the textiles and building industries unemployed. Grave reports from the Uffizio della Sanità informed Ferdinand II that fresh water was in short supply throughout Florence, a situation that contributed greatly to the suffering of the sick and the poor. Closer to home there were signs of water shortage in the Boboli gardens, where some of the pools were dry. Ferdinand was obliged to take some action to prevent mass starvation and relieve suffering in the city. Traditionally this obligation could be fulfilled by the distribution of alms. Ferdinand sanctioned alms-giving in the usual way, but he also took hundreds of unemployed silk and wool workers on to

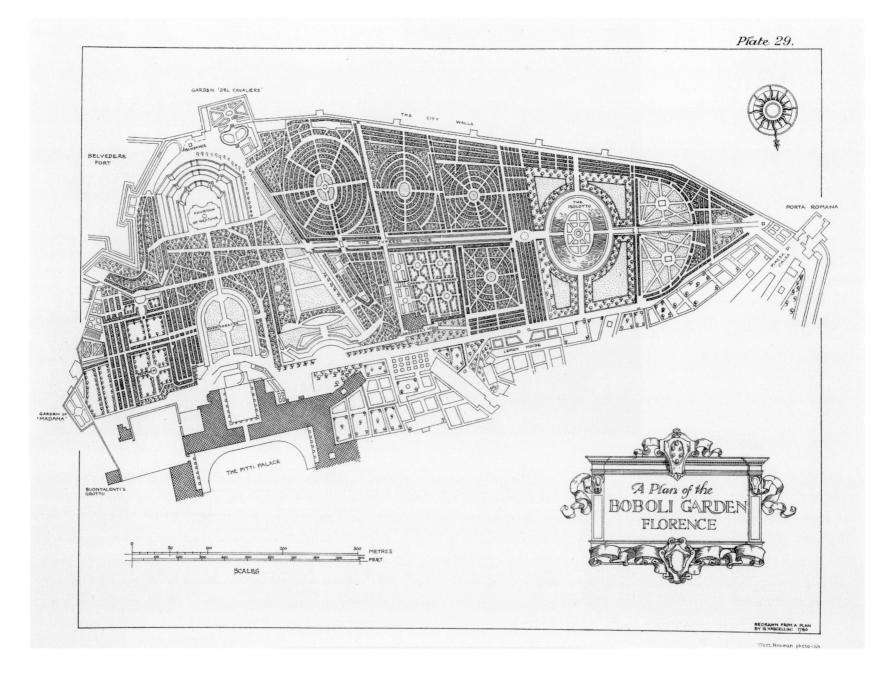

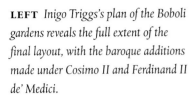

LEFT *Inigo Triggs's plan of the Boboli gardens reveals the full extent of the final layout, with the baroque additions made under Cosimo II and Ferdinand II de' Medici.*

RIGHT *An unusual, aerial view of Florence, with the Boboli gardens in the foreground. The gardens cover 79 acres (32 hectares) in the heart of the city.*

the payroll. In their own industry these workers were probably highly skilled. Now strength was the only qualification required of them. Ferdinand's workforce consisted of men, women and even children with one thing in common: they could all hoist a wicker basket full of earth on to one shoulder and carry it. Elsewhere in Italy garden building ground to a halt during the plague years. In Florence the 1630s saw the building of Ferdinand II's new aqueduct which brought fresh water to the city from the slopes of Mount Montereggi, and a new construction phase in the Boboli gardens.

The textiles workers were joined by unemployed sculptors, masons and stone cutters in the gardens. The *prato* behind the palace was cleared in preparation for the construction of the new amphitheatre. This was done by moving Giambologna's statue of Oceanus from the *prato* to the centre of Cosimo's Isolotto. Here Oceanus, father of three thousand rivers, became part of a sustained celebration of the Acqua Ferdinanda brought to Florence by Ferdinand's new acqueduct. The large stone amphitheatre became the key feature in a garden that was now recast to celebrate Ferdinand as benefactor and author of peace and prosperity. It provided a permanent setting for pageants designed to mark every social or political event in the life of the Medici court. Its design may have been inspired by Pliny the Younger's description of the hippodrome in the garden of his Tuscan villa, a feature said by him to 'greatly surpass' the beauty of the villa itself. The classical association was certainly perceived by William Beckford, who wrote a vivid account of the Boboli gardens in a letter dated 14 September 1780. Of the amphitheatre he said:

> … [it] brought the imagery of an antique, Roman garden so vividly to mind that, lost in the train of recollections this idea excited, I expected every instant to be called to the table of Lucullus hard by, in one of the porticos, and to stretch myself upon his purple *triclinias* ; but waiting in vain for a summons until the approach of night, I returned delighted with a ramble that had led my imagination so far into antiquity.

Beyond the amphitheatre Tribolo's single axis was greatly enlarged. In its original form, the narrow axis drew the eye to the edge of the garden enclosure. Now it was widened and extended to the top of the hill, so that it appeared to draw the eye to infinity. This move from enclosure to openness automatically altered the nature of the garden, changing it from a Renaissance to a baroque landscape.

Much of the work done for Ferdinand II in the Boboli amounted to little more than a recycling and recasting of existing materials. Giambologna's sixteenth-century statue of Francesco I de' Medici's wife, Johanna of Austria, had lain unfinished and abandoned for decades. Now she was resurrected, given a golden wheatsheaf, a cornucopia and a new identity as Dovizia – or 'Abundance'. The inscription on her base spelt out a joyful message celebrating Tuscany's young duke:

> May the memory last forever that while most of Europe was consumed with grievous wars and Italy was struggling from a lack of grain, Etruria, under Ferdinand II, because of the kindness of his will, was enjoying peace, the best of affairs and prosperity. O passer-by, go your way, urgently request that your most excellent ruler may be safe, and wish joy for Tuscany.

Below Dovizia, Stoldo Lorenzi's sixteenth-century bronze Neptune was installed on a rocky mound at the centre of the Vivaio Grande, an oblong sixteenth-century pool. Like Oceanus, Neptune celebrated the supply of fresh water brought by Ferdinand to the city. A new two-tier fountain dubbed the Fontana del Carciofo (artichoke fountain) was designed by Giovanfrancesco Susini to stand on a terrace between the palace and the amphitheatre and installed in about 1642. Cherubs perch on the sides of the bowl and ride turtles and swans in the water. Originally made twenty years earlier, the cherubs began life on Cosimo II's Isolotto. Now they were recast to become part of the general theme of joy and abundance.

The Boboli amphitheatre was constructed on the grand scale of a civic building. At Villa Cetinale there was also a purpose-built theatre,

but it was constructed on a small scale for private entertainment. Carlo Fontana designed the Cetinale theatre for his patron, Cardinal Flavio Chigi. Despite constant disapproval and stinging criticism from the Vatican, Flavio Chigi was Rome's leading impresario, and he had a theatre built for him in every property he owned (see Chapter 8). At Cetinale the theatre stands at the base of the hill, on the garden's main axis. The stage is backed by a curved wall that was originally decorated with busts by Mazzuoli.

Flavio Chigi and Ferdinand II de' Medici were driven by passion or politics to create purpose-built areas for performance within their gardens. The majority of seventeenth-century garden owners were content with suggestive spaces in the garden that could be adapted for dramatic purposes, concerts or pageants as required. Garden architects created theatrical structures that were borrowed from classical architecture, but not always directly associated with the theatre. For example, both Villa Aldobrandini and Isola Bella, on Lake Maggiore in

Piedmont, have a water theatre, a tall, semicircular structure decorated with statues and fountains. Despite its name, the water theatre probably took its semicircular shape from the hemicycle, a structure that had been excavated in the Emperor Hadrian's classical gardens in Tivoli.

At Villa Aldobrandini, Della Porta's semicircular water theatre stands at the base of the hill, below the water staircase. Della Porta's death meant that Carlo Maderno completed the theatre, with technical assistance from Giovanni Fontana (1546-1614) as hydraulic engineer. The theatre was the final destination for the torrent that tumbled down the staircase, gathering momentum as it fell. The base of the staircase is flanked by the Pillars of Hercules, decorated with the

ABOVE *Hubert Robert's evocative, eighteenth-century view of Villa Aldobrandini's Water Theatre in full working order.*

RIGHT *Atlas struggling beneath the weight of the heavens at the centre of the Water Theatre. The face of Enceladus is just visible at the base of the fountain.*

Aldobrandini *imprese*, or emblems, picked out in mosaic. Ribbon-like watercourses encircle the pillars, making them appear twisted. The water staircase has not worked properly for centuries, but originally a portion of the falling water was driven up through the cores of the two pillars. Re-emerging through their crowns, it span down the external watercourses to re-join the main flow. The water entered the theatre with a deafening roar and a force that gave Giovanni Fontana the ability to generate a storm of intensely theatrical and constantly changing effects. These effects were described by Richard Lassels in his *Voyage or a Compleat journey through Italy* (1670), as 'Rain, Hail, Snow and Thunder'. The centre of the theatre lies opposite the villa's front door. It is marked by Jacques Sazzarin's muscle-bound figure of Atlas supporting the watery, azure-blue globe of the heavens on his shoulders. Hercules originally stood below Atlas, his foot planted firmly on the head of Enceladus, a defeated Titan. Water brought the architecture and the statues to life, transforming the theatre into the setting for a real performance by forcing Enceladus to roar and spit, Pan to play his pipes, the centaurs to sound their horns, and the lion and tigress to roar and hiss.

Fountains, terraces and a water theatre are the principal ingredients of Isola Bella, the island garden built for the Borromeo family on Lake Maggiore in Piedmont. Isola Bella is both the most ambitious and the most theatrical of Italy's baroque gardens, a perfect expression of the confidence and power of the Borromeo. It was built between 1632 and 1671 on the instructions of Count Carlo Borromeo III, who wanted to transform a jagged rock in the lake into his own version of the Garden of the Hesperides. His vision was quite clear, the garden was to be built from 'a pyramid of terraces' that would transform its rough contours into the shape of a great baroque galleon at anchor on the lake.

Work began in 1632 under Angelo Crivelli, an otherwise obscure architect and engineer from Milan. Unfortunately the count's vision was not shared by all of the island's inhabitants. It was especially unpopular with people who were asked to move out of their homes in the village on the western shore in order to make way for the new palace. Most of them refused, and as a result the palace had to be designed to an irregular T-shaped plan. This prevented Crivelli from creating a central axis that would link the palace to the terraced garden. In addition to this irritation, the Borromeo had to negotiate with the Church about a chapel inconveniently placed on the site of the garden. The problem was eventually resolved after Carlo III's death by his son, Count Vitaliano Borromeo VI. He bought the chapel and the road leading to it, promised to build a new church and to allow processions across his garden on saints' days.

For many years traffic was heavy between Isola Bella and the shore. The first cargo was soil, transported in massive quantities from the mainland. This was followed by marble from Baveno, stone from Viggiù and rock from Migliardo. Later on the boats were packed with young lemon trees, many of them imported from Spain. Over months, years, decades, the view from the shore of the lake gradually changed. Living and working on the water's edge, local people witnessed the change, but Carlo Borromeo had not shared his vision with them, and they had no idea what the outcome of all the hard work and expense would be. Perhaps it became clear one summer morning, when mist could have clung to the water of the lake and most people in Baveno were still asleep. The fishermen may have been up, and the baker, and perhaps a young woman sitting at a window to feed her baby. As the sun rose over the lake, the fishermen might look up from their work to watch the haze burn off the water. As the view cleared, perhaps they shared Carlo Borromeo's vision, just for a moment. In place of the island that they had known all their lives there was a great boat, a gleaming baroque galleon, anchored peacefully on the water. The woman might have seen it too, wrapped her baby in a shawl and rushed out of the house. They would all stand on the water's edge, the baker, the fishermen and the young woman, and explain the view to each other. Now they understood that the earth, shipped out in such quantity, had been used to clothe the rocks, levelling the rugged contours of the island. The stone had been made into galleries that transformed the uneven coastline, rendering it sleek and regular. They looked at the ten terraces rising steeply from the water, and saw that the island's southern end formed a stern for the galleon.

Building work continued until 1650, when progress was interrupted by an outbreak of plague. In 1652 Carlo III died, leaving the island to his sons. Count Vitaliano Borromeo VI, the youngest son, took on responsibility for Isola Bella, and work resumed in 1654 under a large team of local artists and architects. Carlo Fontana, who had been in Rome for many years, returned home to work for the Borromeo on Isola Bella. In addition to his enormous success as an architect, Fontana was the seventeenth-century authority on hydraulic engineering in all its forms. In 1696 he published a treatise on all aspects of water use and management called *Utilissimo trattato dell'acque correnti* (The extremely useful treatise on running water). Fontana's semicircular water theatre stands just below the bridge of the galleon. According to Vitaliano VI, its site was selected because, being north facing, it was the one place that you could not grow lemons. The theatre is a delicate, almost rococo confection of niches that house enormous scallop shells and statues of Mars, Vulcan, Agriculture and the Arts. Waving *putti* and noble obelisks stand against the skyline, and the whole structure is topped by the Borromeo unicorn. The water theatre may have been used as the backdrop for performances, but it is important to remember that the Borromeo also built another theatre on the island that was subsequently demolished. This theatre was in one of the cool

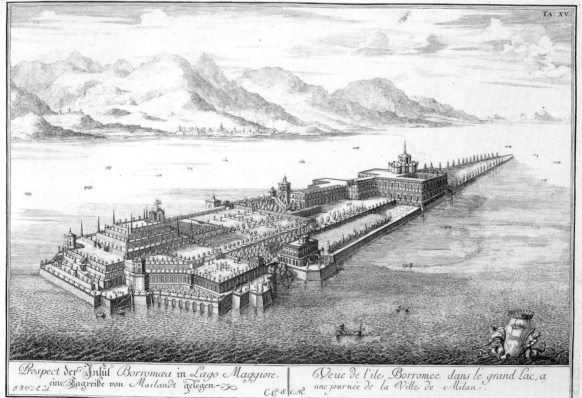

Prospect der Insul Borromæa in Lago Maggiore.
eine Tagreike von Mailandt gelegen.

Veüe de l'ile Borromee dans le grand Lac, a
une journée de la Ville de Milan.

ABOVE Isola Bella rises from the waters of Lake Maggiore, its terraces built to resemble the stern of a galleon. The tower on the right of the picture houses a pump, providing lavish quantities of water for irrigation in the garden.

LEFT Fischer von Erlach's eighteenth-century engraving shows the northern end of the island transformed into a sharply pointed prow of the galleon. However, this part of the project was never completed.

RIGHT The two reclining figures at the centre of the Water Theatre represent Toce and Ticino, the two principal rivers that feed Lake Maggiore. The female figures flanking the theatre represent Art and Agriculture.

subterranean garden rooms that also housed a collection of marine curiosities. It was large enough to seat an audience of 300, and the entertainment was usually provided by Carlo Maria Maggi, the Borromeo family's resident playwright.

Steps to each side of the theatre lead to the bridge of the galleon, a huge marble terrace surrounded by a balustrade. Beneath the bridge there is a reservoir filled with water pumped up from the lake. The garden terraces descend steeply from the southern end of the bridge, each one enclosed by a balustrade and decorated with statues, obelisks and pots of lemons. Gilbert Burnet, the French diarist and bishop, visited Isola Bella in 1685, and wrote: 'The fragrant smell, the beautiful

Prospect, and the delighting Variety that is here makes such a habitation for Summer that perhaps the whole world has nothing like it.' The vision had taken forty years to realize, but it was one of art's greatest victories in the ongoing contest with nature.

In 1671 the builders, sculptors and masons left Isola Bella. The family continued to build on the botanical collection during the nineteenth century, importing and naturalizing exotic plants from all over the world (see Chapter 10). However building work on the palace was not resumed until the 1950s, when the palazzo was completed under Prince Borromeo-Arese, using the original plans.

VII | Horticultural extremes
Plant collections 1600-1700

DURING THE SEVENTEENTH CENTURY Italy was overwhelmed by an irresistible passion for rare and exotic plants. Enthusiasm for collecting and cultivating exotics was rooted in the sixteenth century. The discovery of America and the development of trading links with South East Asia, Africa and the Far East brought an extraordinary influx of strange and wonderful seeds, bulbs, tubers, rooted plants and trees. The first botanic gardens were founded in the mid-sixteenth century by scientists and doctors as open-air laboratories where foreign plants could be cultivated, studied and classified (see Chapter 3). Although the directors of these gardens were academics or physicians, they were often dependent for collaboration and funding upon aristocratic patrons with an amateur enthusiasm for horticulture. It was through figures such as Cosimo I de' Medici and his sons Francesco I and Ferdinand I that plant collecting ceased to be the preserve of academics and professional scientists. Cosimo I funded the botanic garden in Pisa and the Giardino dei Semplici in Florence, but he also collected and displayed exotic plants in his own gardens. According to Agostino del Riccio in *Il Giardino di un re* (1589) Cosimo I enjoyed pruning and grafting these specimens himself. Del Riccio lists the plants growing in Florence between the end of the sixteenth and beginning of the seventeenth centuries, providing us with the vignette of a planting palette that is already very varied. The list includes fourteen varieties of lemon tree, six kinds of jasmine, five of narcissus, sixteen varieties of carnation, dwarf apple trees and Indian figs. This image is reinforced by the work of Jacopo Ligozzi, court painter to both Francesco I and Ferdinand I de' Medici. Between 1577 and 1603, Ligozzi was commissioned to paint the plants and animals in the ducal gardens

and menageries. Once again the variety of plants, exquisitely drawn and coloured, confirms that plant collecting was already well established by the end of the sixteenth century.

The Medici family continued to be fascinated by exotic or otherwise unusual plants. In the latter half of the seventeenth century the first pineapple ever grown on Italian soil was picked in the Boboli gardens for Cosimo III de' Medici. Cosimo commissioned Bartolomeo Bimbi to document the plants that grew in the Medici gardens and, more generally, on Tuscan soil. Bimbi's paintings reveal a typically seventeenth-century delight in gigantic or otherwise spectacular forms of fruit and vegetables. One of his most striking pictures depicts a gigantic pumpkin raised in the ducal gardens. It is set against the skyline of Florence, dwarfing the Duomo and Baptistery (see page 119).

By the beginning of the seventeenth century plant collecting had gathered force and developed into a full-blown mania that extended as far as Naples in the south and Venice in the north. A plan of Rome made by Giovanni Maggi in 1625 shows a profusion of gardens of every dimension. Some are attached to palaces, but others belong to the smaller houses of middle-ranking nobles, or even those of ordinary Romans caught up in a local addiction to horticulture. Plant catalogues of the same period reveal that New World species such as passion flowers, yuccas, sumachs, morning glory and trumpet vine were all being grown in Italy, alongside plants from the East, such as aubergines from tropical Asia, rhubarb from central Asia, *Anchusa azurea* from the Caucasus, tulips from Persia and *impatiens balsamica* from the East Indies.

The seventeenth-century Italian garden can only be properly understood by trying to imagine the workings of a plant collector's mind, and by sympathizing with his compulsion to be the very first person to own a plant from a country so distant and strange that its mere presence could imbue the garden with magic, evoke wonder

LEFT *An illustration from Giovanni Battista Ferrari's* Hesperides, *an epic, seventeenth-century work on every aspect of citrus cultivation. The woman in the foreground holds a citron, a favourite among citrus collectors.*

and admiration from visitors, and endow him with real social and intellectual prestige. The feverish desire to own such a plant could compel the garden owner to spend as much on a single bulb from Persia or Constantinople as he paid his head gardener or chef for a month's work. Plants as valuable as this had to be kept behind the locked door of a *giardino segreto*, a walled garden that was cared for by gardeners during the day and patrolled by dogs at night. By imagining all these things it may be possible to feel the heat of passion that burnt at the heart of baroque garden culture in the seventeenth century.

Although there was a fashionable and faddish aspect to plant collecting, seventeenth-century gardens were part of a wider intellectual landscape. They were the outdoor extensions of cabinets of curiosities, or private museums, established by educated and affluent patrons. Indoors the museum was often housed in the *studiolo*, or study. The walls were lined with cabinets containing countless tiny drawers where natural (*naturalia*) and man-made (*artificalia*) 'curiosities' were stored. Galileo made a disparaging but rather useful comparison between the works of the sixteenth-century epic poet Torquato Tasso and a small and somewhat insignificant cabinet of curiosities. His description of the disparate contents of the collection reflects a deep derision for Tasso's work, but it also provides us with a very vivid account of the kind of natural and man-made objects that might form the collection of an educated gentleman anywhere in Europe during the second half of the sixteenth and the early seventeenth centuries:

> …things that have something exotic about them, either because of age or rarity or some other reason, but are in effect bric-a-brac – a petrified crayfish; a dried-up chameleon, a fly, and a spider embedded in a piece of amber, some of those little clay figures said to be found in the ancient tombs of Egypt, and (when it comes to painting) a sketch or two by Bandinelli and Parmigiano and other similar trifles.

The purist views of scientists such as Galileo did nothing to diminish the popularity of cabinet collections. Cardinal Flavio Chigi, one of Rome's leading patrons and owner of the Villa Cetinale and its baroque garden (see pages 98, 99), kept one of the most esteemed collections in Rome. It was housed in a garden room in his palace at Quattro Fontane, and the inventory of its contents is as varied as Galileo's imaginary collection. There were strange tools, Turkish costumes, Japanese weapons, Chinese fans and porcelain and other peculiar objects brought back by Jesuit missionaries to China and the New World. Among the natural curiosities were stuffed birds of paradise, fossils and a fish's jaw with four rows of teeth.

The garden was also a museum of curiosities. The scientific and didactic element of the cabinet was stored in the *studiolo*, while the garden housed the sensual part of the collection. It contained exotic plants that formed a living and exciting link between the observer and the alien and distant landscapes where they had originally been discovered. It was also a gallery where antiquities could be displayed. The walls of the *giardino*

Within the painting:
Zucca nata in Pisa
nel Giardino di S.A.R.
detto di S. Francesco
l'Anno 1711 Pesaua ℔160.

segreto, of the palace or the garden loggia were often used to display antique bas-reliefs, or fragments of epitaphs once inscribed on the lids of Roman sarcophogi. In Rome it was traditional to make these open-air collections accessible to the public. The collector would acquire and restore antiquities, and then invite scholars and artists to see them. Together the plants and statues formed a political instrument used by the garden owner to win the support of learned and influential visitors. Rare bulbs and *objets d'art* could often be bought from the same dealer, who would work indiscriminately in *naturalia* and *artificalia*, feeding the competition between his clients and furnishing their cabinets with curiosities from all over the known world. A menagerie of strange animals and a series of fresh and saltwater pools stocked with fish completed the museum and the attempt, in the words of Francis Bacon, to 'have in a small compass a model of universal nature made private'.

LEFT *A pineapple by Jacopo Ligozzi, painter to the Medici family. The first pineapple ever cultivated in Italy grew in the Medici gardens at Boboli.*

ABOVE *This giant pumpkin was one of the curiosities of the Medici gardens. By painting Florence's skyline as a backdrop, Bimbi gave some idea of its monstrous size.*

The design of the flower beds reflected that of the *studiolo*. The space was divided into equal sections, rather like the cabinets indoors. These sections were then split into small compartments that were sometimes referred to as *cassette* or 'boxes'. Private patrons followed the example of the botanic gardens, identifying each compartment with a letter or symbol, and then marking the plants, bulbs and tubers with numbered canes (see Chapter 3). These details were then recorded on a carefully drawn and bound planting plan, or in an index book. This orderly system, which minimized the risk of losing any of the garden's precious specimens, was advocated by Giovanni Battista Ferrari, author of *Flora overo cultura dei fiori*, the most influential florilegium of the seventeenth century. The desired result, in Ferrari's words, was 'an almost military accommodation of the floral ranks', although he made it clear that this should not eliminate aesthetically pleasing planting. An example of seventeenth-century display beds survives on the upper terrace of Villa Buonaccorsi near Ancona, where four stone-edged beds are laid out around a pool. Each bed is divided into a variety of complex shapes, including stars and lozenges. Some sections are planted, and others contain lemons in pots or eccentric little obelisks with ball feet.

RITRATTO DEL MVSEO DI FERRANTE IMPERATO

Cabinets of curiosity were a wonderful expression of contemporary thought. Both the *studiolo* and the garden reflected the desire to embrace an ever-expanding world and to understand man's place in it. Bizarre plants – a lemon shaped like hands clasped in prayer, a plant thought to be poisonous or one said to be invested with magical properties, took pride of place. The seventeenth-century flower garden had so many roles to fulfil – it must astonish, instruct, amuse and delight the eye of the visitor.

Many of Italy's most important seventeenth-century plant collections were in private gardens in Rome, which became a European centre for scientific research of all kinds and amassed particular expertise in botany. In 1603 the Accademia dei Lincei was founded, a scientific academy that pre-dates both the Royal Society in England and the Académie des Sciences in France. It was named both for the lynx (*lince*) identified by Pliny as the animal with the keenest sight, and for Lyncaeus, the sharp-sighted Argonaut. There is something boyish about the name and this may be due to the fact that Prince Federico Cesi, founder and patron of the Lincei, was only eighteen years old in 1603.

He founded the academy with three friends with the express purpose of studying every aspect of natural history through direct observation, a process that would inevitably lead them to test, question and revise the classical theories that had formed the basis of knowledge throughout the Renaissance. At first the academy grew slowly. When Galileo was invited to join in 1611, he was only the sixth member. However from 1611 onwards membership expanded rapidly and soon encompassed several nationalities. The Lincei agreed that if only Francis Bacon had lived in Italy, they would have 'made every effort to make him one of us'.

As soon as the Academy was formed in 1603 the Lincei began to correspond with students, doctors and scientists all over Europe.

ABOVE *This is the earliest picture of a cabinet of curiosities. It belonged to Ferrante Imperato, a Neapolitan apothecary, who used the collection for his research. He is here with his son Francesco, showing the collection to visitors.*

RIGHT *These knives illustrate a section devoted to the tools used for successful citrus cultivation in Giovanni Battista Ferrari's* Hesperides, sive, de malorum aureorum cultura et usu *(1646).*

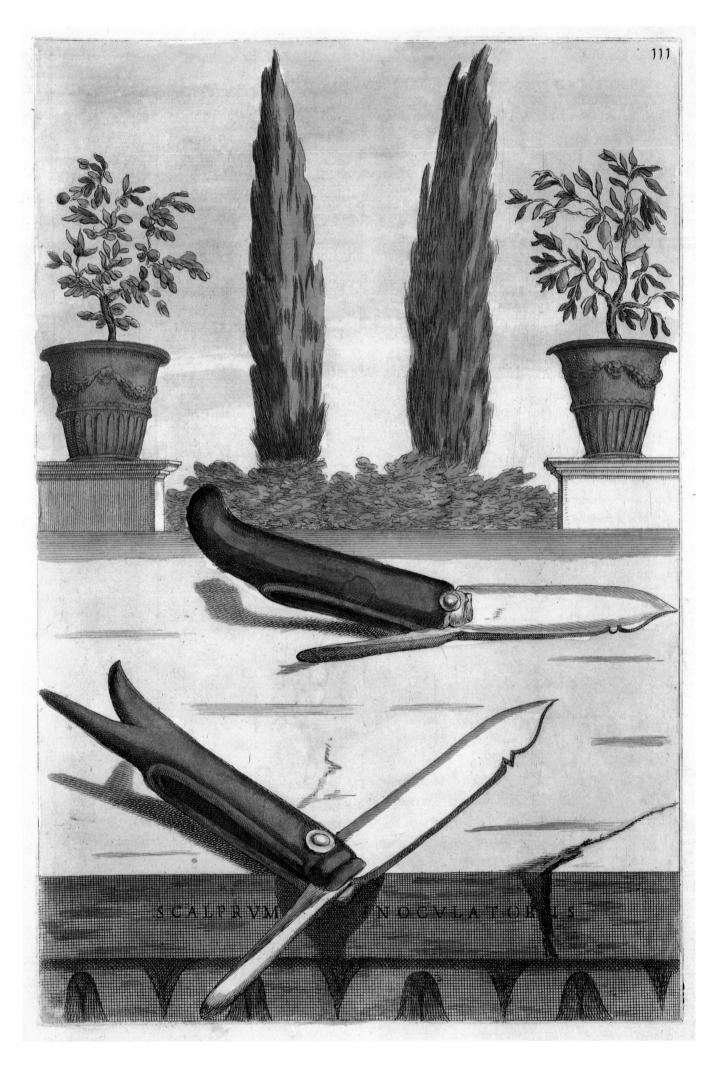

SCALPRVM   INOCVLATORIS

The greatest botanists of the day, like Clusius in Leiden and Jean Robin in Paris, were among their correspondents, and they rapidly received an avalanche of information about exotic plants never recorded by Pliny, Theophrastus or Dioscorides. The Lincei made their own expeditions into the countryside surrounding Cesi's home in Umbria, taking samples of everything they found – plant, mineral and animal. Unlike their sixteenth-century predecessors, they were not content to examine the surface of these things. Working in their simple laboratories, they cut open seedpods, counted seeds and dissected flower buds and fruits. Their botanical work was greatly enriched in 1624 when Galileo donated his microscope, subsequently known as 'the Lincean explorer', to the academy.

The greatest work ever published by the Lincei was *The Mexican Treasury*, a vast treatise on the plants, birds and animals of Mexico. The treasury was derived from work originally done by Francisco Hernández, personal physician to Phillip II of Spain. Hernández was sent to Mexico by the king in 1570 in order to record medicinal plants, birds and animals. He created a huge and chaotic compendium

of text, including several thousand completely new plants, and made beautiful illustrations. The academy finally published an amended form of Hernández's great work between 1649 and 1651.

There was a close association between the Accademia dei Lincei and the Barberini court of Pope Urban VIII. The Pope and his nephew, Cardinal Francesco Barberini, were at the centre of an intellectual circle united by a common passion for horticulture. Bulbs and seeds may have been swapped among members of the Barberini court, but competition for the newest and most remarkable arrivals from the New World was fierce. The court gave employment to botanical artists drawn to Rome from all over Europe, and the city soon rivalled Florence as a centre for botanical illustration. Francesco Barberini was patron to both Nicolas Guillaume Delafleur, soon nicknamed Monsú Fiore (Mr Flower), and Mario Nuzzi, generally known as Mario dei Fiori (Mario of the Flowers).

Francesco Barberini was no amateur. He studied botany at the University of Rome under Johann Faber. A physician and botanist, Faber was one of a small but important group of German members of the Accademia dei Lincei. Francesco's link with the academy was strengthened by his friendship with Federico Cesi, and his choice of Cassiano dal Pozzo, an academician and one of the best-known antiquarians, collectors and artists' patrons in Rome, as his secretary and special advisor. Cassiano's advice extended to the layout of the Orti Barberini, Francesco's garden on the Quirinal hill. In a letter written in 1627 he suggested that it should be divided in two, one part sunny and formal, the other shady and more rustic. The sunny part of the garden was to be divided again into sixteen smaller compartments decorated with orange trees, fountains and flowering plants. He also wrote of the necessity of creating a private flower garden, or *giardino segreto*, where the cardinal's valuable plants would be safe, 'since no one will ever have any need to enter there for any other reason, nor without the gardener or the owners will one be able to do so, whereby the plants will remain secure'. Despite these very valid anxieties about security, Cardinal Barberini did allow a number of botanical scientists to work in the garden. Among this distinguished entourage was Giovanni Battista Ferrari, Jesuit priest, professor of Hebrew and Syriac at the new Jesuit Collegio Romano, where he also taught rhetoric and pursued his interest in humanism, oriental studies and, above all, botany. These diverse and demanding activities did not prevent Ferrari from becoming

LEFT *Mario Nuzzi's powerful sense of design, his use colour and of the contrast between light and shade made him the most successful flower painter in Rome.*

RIGHT *Johann Friedrich Greuter's engraving illustrating the sad tale of Bruco and Limace in Ferrari's Flora. Bruco is shown at the outset of his transformation into a slug.*

head gardener and chief horticultural advisor in the Orti Barberini, where he added greatly to the prestige of the garden by cultivating numerous new and exotic plants for the first time on Italian soil.

In 1633 Ferrari published *Flora de florum cultura*, the most influential florilegium of the seventeenth century. In 1638 an Italian translation was produced under the title of *Flora overo cultura dei fiori*, and dedicated to Francesco Barberini, who appears to have paid most of the production costs. Ferrari's book was one of a great wave of florilegia published in the seventeenth century. Unlike the herbals of the previous century, florilegia recorded plants that were of no practical use. Ferrari's *Flora* was the first book ever written about plants cultivated for purely ornamental purposes. Florilegia were often commissioned by aristocratic patrons intent on recording the contents of their plant collections for posterity, and they were read by collectors and amateurs. Ferrari's florilegium is divided into four books, and again into chapters written in a loose discursive style. He tackles every imaginable aspect of floriculture, from the choice of a garden guard dog (vigilant, sinewy, robust, a dog with no time for strangers and no ear for flattery), to the modification of flower colour, scent (a flower with an unpleasant scent is like a person with bad breath) and form. Ferrari leavens the informative tone of his text by inventing mythical stories about Flora, goddess of the garden. The most engaging of these is the sad story

LEFT *Cornelis Bloemart's copperplate engravings in Ferrari's* Flora *were executed from life. This is 'Gelsiminum indicum', one of the plants that Ferrari described growing in the Orti Barberini in Rome.*

RIGHT *Cornelis Bloemart's engraving of the fruit and a section of the fruit of a Chinese rose (*Hibiscus mutabilis L.*) in Ferrari's* Flora.

FAR RIGHT *The use of the microscope revolutionized botanical studies. This is Bloemart's engraving of the magnified seeds of the Chinese rose. To Ferrari's eye they resembled 'the kidneys of a baby goat'.*

of Bruco and Limace, which Ferrari inserts at the end of a solidly practical section on garden pests. Bruco and Limace are two gardeners in Flora's team, one too lazy to work and the other a thief. Flora loses her patience and transforms Limace into a slug and Bruco into a caterpillar. The story is illustrated with a powerful engraving of Flora standing over Limace, who has already grown a horrifying blunt head and eyes on stalks. In a minute Bruco's thieving hands will be replaced by 'a multitude of feet'.

Ferrari devoted the whole of the twenty-first chapter of Book Three to the plants in the Orti Barberini. The lengthy list includes several narcissi, cult plants in the seventeenth century, an 'Indian' yucca, jasmine – yellow and white – exceptionally large strawberries, Brazilian beans, acacia, hibiscus, Egyptian papyrus, the American coral tree, the tamarind and numerous bulbs and tubers. Many of these plants would have been bought at an exorbitant price, either from dealers, or directly from sailors, missionaries or explorers returning from long journeys to almost unimaginably distant lands. Although Ferrari was never invited to join the Lincei, it is clear from his plant descriptions that he has joined them in their search for a means of classifying the torrent of new plants pouring into Rome from the New World.

Some of the plants in the Orti Barberini may have been the first living example of their kind in Italy – or even Europe. It was vital that the florilegium should be illustrated with plates that did credit to their subject, revealing the exotic and wonderful beauty of form, flower or fruit. Francesco Barberini paid for the copperplate engravings that illustrate Ferrari's *Flora overo cultura dei fiori* himself. The beautiful plates depicting bulbs and flowering plants were the work of Cornelis Bloemaert, a Dutch artist resident in Rome. Some of them show only the flower, and others the whole plant with flowers or fruit. Each plant is labelled with a flowing banner inscribed with its Latin name. Six additional engravings illustrating the antics of Flora were made by Johann Friedrich Greuter, a favourite of the Barberini family, Claude Mellan and Anna Maria Vaiani, working from drawings by Guido Reni, Pietro da Cortona, Giovanni Lanfranco and Andrea Sacchi.

Although he acknowledges the beauty of the Gonzaga gardens in Mantua, the Farnese gardens in Parma and the 'flowering of Florence', Ferrari is in no doubt that Rome's gardens outshine all competitors. He dwells particularly on the Barberini gardens, but he also refers to Villa Borghese, where 'a wall embraces all the delights of the Hesperides', and the Borghese eagle takes the place of a dragon at their door.

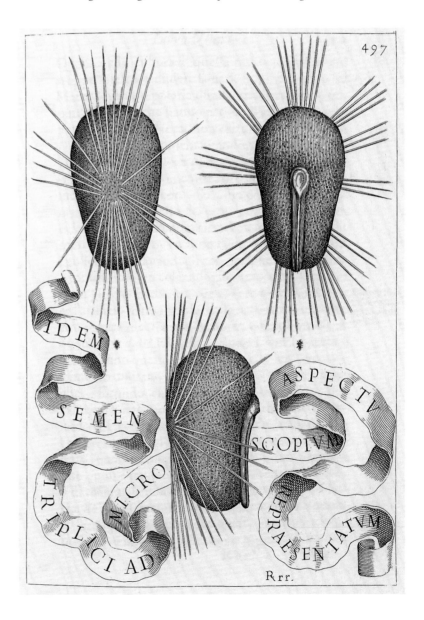

Villa Borghese, at the foot of the Pincian hill, was surrounded by a large park. The park was open to the public, and the Latin inscription of the *Lex Hortorum* read:

> I, custodian of Villa Borghese on the Pincio, proclaim the following: Whoever you are, if you are free, do not fear here the fetters of the law. Go where you wish, pluck what you wish, leave when you wish. These things are provided more for strangers than the owner…

Cardinal Scippione's invitation certainly did not extend to the *giardini segreti*, walled, private gardens that could be reached directly from the reception rooms of the villa. The villa has three secret gardens, the first two were built in about 1610 for Scipione Borghese. They were open-air drawing rooms, furnished with stone seats and decorated with classical statues, African marble wall fountains and a breathtaking display of fascinating flowers and bizarre citrus fruits. In 1650 Jacopo Manilli, keeper of the Borghese wardrobe, wrote a description of the garden that runs from the north-west façade of the villa, and has the wonderfully ornate façade of the aviary pavilion as its far boundary. This garden

was generally called the 'Giardino delle Cipolle' – or onion garden – a reference to the predominance of bulbs in the planting:

> The two long walls are covered in oranges and two small fountains… The garden is split into ten compartments, and these are divided once again, lengthways, and enclosed by low myrtle hedges. In each compartment six bitter orange trees are planted, and all around them are little squares filled with tulips, anemones, jonquils, hyacinths and other rare and wonderful flowers.

In 1700 Domenico Montelatici remarked that the garden was 'embellished still further' by 'eighty-eight stone pedestals [that] have been arranged along the paths, and the pots of lemons placed on them'.

Fifty years after the creation of the first two *giardini segreti*, a third garden was built by Giovan Battista Borghese beyond the aviary. The space had originally been used as a hen run, and the hen house was now converted into an elaborately decorated pavilion and renamed the Meridiana, a reference to the sundial on its façade. Giovan Battista Borghese was an ambitious plant collector, with a particular passion for tulips. The garden was cut into sections by four paths, and each section was then subdivided into forty-three compartments. The garden's most exciting feature was a plant theatre that ran the length of each side of the central axis. It consisted of four steps supported by beautifully carved balustrades and protected from sun and rain by an awning on a metal frame. The steps were used to display pots of scented bulbs as they came into season. Montelatici refers to anemones, hyacinths, tulips, carnations and 'other, rarer plants', and comments that 'their prettiness is equalled by the wonderful scent that fills the air'.

Giovanni Battista Ferrari's warmest praise is reserved for the garden of Duke Francesco Caetani in Cisterna, about seventy-two kilometres (forty miles) south of Rome. Caetani was governor of Milan and Viceroy of Sicily and, in Ferrari's view, he was 'as skilled a governor of flowers as of men'. In an unfinished manuscript about his garden Caetani revealed that he had contacts with plant dealers in Amsterdam, Constantinople, Paris, Avignon, Brussels, Frankfurt and Vienna, exposing the highly international character of seventeenth-century garden culture. His collection was made up almost exclusively of bulbs and tubers. He specialized in the cultivation of anemones, one of the most fashionable flowers of the seventeenth century, and for this part of his garden alone he achieved international fame. Nor was he immune to tulip fever, and by 1651, in a garden containing over 62,000 plants, he had 15,000 tulip bulbs. Ferrari admired this 'ingenious mixture' of plants, but seemed even more impressed by the style of the planting. Each compartment was planted with only two or three kinds of plant, compatible in both form and colour, so that the garden as a whole created a very harmonious impression. Pots were sunk at the centre of the larger compartments and planted with tuberoses. This arrangement enabled Caetani to give the tuberoses all the water they needed during the flowering season, without harming the other plants in the compartment.

LEFT *Ludovico Pozzoserrato's* View of a Villa *is an impression of* Villa Borghese, *where public access made the park a setting for a myriad of different amusements.*

RIGHT *The plan of Duke Francesco Caetani's garden at Sermoneta, which is described in great detail by Ferrari in* Flora ovvero cultura dei fiori.

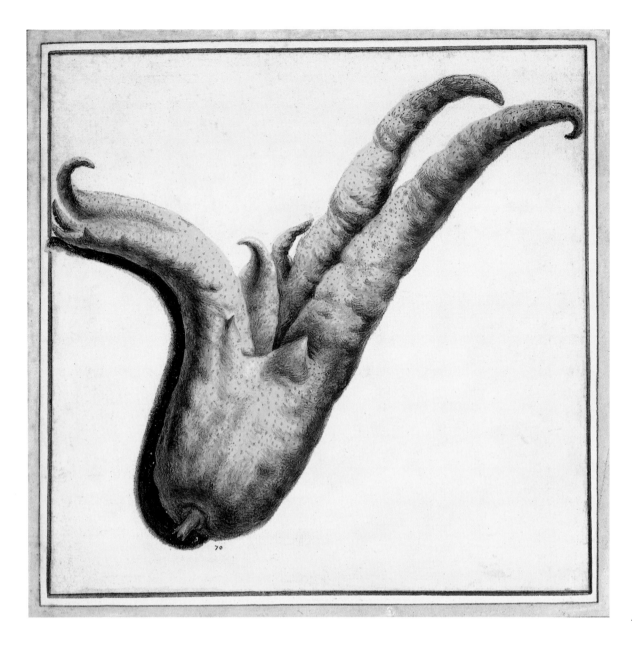

Ferrari paid a final compliment to Francesco Caetani by including a plan of his garden in his *Flora*, and there can be little doubt that he also used the Caetani garden as the inspiration for his own detailed instructions. He assures the reader that the result of careful planning and planting will be a garden with something blooming all year round, so that the 'ordered confusion of flowers will look like a tapestry, carpet, or beautifully embroidered cloth'.

The seventeenth century was marked by great enthusiasm for all things anomalous, bizarre or distorted. In the garden this translated into a fashion for flowers with double or otherwise surprising forms – crinkled petals perhaps, or unexpected colours. Giovanni Battista Ferrari devoted part of the fourth and final book of *Flora* to the artificial creation of 'marvels' in the garden, divulging 'secrets' that would persuade a plant to flower out of season, turn a flower an unnatural colour (blue, black or green), change its appearance (by giving it crinkled petals, for example), or improve its scent. Almost without exception, the first stage of these processes involved the creation of a solution of sheep droppings in vinegar. In order to produce black flowers, alder cones were dried, ground and added to the solution in a proportion of one to

three. This mixture was then poured into the pot or the hole in which the bulb was to be planted. If the bulb was watered and cultivated as usual, Ferrari assured his readers that it would produce sensational black flowers. Green flowers could be produced by adding the juice of rue to the solution, and blue with the addition of ground cornflowers. By pouring a strong scent, such as musk, into the same sheep-dropping-vinegar solution, Ferrari improved the scent of flowers. This was an important 'secret', for a poor scent, like bad breath, 'renders every other beauty insipid'. Ferrari also passes on the method for artificially creating flowers with highly desirable wrinked petals. All you have to do, he claims, is crush the seeds in a mortar before planting, 'for the petals of a flower from a crushed seed will be distorted as surely as water from a twisted pipe'.

Encouraged by the extraordinary success of *Flora*, Ferrari went on to publish a second book in 1646, this time devoted to the cultivation of citrus fruits of all kinds. *Hesperides, sive, De malorum aureorum cultura et usu* (On the cultivation and use of golden apples) was the longest book ever written on a subject that had become immensely popular in the second half of the sixteenth century. In the garden citrus trees could be espaliered against walls or trained over pergolas, but the collector's items were always grown in terracotta pots and displayed in prominent positions throughout the summer. In winter they were taken into the shelter of a *limonaia*, or lemon house. Certain kinds of lemon qualified as 'curiosities' on account of their strangely shaped fruits. They were known as *bizzarrie*, or 'bizarres' and were highly prized. Several of these specimens found their way into Cassiano dal Pozzo's Paper Museum, a vast collection of drawings, prints and watercolours that recorded classical artefacts and documented and classified the natural world, both at home and abroad. Paintings of monstrous or anomalous fruits were filed alongside other oddities, such as a picture of a dolphin brought to the fish market in Rome, the plant that grew out of a Spanish man's side in 1626, and a saw used to put martyrs to death. Many of the strange citrus fruits in Cassiano's collection had shapes reminiscent of parts of the human body. One of the most benign in this respect was the *Citrus medica digitata*, a thick-skinned citron bizarrely formed to resemble a human hand with far too many long tapering fingers. There were also oranges which had warty excrescences, or were 'pregnant' with a second fruit inside them.

There is a striking similarity between the bizarre fruits in the Paper Museum, and the illustrations in *Hesperides*, which has eighty-two engravings of oranges, lemons, citrons and limes and their varieties. Cassiano was a close friend and supporter of Ferrari, and it is likely that he invited Cornelis Bloemaert to make the engravings of fruit for *Hesperides* from drawings by Vincenzo Leonardi, the artist that he used to document many of the exhibits in his Paper Museum. Pietro da Cortona, Andrea Sacchi, Francesco Albani, Nicolas Poussin, Domenichino and Giovanni Lanfranco were also commissioned to produce the drawings that illustrate Ferrari's allegorical tales about the arrival of the different kinds of citrus fruits in Italy, and these were made into fine engravings. Ferrari also listed the tools needed for the successful cultivation of citrus fruits and, once again, these are beautifully illustrated and labelled with flowing banners. He gives descriptions, plans and sections of several *limonaie*. These include the wooden housing built over the Duke of Parma's orange grove on the Palatine hill, the orangery at Villa Aldobrandini, and the protective roof erected each winter over Cardinal Carlo Pio's orange pergola in Rome.

Plant collecting had reached a crescendo in the middle of the seventeenth century. A long period of diminished enthusiasm followed during the late seventeenth and eighteenth centuries. It was not until the nineteenth century, when a huge influx of new plants reached Europe, that horticulture became fashionable once again.

VIII | Watering the guests
Garden entertainments 1530-1850

TODY THE RENAISSANCE or baroque garden is an empty stage. The set may be intact and, provided the trees have not grown too tall, the lighting will still work. However the stage is bereft of the actors who brought it to life with their parties, plays, concerts, banquets, games and other light-hearted amusements. Fortunately these activities are well documented in visual and written sources, and sometimes preserved in the structure of the garden itself. Drawing on this evidence, it is possible to visualise the garden as it was intended to be seen – the setting for any number of entertainments and a focus for social and cultural life.

The garden played a crucial role in *villeggiatura* – a revival of the ancient Roman tradition of abandoning the city to the summer heat and withdrawing to the country – and in the concept of *otium* (see Chapters 1 and 6). It was a sculpture gallery, a museum, a menagerie, a laboratory, a theatre, a concert hall and a dining room. It offered opportunities for strenuous exercise and encouraged absolute indolence. Plato had made the garden into the accepted venue for philosophical discussion among friends, but an equally potent tradition associated it with private meetings between lovers. It satisfied the senses with the beauty of its structure, the sound of birdsong and falling water and the scent of flowers, and it engaged the mind with the iconography of its statues and fountains.

Exercise was a vital component of the complex condition of *otium*. In 1443 Leon Battista Alberti, author of the first Renaissance treatise on architecture, wrote a slim work on domestic life called *Della famiglia*. In it he warned of the dangers of indolence:

Through inactivity the veins become filled up with phlegm, becoming waterlogged and flaccid, and the stomach becomes finicky, the nerves dull and the whole body sluggish and drowsy; and furthermore with undue laziness the mind gets clouded and dim, and every spiritual force becomes stagnant and feeble.

LEFT *Music added another layer to the sensual experience of garden visitors. This is Ludovico Pozzoserrato's* Concert at the Villa.

ABOVE Giochi d'acqua, *or water jokes, featured in many of Venturini's engravings for* La Fontane di Roma *(c.1675) by Falda.*

787

The benefit of country air was also understood, and clearly explained by Antonio Guevara in his *Il dispregio della corte, e lode della villa* (Contempt for courtly life and praise for the villa, 1601):

> It is the privilege of those who stay at country houses to live in better health, with less illness, which does not turn out thus in cities, where, since the dwellings are high and rooms bleak, and the streets dark, the air gets infected more rapidly, and people fall ill frequently.

As well as contributing to health and wellbeing, *villeggiatura* had the additional purpose of giving the landowner an opportunity to supervise the harvesting of his crops. However, if Filippo in Carlo Goldoni's comedy *Le Smanie per la villeggiatura* (1761) is to be believed, *villeggiatura* gradually evolved to become an end in itself, devoid of any practical purpose. Filippo comments that in his youth everyone would return to the city as soon as the grapes were harvested and the wine made. 'In those days', he says, 'one went to make the wine, but now one goes for fun and stays until the cold weather sets in and the leaves turn on the trees'. By the eighteenth century much of this 'fun' was derived from card playing, but the garden, with its green theatre, labyrinth and bowling alley (along with the water tricks, treehouses and grottoes seen in previous chapters) continued to be a great source of entertainment.

During the sixteenth century free time in the country was inevitably occupied by a good deal of hunting. The villa and garden were often set within a *barco* or hunting park stocked with game. Although canon law had forbidden the clergy to hunt since the twelfth century, the park surrounding the Villa Borghese and its gardens in Rome was enclosed by two miles of wall and stocked with roebuck, fallow deer, ducks, hares, peacocks and stags. Similar creatures inhabited Cardinal

ABOVE *Ludovico Pozzoserrato's Labyrinth of Love is a wonderful image of the garden 'stage' occupied by innumerable players engaged in a variety of different activities.*

RIGHT *Sebastien Vrancx depicts food, music and love among the attractions of the Duke of Mantua's garden.*

OVERLEAF *In Antonio Visentini's Concert at the Villa the garden is the theatrical setting for an informal concert.*

Gambara's park surrounding the Villa Lante at Bagnaia. Other villas, like Cetinale in Tuscany for example, were surrounded by wooded hills that continued to be rich in game long after the Roman Campagna had become too tame, cultivated and over populated to shelter anything much larger than a rabbit. It is no coincidence that Cardinal Flavio Chigi chose Saint Eustace as the patron saint of his chapel in the *giardino segreto* at Cetinale (see Chapter 6). Flavio Chigi was another hunting cardinal and St Eustace was the patron saint of the chase.

Although full-scale hunts were confined to the park, smaller events were staged within the garden enclosure. These miniature hunts were theatrical performances timed to entertain the guests at the end of a garden banquet. The spectators were invited to sit in a raised pavilion or loggia and watch as professional huntsmen and their dogs slaughtered hares, rabbits, herons, ducks and other innocuous creatures. This practice is imprinted upon the structure of gardens such as Castello or Boboli in Florence, where groves of fruit and berry-bearing trees were planted to feed and shelter small game.

When the English traveller Fynes Moryson visited Italy at the beginning of the seventeenth century he commented on the importance of birding, which had replaced hunting as the most popular outdoor sport. Birding was the ideal sport for the garden. The tiny song birds that were its prey did little damage to the plants, and the *ragnaia*, or fowling grove, could be incorporated into the layout. Birding was particularly popular in Tuscany. The Medici gardens of Boboli, Castello and Villa Medici in Fiesole all had fowling groves, as did the smaller and more private gardens of Villa Geggiano and Villa de' Gori near Siena.

Birds could be lured to a garden by food and fresh water. In 1619 Cosimo II de' Medici commissioned Romolo Ferrucci del Tadda to build a water chain among the trees of the *ragnaia* at Boboli. Del Tadda responded to the commission by designing a series of monstrous water-spouting faces.

A *ragnaia* consisted of stands of trees divided by broad *viali* or avenues. Fine nets were suspended from poles across the avenues. The birds – mostly garden warblers, thrushes and sparrows – were scared out of the trees by the hunters who then drove them into the nets, where they became entangled and could easily be picked off and sent to the kitchen. Another form of fowling grove was known as a *frasconaia* and used mainly for catching finches. Two nets were stretched over rectangular frames at the centre of a circular clearing. The frames were lent against each other to make a tent shape and then concealed with leafy branches (*frasche*). Decoy birds were tied to the branches and, as soon as they lured other birds inside, the fowler collapsed the net by pulling a cord. Hides were built close to the nets as birding was a very popular spectator sport. Another variation was birding at night, when screech owls might be employed to flush out smaller birds, or a covered lantern used to dazzle blackbirds, wood pigeons or thrushes so that they could be lifted off their nests.

Although hunting on horseback was generally confined to the park, horses were not entirely excluded from the garden. In *De re aedificatoria* (1453), Leon Battista Alberti recommended the creation of 'a large open area for chariot and horse races, its dimensions greater than a young man could hurl a javelin or fire an arrow'. This feature, which was undoubtedly inspired by the Pliny the Younger's description of the hippodrome in his own garden, translated in the Renaissance and baroque garden as an open space in front of the house, overlooked by the windows and balconies of the *piano nobile*. The area served as a *manège* for schooling horses and a venue for numerous equestrian games, archery, javelin throwing and other entertainments. In *Villa civile, da Re, da duce, et da potente signore* (A respectable villa for kings, dukes or powerful gentlemen) Antonfrancesco Doni describes a royal villa with a loggia overlooking a large open space where local peasants were assembled to engage in wrestling contests, horse races, football games and tilting matches for the amusement of the family and their friends.

In the eighteenth century, over 200 years after the publication of Alberti's text, Francesco Muttoni incorporated an unusual raised or 'hanging' *manège* into his complex design for the gardens of Villa Trissino near Verona. Muttoni had been commissioned to redesign the villa and create a garden on the steep site in 1722. The area outside the villa was dominated by an outcrop of rock that was much too large to break up or move. Muttoni ingeniously resolved the problem by using the rock as the foundation for the 'hanging' *manège* that he built at the same level as the *piano nobile* of the villa. The space between the villa and the retaining wall of the *manège* became a walled garden. He then linked the *manège* to the *piano nobile* with a path along the top of the wall enclosing the garden. Horses reached their schooling ground from the lower garden by going up an ingenious enclosed ramp. For humans the descent to the lower garden was via a spiral staircase inside a minaret.

During the sixteenth-century the revival of chivalry, reflected in the epic poetry of Ludovico Ariosto and Torquato Tasso, had brought new popularity to jousting, tilting and tournaments, providing entertainment for both participants and spectators. The stone amphitheatre built between 1631 and 1634 by Giulio Parigi in the Boboli Gardens was designed to accommodate equestrian events on a grand baroque scale. Equestrian ballet – which perhaps translates better as 'dressage' to the modern ear – was popular among the ancient Romans. It was revived largely by the Medici, who built it into every festival from 1600 onwards.

Comparía del Ser.mo Principe di Tofcana Figuran Ercole Accompa.to dai Carri del Sole e della Luna e seguito de Caualieri d'Europa America Afia ed Affrica Nella Festa a Cauallo Rapprel Per le Reali Noze dell A. SS.me
Il Sig.r Alessandro Carducci In.tor del Ballo e Banog   Nel Teatro Congiunto Al P.lazzo   Del Ser G.D.   Fran.co Tacca Ing.tor

The first great event to be staged in the amphitheatre was the last in a long series of celebrations for the marriage of Ferdinand II de' Medici to Vittoria della Rovere, Princess of Urbino.

The performance took place after dark on 15 July 1637. It was built loosely upon the story of Armida, the wicked enchantress in Torquato Tasso's *Gerusalemme liberata*, but it was not this familiar story that aroused the admiration of the audience. Eyewitness accounts evoke a spectacle so rich that it banished the memory of all the other wedding celebrations. Although darkness had fallen, the stage was dazzlingly illuminated by torchlight reflected and intensified by a tin lining attached to the wall of the amphitheatre. The horses, their heads decked with brightly coloured plumes, moved in perfect formation, sometimes at a stately walk and sometimes a controlled canter, the sequence of their movements choreographed by Agniolo Ricci. The riders' elaborate costumes were made from rich and intensely coloured cloth, and several of them wore silver surcoats that would have appeared almost incandescent by torchlight. Armida, also fabulously dressed, appeared on a float pulled by four elephants, preceded by ten trumpeters on horseback and flanked by a hundred torchbearers. Her float was an ingenious machine designed by Felice Gamberai. After she had sung to the bride and groom, Armida worked her magic and the float was divided in half. The lower part of it became her chariot and the upper part, now detached, became a terrible mountain, complete with a fire-belching cave that was inhabited by a monstrous snake. All the different elements of the performance were brought together under the direction of Ferdinando Saracinelli to create, according to eyewitness accounts, an experience that wiped the mind clean of all that had gone before and lodged itself in the memory forever. The extravagant sets, ingenious machinery and lavish costumes of Saracinelli's *festa a cavallo* left the audience awestruck and mystified, unsure whether the scenes that they had witnessed were the product of machinery or magic. The inspiration for the performance was classical, and yet the audience reaction was a perfect realization of the aims of baroque theatre.

The Medici family traditionally took inspiration for their lavish entertainments from ancient Rome. In 1589 the garden courtyard of the Pitti Palace had been the setting for a classically inspired *naumachia*,

ABOVE Il Mondo Festeggiante (1661) was an 'equestrian ballet' staged to celebrate the marriage of the future Cosimo III de' Medici to Margherita Luisa d'Orleans.

RIGHT The garden courtyard of the Pitti Palace flooded and packed with miniature warships during the naumachia that was staged in 1589.

or mock sea battle, and once again the eyewitness accounts are very detailed and evocative. The courtyard was covered with sailcloth and seats were arranged on the balconies of the first floor and in tiers under the ground floor loggia. When two sluice gates were opened, the courtyard filled with water to a depth of two metres. The guests had no idea what was happening and several of them had to be prevented from running away. Suddenly – and as always 'suddenness' was the vital element – warships began to sail into the courtyard from all directions. The majority of the ships were Christian and the others Turkish. The Turks defended a castle that had been erected at the garden end of the courtyard and six Christian ships were seen to overcome four of the Turkish fleet. The air was filled with terrible trumpeting, battle cries and screams from the wounded Turks. The water seethed with bodies and wreckage. As a finale, the Christians set fire to a Turkish frigate, conquered the castle and raised their flag over its walls. As soon the battle was over the galleys disappeared, the courtyard was drained and dried with sawdust in preparation for the next event.

The garden was the ideal venue for performances on this grand scale. On 15 August 1668 Flavio Chigi invited his friends to a spectacular performance in the garden of his palace at Quattro Fontane in Rome. Chigi was an intriguing character. A cardinal at the age of seventeen, he was sent by his uncle Pope Alexander VII to the court of Louis XIV in 1664. At Versailles he witnessed theatrical events so inspiring that he braved Vatican disapproval to become one of Rome's leading impresarios, and the founder and patron of several theatrical academies. He built theatres in every villa and palace he owned. At Cetinale, his villa in Tuscany, Carlo Fontana included a brick-built theatre in the layout of the garden (see Chapter 6). Fontana was the Chigi family architect, but he was also drawn into Flavio's theatrical world as a designer of sets, costumes and machinery.

The performance in Chigi's Roman garden in August 1668 was designed entirely by Fontana, who transformed the garden into the set for an extraordinary play, a party within a party, with guests as actors. The event was so successful that Fontana was commissioned to write a description of the evening and make a set of engravings to accompany it. The commission came from the friends who had failed to attend and then been driven wild by the gossip and reverie that followed the performance. According to Fontana's description, the guests were

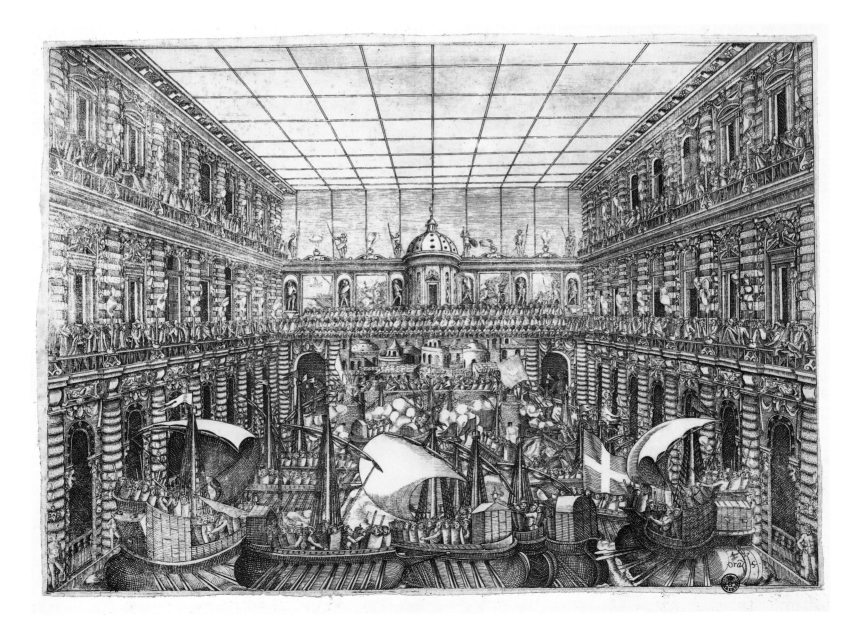

invited to arrive in the garden at dusk. Torches had already been lit, creating a mysterious atmosphere. The garden itself seemed strangely altered. A grove of mature trees had sprung up, and among them the guests could make out pretty fountains and grassy slopes. They found some chairs in a clearing and sat down. Suddenly Flavio Chigi's old gardener appeared, a man that many of them had known by sight for years. He seemed very flustered and he began to tell them, in verse, that they had arrived too early, that nothing was ready, and that all he could offer them for dinner was the simple snack that he had brought for his own tea. Then their attention was caught by the appearance of the real actors, Bacchus, Flora and Pomona, among the trees. They may have been distracted, but how could they have missed the arrival of two massive dressers, one laden with exotic food, all of it elaborately sculpted from sugar, and the other with jugs, bowls, goblets and even fountains of wine? And now two tables appeared, as if by magic, spread with embroidered cloths and laid with the finest silver and glass. By this time the guests were on their feet, astounded by the open air dining room that had materialized around them. It finished as suddenly as it

had begun. There was a clap of thunder and then the air was filled with a storm of confetti and rose water. They may have been invited to dinner, but there was no question of food or drink. Everyone went home hungry, thirsty and completely satisfied.

Flavio Chigi's garden theatre at Cetinale stands at the end of the *viale* on the northern side of the house, close to the original entrance from the old road to Siena. The semicircular stage is enclosed by brick walls that were originally decorated with classical busts. During the *villeggiatura* season Flavio would stage comedies at Cetinale that had already been performed in his palace in Rome, or at the Palazzo Chigi

ABOVE *The Obizzi family, owners of Villa Cataio in the Veneto, played an important part in Venice's victory over the Turks at the Battle of Lepanto. Thereafter, this courtyard was regularly flooded and used as the setting for* naumachie *that recreated their finest moment.*

TOP RIGHT *This engraving, after Carlo Fontana's design, shows the tables and dressers that appeared, as if by magic, during the extraordinary performance in Flavio Chigi's garden.*

BELOW RIGHT *The simple enclosure of Cetinale's open-air theatre.*

Carolus Fontana inven. delin.

Theresia de' Po sculp.

in Ariccia. Fontana's brick-built theatre was quite unusual in the seventeenth century, when *teatri di verzura* or 'green theatres' were just becoming fashionable. Several examples of green theatres fashioned from clipped box, cypress or yew still survive. At Villa Reale (originally the Villa Orsetti), near Lucca, the stage and auditorium are enclosed by yew hedges of an enormous height. The footlights, orchestra pit and prompter's box are all cut from box or yew. Niches cut in the yew backdrop are furnished with life-size, terracotta statues of stock characters from the *commedia dell'arte*, light-hearted, informal plays that were perfectly suited to a garden setting.

In 1806 Villa Reale was subject to compulsory purchase by Napoleon, who gave it to his sister, Elisa Bonaparte. In 1809 Tuscany was annexed to France and Elisa was named Grand Duchess. It was at this moment that Villa Reale (the 'royal' villa) got its name and became the seat of Elisa's court. Count Felice Bacchiocchi, Elisa's Corsican husband, became commander of the tiny Luccan army and Niccolò Paganini was appointed royal director of music. During that brief and glamorous period of Villa Reale's history, it is said that Paganini gave regular concerts in the green theatre.

The *teatro di verzura* at Villa Geggiano, near Siena, was built during the renovation of villa and garden prior to an important wedding in 1768 between Anton Domenico Bianchi Bandinelli, whose family owned Geggiano, and Cecilia, a daughter of the powerful Chigi Zondadari family. Their two coats of arms decorate the brick-built, baroque arches that flank the stage of the garden theatre. Niches in the side wall of each arch contain statues of Tragedy and Comedy by Blosio, a Maltese sculptor. The stage is a raised semicircular lawn enclosed by clipped hedges that form a backdrop and flats. Vittorio Alfieri, the Piedmontese playwright, was a close friend of the family, and such a frequent visitor to Geggiano that an early nineteenth-century inventory refers to an exquisitely decorated bedroom on the first floor as 'Count Alfieri's room'. In his *Rime* Alfieri makes a specific reference to the entrance hall of the villa, a wonderful barrel vaulted room. Ignazio Moder, an itinerant artist from Austria, was commissioned to decorate the villa before the wedding, creating the happy carefree atmosphere appropriate to the summer villa of a fashionable young couple. He painted the hall with bucolic scenes to represent every month of the year. Among these rural figures is an elderly man traditionally described as Perellino, the popular eighteenth-century musician. He is shown eating a songbird – perhaps caught in Geggiano's own *ragnaia*. His three actress daughters stand at his side. There is no archival evidence to prove that Alfieri staged his plays in Geggiano's *teatro di verzura*, but the playwright's frequent visits and the presence of the Perellino sisters among Moder's paintings suggest that this was the case.

LEFT *Signor Perellino and his three, actress daughters who may have graced the stage in the garden of Villa Geggiano, Tuscany.*

RIGHT *The auditorium of Trezza's green theatre at Villa Rizzardi. The theatre was probably used to stage light-hearted entertainments by local playwrights such as Carlo Goldoni.*

One of the largest green theatres in Italy belongs to Villa Rizzardi near Verona (see page 177). The garden was laid out in 1783 by Luigi Trezza, whose plan of the theatre was labelled 'teatro a similitudine degli antichi' – a theatre built to the classical model. It is said that Trezza spent many months studying the acoustics of the site before choosing a position for the theatre on the garden boundary. A beech hedge encloses the stage and auditorium, and niches cut in the hedge contain statues by Pietro Muttoni. The raised stage is twenty-seven metres (85 foot) wide, with a beech backdrop and flats. The space between the flats and the encircling hedge was designed as dressing rooms for the actors. The auditorium of Trezza's green theatre must be the largest in Italy, but the seven ranks of raked seats were never intended for use. The audience found much more comfortable accommodation on sofas dragged out from the villa and arranged on the flat ground immediately below the stage.

During the hot Italian summer the garden became an open-air dining room. In *La nuova vaga e dilettevole villa* (1559) Giuseppe Falcone celebrates the informality of eating outside:

> In your villa you eat what is at hand – dry bread seems cake – at any time you please, and as much as suits you, outside under the pergola or under the loggia of the portico, or in the open air, or in the kitchen garden, or the ornamental garden, or at the fountain…

During the golden days of Pope Leo X's reign (1513-21) the gardens of Rome became the venue for meetings between groups of scholars, poets and artists. The business of these garden academies was traditionally conducted over a meal. The most famous academy under Leo X met in Johannes Goritz's garden, a simple citrus grove overlooking Trajan's Forum, where ancient statues, inscriptions and sarcophagi were scattered among the trees. Jacopo Sadoleto, Pietro Bembo and

Baldassare Castiglione were all members of Goritz's academy, and after the terrible Sack of Rome in 1527 Sadoleto looked back on their meetings as the happiest time of his life. In 1529 he wrote a nostalgic and evocative letter to Goritz (or Coricio, as he was known to his humanist friends) from Carpentras, where he was bishop:

> Oh if I think again of times past, when so many of us used to gather together, and our age was much more readily disposed to hilarity than today. How many times those meetings and suppers that we held so often return to my mind. When in your garden outside the walls, or in mine on the Quirinal, or at the Circus Massimus, or on the banks of the Tiber, in the Temple of Hercules, or elsewhere, we held those reunions of gifted and respected men... where after our homely banquets, flavoured more with wit than gluttony, we recited poetry and declaimed orations, among our friends Fera, Beroaldo, Porzio, Capello, Donato and Coricio; now as I write all dead.

Every year Goritz celebrated the Feast of St Ann on 26 July with a reading of specially commissioned poems by Rome's leading writers. Once again a garden banquet formed an important part of the proceedings. In 1524 the poems written for the feast day were published in a book called *Coriciana*. The collection includes an endearing eyewitness account of Goritz, the 'happy host' who 'runs here and there among the tables and fills cups of wine with liberal hand, arousing raucous laughter'.

The plays and concerts performed in the garden theatre and the banquets served beneath the loggia or arbour were an irregular source of entertainment. The garden offered other more enduring amusements. *Giochi d'acqua*, or water tricks, rediscovered during the Renaissance, provided a reliable form of entertainment that lost none of its popularity in the baroque garden. Some of the finest examples of hydraulic engineering and *giochi d'acqua* were to be found at Villa Aldobrandini (see Chapter 6), where the rooms at either end of the

LEFT *A classical figure glows against the foil of the trees at Villa Rizzardi.*

RIGHT *In Benedetto Caliari's sixteenth-century painting of a Venetian garden, the cool shade of the loggia made an ideal setting for a meal. The water in the foreground cools the air, and offers the ladies of the house ample opportunity for entertainment.*

water theatre had been decorated between 1615 and 1621. The room on the left-hand side became the family chapel, while the one to the right was transformed into a hall of wonders known as the Temple to Apollo and the Muses. Mount Parnassus was constructed at one end of the room, complete with Pegasus and wooden automata of Apollo and the nine Muses designed by Giovanni Guglielmi, an organ master employed at the villa between 1617 and 1621. Guglielmi built a water organ and installed it beneath the hill. All of his wooden figures appeared to be playing musical instruments, but their music was actually generated by the water organ. The other great wonder in the room was a spinning copper ball suspended just above the floor, an effect that greatly impressed the English traveller John Raymond:

> Underneath this hill are Organs, which plaid divers tunes so distinctly, that we conceive'd some Master was playing on them, but looking we saw they went of themselves, the cause of all this wee afterwards saw; In the midst of the roome, there being a Hole out of which winde issueth so violently, that for halfe a quarter of an houre it beares up a Ball…

The water from the theatre entered the chamber of the organ with such force that the air in the chamber was forced into the organ pipes, making them play, and also into the channel beneath the ball, so that it remained suspended on air as long as the organ played.

Elsewhere, the garden was peppered with *giochi d'acqua*. The victims of these tricks unwillingly staged an impromptu performance perfectly attuned to their companions' seventeenth-century sense of humour. Little had changed by the mid-eighteenth century, when French historian President Charles de Brosses visited Frascati with a group of young companions. His description gives a marvellous sense of the physicality of visiting a baroque garden that was still functioning as its architect intended. Their day began at Villa Mondragone:

> …around a polypriapic pool, where the edge of the basin is fitted all round with hosepipes, made from leather, and with copper nozzles at the end. These pipes were lying there, idle and innocent, when – after the tap had been turned on – these fine creatures began to stand up in the oddest way, and, as Rabelais says, began to piss fresh water non-stop. Migieu grabbed one of these weapons and squirted it straight in Lacurne's face; he shot back, and we all joined in this excellent sport, and went on for half an hour until we were drenched to the skin. You'd think winter was not the best season for this little game, but the day was so mild and fine that we couldn't resist the temptation.

LEFT *The lemon garden of Villa Rospigliosi on the Esquiline Hill in Rome depicted as the setting for a* *riotous party to mark the end of the grape harvest.*

De Brosses and his friends returned to their inn for a change of clothes, and then set off for Villa Aldobrandini for more sport:

> …we were sitting behaving ourselves, by the Belvedere of the Villa Aldobrandini…and didn't notice a hundred, treacherous little pipes distributed between the joints of the stones, when suddenly they went off in jets all over us. Well, we had no dry clothes left after the games at Mondragone, and so we plunged boldly into the wettest corners of the place, where we spent the rest of the evening playing the same sort of tricks. There is an especially good little curving stairway where, as soon as you are part way up, the water jets shoot out, criss-crossing in every direction, from above, from below, and the sides. At the top of these steps we got our revenge on Legouz, who had been responsible for our wetting by the Belvedere. He had intended to turn on a tap to squirt water at us, but the tap was designed to trick the tricker. It shot out a torrent of water, thick as your arm, and with ferocious force, straight into Legouz's stomach. Legouz bolted off, his trousers full of water, guttering down into his shoes.

LEFT *Mount Parnassus in the Temple to Apollo at Villa Aldobrandini. Wooden automata people Mount Parnassus at the end of the room. The figures in the foreground are gathered around the spinning copper ball suspended in mid air.*

RIGHT *A victim is chased down the 'especially good little curving stairway' at Villa Aldobrandini by jets of water.*

We all fell over with laughing, and that was enough. But the end wasn't as funny as it had been in the morning. We had to stay in with nothing to wear but our dressing gowns, eating a vile supper, while they dried our clothes.

Gardens also had a much more serious, didactic function. By the seventeenth century many of them were used as showcases for the living portion of a collection of curiosities (see Chapter 7). These collections, or private museums, were compendia of carefully catalogued exhibits drawn from sea, earth – both above and below the ground – and sky. The rare or exotic plants in the *giardino segreto* formed an important part of the collection, but animals, birds and fish were also included among the living exhibits (see Chapter 4 for the fish pools at Villa d'Este). The inspiration for garden menageries, aviaries and fish pools came from ancient Rome, but they were also an expression of a much more general and academic interest in natural history. Particularly fierce or precious animals were caged, and others were allowed to wander freely in the park. Animals and birds brought back to Italy from abroad by merchants, missionaries, diplomats and explorers found their way into the collections of aristocratic patrons. Before long the garden menagerie began to house creatures unrecorded by Aristotle in *On the animals,* or Pliny the Elder in his encyclopaedia of natural history, and this provoked a reassessment of the ancient wisdom that had always formed the basis of scientific thought. Some of the creatures in the menageries of powerful political families were sent as diplomatic gifts. The Medici were particularly favoured in this respect. Lorenzo the Magnificent was given a giraffe and a dromedary by the Sultan of Egypt in 1487, and in 1514 Leo X received Hanno the elephant from the King of Portugal. Under Ferdinand I de' Medici, the garden of the family villa in Rome was home to bears, ostriches, lions and tigers.

In 1603 the Academy dei Lincei was formed in Rome with the aim of studying every aspect of natural history (see Chapter 7). In 1622 Giovan Pietro Olina was invited to join the academy on the strength of a treatise on birds and garden aviaries. Much of his research was done in the aviary of Villa Borghese in Rome. The treatise was entitled *Uccelliera, overo discorso della natura e proprietà di diversi uccelli, e in particolare di que'*

che cantano, con il modo di prendergli, conoscergli, allevargli e mantenerli… (The aviary, or a discussion of the nature and habits of various birds, particularly songbirds, and how to obtain them, know them, breed them and look after them…), and in it he defined the importance of both the menagerie and the aviary in the princely garden:

> The keeping of a variety of animals, and in particular of birds, is one of those things that can give great pleasure while communicating a certain degree of magnificence and splendour. Few princes fail to include an aviary among the delights of their gardens. The birds are amusing, watching them is an excellent pastime and the contribution made by the aviary to the palace table is far from trivial.

LEFT *Vernet's mid-eighteenth century painting depicts the garden of Villa Ludovisi in Rome, where unsuspecting female visitors are the new victims of the giochi d'acqua. They are shown in the aftermath of the attack, trying to wring the water from their heavy silks.*

BELOW *A cabinet of curiosities belonging to Venetian collector Luigi Vendramin. Most of the exhibits were antiquities or vases from southern Italy, and they were displayed in this tailor-made wooden case.*

John Evelyn describes a large aviary at Palazzo Doria in Genoa:

> where in grow trees of more than 2 foot in diameter, beside Cypresse, Myrtils, Lentiscs & other rare shrubs, which serve to nestle and pearch all sorts of birds, who have ayre, & place enough under their wyrie Canopy, supported by huge Iron Worke very stupendious to consider, both as to the fabrick & the Charge.

However, it was Villa Borghese that had the largest and most elaborate aviary of the seventeenth century. It was built between 1617 and 1618 for Cardinal Scipione Borghese, and has recently been beautifully restored. Cardinal Borghese's magnificent collection of rare and exotic birds was housed in two large rectangular rooms joined by an elaborately carved tympanum. The ceiling of each room, or cage, opens into a large wire-clad cupola. The covered corridor between the rooms has wire sides. This allowed the cardinal and his friends to observe the birds from close quarters as they flew about, fed or drank from two pretty fountains. Annibale Durante was commissioned to decorate the walls with frescoes. He created an elaborate *trompe l'oiel* trellis on the

ceiling and set it against an infinite blue sky. Durante used specimens from the cardinal's own collection as models for the birds that perch elegantly on the arabesques and finials of the trellis and fly high up against the azure sky. Durante decorated the walls with rural landscapes in different lights and seasons of the year.

Sport was another ongoing source of entertainment. By the seventeenth century it was common for a bowling alley to be incorporated into the design of the garden. In its earliest form bowls, or *boccie*, was played with stones tossed at a target. The stones were gradually replaced by wooden and then metal bowls. This transition may not have been universal, however, for at Villa della Torre near Verona the bowling alley is still equipped with stone bowls (see Chapter 5). Giovanni Battista Falda's engraving of Villa Doria Pamphilli in Rome marks an 'alley for the game of Pall-Mall'. This crude form of croquet originated in France and became very popular in Italy at the beginning of the seventeenth century. At Villa Gamberaia, outside Florence, the long grass bowling alley is enclosed on one side by the retaining wall of the lemon garden and on the other by the villa and chapel. This enclosed space could have been used for ball games of all kinds.

The complexity of Italian garden design and the great variety of spectacles and entertainments made some contemporary visitors feel that they were visiting a series of different gardens. Sir Henry Wotton, the English traveller, diplomat and poet, described this sensation in his *Elements of Architecture*, published in 1624:

> … the Beholder descending many steps, was afterwards conveyed again by several *mountings* and *valings*, to various entertainments of his *sent* and *sight*: which I shall not need to describe (for that were poetical) let me only note this, that every one of these diversities, was as if he had bin Magically transported into a new *Garden*.

The seventeenth century saw the garden beginning to lose some of its intellectual significance. However the reactions of travellers like Sir Henry Wotton show that it had lost none of its power to entertain.

LEFT *The fish pools in the Renaissance garden at Villa Cicogna (Lombardy) are very decorative. However, they once served a practical purpose as stew ponds, providing fish to supplement the household diet.*

RIGHT *A fresco of classical ruins forms an evocative backdrop for the aviary at Villa Corsi Salviati in Florence.*

IX | Foreign influence
English and French style 1696-1783

IN 1679 ANDRÉ LE NÔTRE made the long journey from Paris to Rome. By this time Le Nôtre was a grand old man. Throughout northern Europe his gardens were perceived as the most effective and intrinsically modern expression of wealth and power, and they had already been imitated by the courts of Sweden, Holland, Germany and England, where France had replaced Italy as the inspiration for garden design. Italy was not so quick to bow to foreign influence. When Le Nôtre made his journey in 1679 the Italian baroque was still vigorous and spawning new gardens. Perhaps this was at the root of his withering remark regarding Italian garden design, recorded by Claude Desgots, his great- nephew and companion in Rome. According to Desgots, Le Nôtre said that the Italians had 'no taste in gardens that can approach ours, and they do not know how to make them'. It was certainly true that they had not yet begun to imitate the great open spaces and radiating vistas that defined his own style.

By the early eighteenth century views of Le Nôtre's landscapes at Marly, Chantilly, Versailles and Vaux-le-Vicomte were in general circulation, and Dezaillier d'Argenville's *La théorie et la pratique du jardinage* (1709), in which many of Le Nôtre's designs were codified, had also reached Italy. Now the appeal of French landscape design began to be felt, and during the first half of the eighteenth century the Bourbon king in Naples, the Duke of Savoy in Piedmont and the Doge in the Veneto all commissioned important garden landscapes loosely modelled on the French style. The fashionable 'Frenchness' of these gardens was manifest both in their overall layout and in smaller details, such as the use of wooden Versailles boxes for growing lemons instead of the traditional terracotta pots. The French influence spawned geometrically designed gardens on a much larger scale than even the grandest baroque designs, and in most cases the traditional single axis of the baroque garden was exchanged for Le Nôtre's multiple radiating avenues of deciduous trees across a landscape that was open and uncluttered. Traditional geometrically arranged parterre beds were replaced by the arching arabesques of the French broderie parterre.

Piedmont's geographical position and the political ambitions of the House of Savoy had always laid the kingdom open to foreign influence – particularly from France. Duke Vittorio Amadeo II of Savoy had an ambassador in Paris, and it was by this route that he approached Le Nôtre. His commission was accepted in 1696, despite the fact that France and Piedmont were at war. No real progress could be made until the Treaty of Ryswick was signed in 1697, when Le Nôtre drew up plans for the area between the royal palace (Palazzo Reale) and the city walls of Turin. However, at the age of eighty-five, he chose to avoid the long journey from Paris to Turin by appointing his pupil, De Marne, to realize his plans. De Marne arrived in Turin in October 1697. He was certainly capable of implementing his master's plans, but as a mark of respect he chose to refer any difficulties directly to Le Nôtre. He returned to Paris for the first time in December 1697, and continued to travel backwards and forwards for the next six months.

The garden of Palazzo Reale was completed in 1702, two years after Le Nôtre's death. The site had been divided into three distinct areas, each with its own vista. The first was to the north of the royal palace, immediately in front of the gateway to the inner courtyard. Here Le Nôtre designed long rose beds interspersed with rows of pots. Lime and plane trees were planted to mark the garden boundary. The second area lay at right angles to the rose garden, to the east of the palace. It was occupied by two large parterres and linked to the building by a short flight of balustraded steps. The last of Le Nôtre's three vistas was the most characteristic of his style. It was formed by

LEFT *The garden of the lower villa at Trissino is all that remains of the original complex after the villa was burnt down* *two times. Little remains of the terraces that originally occupied the hillside beyond the statues and the balustrade.*

six grand, radiating avenues. The longest of these ran for 400 metres (1,400 feet) until it was severed by a new road built at the beginning of the nineteenth century.

In 1729 Duke Vittorio Amadeo II commissioned the Sicilian architect and set designer Filippo Juvarra (1678-1736) to build a hunting lodge called the Palazzina di Stupinigi just outside Turin. Juvarra had spent ten years in Rome training under Carlo Fontana. He came to Turin in 1714 and served as Vittorio Amadeo's chief architect, designing churches, palaces and whole areas of Turin, which soon became one of the most modern and architecturally important cities in Italy. Juvarra was also famous throughout Europe as a set designer and he brought this skill to bear on the design of the *palazzina*, maximizing the dramatic contrast between the flat landscape and the elaborate building with its rich interiors. The *palazzina* was a combination of stables, tack rooms, kennels and living quarters laid out around the nucleus of a ballroom and an elliptical, stepped banqueting hall. It embraced three courtyards between the ballroom façade and the main entrance on the road to Turin. Juvarra travelled to France in 1718-19, and again in 1721, and the influence of these journeys was reflected in the design of the buildings and the open gravelled spaces surrounding them.

In 1735 Juvarra left Italy for Spain and in 1740 Duke Carlo Emanuele III of Savoy commissioned Francesco Bernard, a French designer, to landscape the area surrounding the *palazzina*. Bernard designed cut-grass parterres in the interlocking courtyards in front of the main

ABOVE *Juvarra was an immensely successful set designer, and gardens were very often his inspiration, as revealed by this engraving.*

RIGHT *A statue stands among the trees on one of the avenues of the garden that Le Nôtre designed at Palazzo Reale in Turin.*

façade. A single axis ran from the entrance on the road to Turin, through the three courtyards and continued to the rear of the palace. The main feature of the landscape behind the palace was the profoundly French *bosquet*, a circular grove intersected by the central axis of the garden to create a tree-framed vista of the palace. Among the trees Bernard inserted a lake, a maze and a series of radiating avenues and carefully framed vistas. Although the *bosquet* was the product of a French designer for a Francophile patron, it also contained the irregular paths that were the hallmark of the English landscape. The influence of English garden style was already being felt in France, and by the second half of the eighteenth century Italy was embracing English as well as French garden design.

The history of Villa Torrigiani and its garden outside Lucca provides a perfect example of the new internationalism of Italian garden design. The villa was a simple building during the sixteenth century, belonging to the Buonvisi family. During the seventeenth century it passed to the Santini, changing its name accordingly and entering a period of grandeur. Marquis Niccolao Santini, Lucca's ambassador to the court of Louis XIV, chose the house as his summer residence. The simple exterior on the south side was pulled down and replaced with a fashionable mannerist façade. In 1679 André Le Nôtre is said to have spent three days with Niccolao Santini on his way to Rome. During his stay he sketched out an idea for remodelling the gardens. The principal themes of his design are depicted in a late-eighteenth-century fresco inside the villa.

RIGHT *A double staircase links Villa Torrigiani's sunken* giardino segreto *to the 'English' park above.*

A plan of Villa Torrigiani's 'French' garden also hangs in the villa. It shows *broderie* parterres arranged around two circular pools in front of the building. To the rear a fountain formed the focus of a second *parterre de broderie*. A second wave of renovation followed the marriage of Vittoria Santini to Guadagni Torrigiani in 1816, and at this point the 'French' parterres were torn out to make way for an 'English' park. By great good fortune, the seventeenth-century *giardino segreto* and the oblong pool above it survived both of these upheavals and remain intact to this day.

The influence of French garden design, and of Le Nôtre in particular, was also felt in the Veneto, where Alvise Pisani commissioned first Count Girolamo Frigimelica, architect, poet and librettist, and then Francesco Maria Preti to transform a modest family villa on the River Brenta at Stra into a palace with a monumental garden in the French manner. There was nothing casual about Pisani's decision to commission a garden in the style of Le Nôtre. He had been Venice's ambassador to the court of Louis XIV from 1699 to 1704, and lived for five years with the landscape of Versailles. This deeply felt personal experience informed his decision to commission Frigimelica in 1719 to design a palace and garden inspired by Versailles. In 1735 Alvise was elected doge and Frigimelica's plans for the palace were discarded in favour of a new and even more ostentatious design by Francesco Maria Prete. However Frigimelica's original garden design was retained.

Alvise Pisani's Venetian visitors generally took the easy route to Stra. They were rowed across the lagoon to Fusina in a *burchiello*, or covered gondola. At Fusina the *burchiello* was attached to a towrope and dragged along the Brenta towards Stra by a horse. The journey from Venice to Stra takes over six hours even today, travelling by motor boat. When they finally disembarked on the Pisani landing stage, Alvise's guests could look across the road and straight through the monumental hall of the palace to the garden beyond. Frigimelica filled the area immediately behind the building with a swathe of French *broderie*

LEFT *The fashionable, new façade for Villa Torrigiani, commissioned by Niccolao Santini, Lucca's ambassador to France.*

ABOVE *The axial layout of Villa Pisani's garden was accentuated by*

this sheet of water, added in 1911, after the villa came into state ownership.

OVERLEAF *Villa Pisani's impressive façade, as it would appear to Venetian visitors arriving by boat on the Brenta.*

parterres. In 1911 the parterres were removed to make way for a long sheet of water. Although this proved a very pleasing and appropriate addition, it was actually designed with a practical rather than an aesthetic purpose and used to test naval scale models. Beyond the parterres the view was stopped by the ornate façade of Frigimelica's pavilion, converted under Francesco Maria Prete into an unusually luxurious stable block. To each side the parterres were flanked by avenues designed to create vistas along the length of the garden. Additional avenues radiated from the vertical axis and were aligned to lead the eye across the parterres and through the trees beyond. Le Nôtre used avenues and radiating axes in his gardens to overcome their real physical boundaries. By continuing the line of the garden axes across open countryside or through dense woodland he made his gardens appear to encompass the surrounding landscape as far as the distant horizon. Several of Frigimelica's vistas were planned to align with the fine wrought-iron tracery of the gates and windows that pierce the curved wall on the garden's eastern boundary. However the cluttered and intensely cultivated landscape of the Veneto that lay beyond the wall did not lend itself to Le Nôtre's treatment, and Frigimelica could only gesture towards this element of his style. At one end of the vertical avenue on the east side of the garden there was already an elaborate eighteenth-century maze, a survivor from the original garden. Frigimelica designed a circular tower to stand at its centre. At the centre of six radiating avenues, he built a hexagonal belvedere. Stone steps lead up through the building to a viewing terrace overlooking the avenues in all directions. Beyond the belvedere the coffee house stands on a mound containing an ice house. The mound was planted with hedges clipped to resemble steps. Several other topiary features in the garden have been lost, and this makes the landscape look emptier than Frigimelica intended. The avenues on the west of the garden were designed to divide the wood into five distinct areas. One was a lawn with a statue at its centre, another was planted with box hedges, and another filled with winding paths, similar to those in the *bosquet* of the Palazzina di Stupinigi.

The palace and garden of Villa Pisani were complete by 1756, but the Pisani family had only forty years to enjoy their comfort and beauty before Napoleon led his army into the Veneto in 1797, requisitioned their property and gave it to his stepson, Eugène de Beauharnais.

Le Nôtre's style was resurrected once again in 1751, when Don Carlos, the first Bourbon ruler of the Kingdom of the Two Sicilies, commissioned Luigi Vanvitelli to build a new capital for the kingdom with a royal palace and a colossal park at its centre. The king chose the tiny village of Caserta, thirty kilometres (19 miles) north of Naples,

ABOVE AND RIGHT *A statue of Minerva, goddess of wisdom, gives little comfort to visitors lost in Villa Pisani's magnificently effective maze. Restoration has returned the maze to prime condition and there is little to distinguish it now from G. Carboni's eighteenth-century engraving.*

as the site of the new city. In 1756 Vanvitelli published sixteen engravings of his plans for the palace and gardens as the *Dichiarazione dei disegni del Real Palazzo di Caserta* (Design statement for the royal palace of Caserta). In letters to his brother Vanvitelli denied the influence of Versailles upon his plans. However Don Carlos was the great-grandson of Louis XIV and he had been a guest at Versailles. There can be little doubt that his vision for the new capital city was coloured by Le Nôtre's design for Versailles. Vanvitelli's layout seems to reflect the influence of both Versailles and of Dezaillier d'Argenville's standard work on the French garden, *La théorie et la pratique du jardinage*, published in 1709 and rapidly translated into Italian. However the iconography of the garden, which Vanvitelli created with the help of the royal historiographer, Giambattista Vico, was intrinsically Italian.

The plans for the capital city show wide tree-lined streets, majestic buildings and vast airy piazzas. The royal palace at the heart of the city was the fulcrum of Vanvitelli's design. The Via Appia, one of the most important Roman roads in Italy, links Caserta to Naples. The new palace was carefully aligned so that the Via Appia ran straight from the centre of its façade to the middle of Naples. Don Carlos was not blind to the physical link that this created between his own reign and the Golden Age of Roman civilization. The road, which was wide enough to accommodate the full panoply of the Bourbon court in transit, was to be flanked by two canals carrying fresh spring water from Caserta to the fetid streets of the city. Behind the palace Vanvitelli's plans show a series of enormous *parterres de broderie*, while the rest of

the site is divided into garden rooms decorated with fountains, a fish pool with a circular island, an orchard and a pavilion on the crest of the hill opposite the palace. The hunting wood, the feature that had originally persuaded Don Carlos to move the capital to Caserta, was incorporated into the layout of the garden and cut through by a series of wide grassy rides.

Vanvitelli presented his designs for the garden in May 1751, and in November he began to stake out the *parterres de broderie*. By the end of the year the new groves of trees marked on Vanvitelli's plans had been planted, and the covers in the royal hunting wood expanded. The foundation stone of the palace was laid on 20 January 1752, to coincide with the king's thirty-sixth birthday. Vanvitelli focused his attention on the palace, but by the time Don Carlos III left Italy to succeed to the throne of Spain as Charles III in 1759, work was still in its very early stages.

The king made his Italian possessions over to his eight-year-old son, Ferdinand, and set up a council of regents to govern the kingdom until his sixteenth birthday. During the regency period work on the palace continued, but the garden was virtually abandoned. Vanvitelli focused his attention on the problem of finding sufficient water for the garden. The engineering involved in transporting water from Monte

ABOVE AND RIGHT *G. Carboni's engraving shows the clipped, topiary steps that originally clothed the mound* *below the coffee house at Villa Pisani. A few box bushes survive, but the steps have been replaced with cut grass.*

LEFT *This is Luigi Vanvitelli's original design for Caserta. It encompassed the palace, its garden and a new capital city built to a grandiose plan. The broad road leading out of the piazza in front of the palace was the Via Appia, the link between Caserta and Naples.*

Taburno, thirty-three kilometres (21 miles) east of Caserta, was almost as impressive as the garden itself. In 1753 Vanvitelli began a huge programme of hydraulic engineering that demanded the construction of a thirty-three kilometre aqueduct and three viaducts. To achieve this gargantuan goal he had to blast a route through six hillsides. This part of the project was not completed until 1762.

In 1769, two years after Ferdinand came of age, work on the garden began again. Labourers were employed day and night on excavating the fish pool, which had to be completed before King Ferdinand came home for Christmas. The fish to stock the pool were delivered in three batches, on the 17, 21 and, just too late, on 30 December. The pavilion for the island in the middle of the pool was hastily constructed from straw. The following year the pool, which had been built far too quickly, had to be repaired, and the pavilion was dismantled and rebuilt in brick to Vanvitelli's plans.

Despite the feverish activity that produced the fish pool, very few of Vanvitelli's original plans for the garden were realized before his death in 1773. When Carlo Vanvitelli took over from his father, the palace was complete only to the level of the cornice. Carlo was employed by King Ferdinand to oversee the interior decoration of the palace and the construction and decoration of the garden. The character of the garden today owes more to Carlo than to Luigi Vanvitelli. His design has the grandeur and simplicity of a French landscape. Its main feature is the wide canal, excavated in 1777 to run for three dead straight kilometres across the plain that lay between the palace and the foot of Monte Briano. Luigi Vanvitelli's aqueduct brought water to the brow of the hill and released it in a rugged, naturalistic cascade that filled the canal with water clean enough to drink. The water descends towards the palace through a series of deep basins filled with fish, down a number of cascades and past groups of life-size statues carved from pure white marble. Carlo Vanvitelli flanked this startling view with clipped hornbeam hedges, rows of trees and ribbons of turf seeded in the royal cowsheds. This cleverly articulated combination of water, light, foliage and statuary was both the axis of the garden and an extraordinarily successful expression of the power of the Bourbon dynasty.

The canal was a peculiarly French garden feature, but the iconography of the garden tied it firmly to its Italian setting. Water was a potent symbol, both in the traditional Italian garden and in the parched landscape of the Mezzogiorno. In the sixteenth century Cosimo I de' Medici had intended to build an aqueduct from his new garden at Castello to Florence (see Chapter 2). His intention was to relieve the desperate shortage of drinking water in the city, while associating himself in the popular imagination with the classical Roman emperors who had originally brought water to Florence, and simultaneously reviving memories of the city's classical splendour. Don Carlos had much the same intention. By bringing water from Caserta to Naples he had hoped to ease the suffering of his subjects. On another, less practical level he intended to enrich his personal mythology by forging a link between Bourbon rule and the classical Golden Age, when Caserta and the fertile, sheltered plain surrounding it were known as the *campagna felix*, an earthly paradise famous for tranquillity and beauty and sacred to the goddesses Diana and Ceres.

The sculptures on the canal represent scenes from Ovid's *Metamorphoses*. Vanvitelli used Ovid's stories to express familiar ideas about the transformation of nature by art and agriculture, and about good government, harmony and fertility. Untamed nature is represented by Paolo Persico's sculpture of Diana which stands beneath the casacade at the top of the canal. She has already bewitched Actaeon, and although his arms and legs are still human, a rack of antlers has burst from his forehead and his own dogs gather round, preparing to tear him apart. The water from the Fountain of Diana disappears underground below the pool and then re-emerges to form the long basin of the Fountain of Venus, executed by Gaetano Salamone in 1780. This sculpted drama also refers to hunting, the favourite pastime of both Don Carlos and King Ferdinand. This time Venus and her nymphs beg Adonis not to go hunting – the preface to another expedition ending badly. The water disappears once again and re-emerges beneath Ceres, a promising symbol of fertility and abundance. The climax of the canal was to have been the semicircular Fountain of Juno and Aeolus, with sculptures executed by Angelo Brunelli, Andrea Violani, Paolo Persico and Gaetano Salamone. The great cascade was built and the water pours over an archway representing the Palace of the Winds. Aeolus was made to sit with his back to the palace, and the winds, newly released, squirm on the rocks to either side of him. Bas-reliefs set above four of the arched doorways of Aeolus' palace represent Jupiter, the marriage of Thetis and Peleus, the judgement of Paris and the marriage of Paris and Helen. Juno was to have ridden through the great pool in a carriage drawn by peacocks, but by the time the workmen downed tools in 1774, she had not even begun to take shape.

Despite a vast workforce, employed since 1751 and made up in part of galley slaves and Muslims captured by Bourbon ships on the coast of North Africa, much of Vanvitelli's original plan for Caserta went unrealized. The palace, with its 1,200 rooms, its church, seminary, theatre, courts of justice and observatory, was virtually complete, but of the new capital, only two barracks and one piazza had been built. In the garden, the garden canal was made and partially furnished, but none of Vanvitelli's garden rooms or fountains were built. King Ferdinand's chief occupation was hunting. He lacked his father's stature as a ruler and had no interest in developing the mythology of Bourbon rule. His decision to stop work on the city and the garden was due as much to apathy as to lack of funds.

RIGHT *A view taken from the top of the cascade down the three-kilometre canal that forms the main axis of the garden at La Reggia. The palace stops the view at its far end. Groups of statues depicting classical scenes punctuate the length of the canal. They are just visible in this picture.*

Caserta provides the perfect example of the internationalism of Italian garden design in the eighteenth century, for in 1785, only eleven years after Vanvitelli's original Italo-French project reached its conclusion, plans were afoot for a new, English addition to the garden. There was already a strong, Anglo-Saxon influence on the court of King Ferdinand. Sir John Acton was prime minister, and King Ferdinand and Queen Maria Carolina spent much time in the company of Sir William Hamilton, the British ambassador to Naples. Hamilton was a charming companion and an expert antiquarian, collector and vulcanologist. His wife, Emma Hamilton, was a close friend of Queen Maria Carolina. The idea for building the English garden at Caserta can be traced back to Hamilton. He was a close friend and correspondent of Sir Joseph Banks, the English naturalist who had accompanied Captain Cook on his voyage around the world, made a vast collection of seeds from Tahiti, Australia and New Zealand and become director of the Royal Society and of the royal gardens at Kew. Hamilton's vision was of an English landscape set against the dramatic backdrop of Vesuvius. His friendship with Banks put him in touch with the exciting, botanical discoveries made on Cook's voyage. He saw that exotic plants could be cultivated in the southern Italian climate and made to thrive with Caserta's copious water supply. Using well-honed diplomatic skills, Hamilton bypassed the rather dim and parochial king, going directly to his more sophisticated wife for funding.

Queen Maria Carolina's sister, Marie-Antoinette, had already commissioned the informal landscape of the Petit Trianon at Versailles, and this may well have helped Hamilton's case, sealing the queen's decision to provide funding for an English garden in the landscape of her own palace. A twenty hectare (50 acre) site was rapidly chosen to the east of the great canal, but no progress could be made until the owners of the land had agreed to relinquish it. Once this had been achieved, a team of 500 men were set to building a wall that enclosed the site. Another eighty men began work on the garden itself. Sir Joseph Banks helped Hamilton by selecting a head gardener for him in England. He chose Joseph Graefer, an experienced gardener who was currently employed by Thompson and Gordon, a well-known nursery in London's Mile End. He had trained under Philip Miller, curator of the Chelsea Physic Garden, and worked in several important private gardens in England. Graefer, a widower, arrived in Naples in April 1786 with his three sons, and set to work at once. Sir Joseph Banks continued to take an interest in the project, sending Graefer the seeds of plants and trees that he had collected during his voyage with Cook on the *Endeavour*. Unfortunately the queen, whose enthusiasm for the new garden had seemed boundless, rapidly lost interest. After only two years she withdrew her funding and Hamilton was forced to approach the king

after all. King Ferdinand had absolutely no understanding of the concept of an English garden. The first order that he gave Graefer concerned the planting of a labyrinth 'where he might lose his courtiers'. This was awkward, as Graefer had no idea how to design such a feature, and he turned to Sir William Hamilton for guidance. Hamilton was also at a loss, and offered Graefer a classical coin from his collection that had a labyrinth design on one side of it.

Caserta's English garden evolved as an undulating park scattered with exotic trees and plants, false ruins, genuine archaeological remains and classical sculptures. Some of the sculptures were taken from the Farnese collection that Don Carlos had inherited from his mother, Elisabetta Farnese, and others came from Pompeii, where Hamilton had organized the first formal excavation. From 1790 Carlo Vanvitelli worked alongside Graefer, designing the romantic ruined temple on the island of the lake, a Chinese pagoda and a circular temple at the heart of the labyrinth.

The trees and plants in the English Garden grew with extraordinary speed. When Count della Torre Rezzonico was shown round by Sir William Hamilton in 1790 it was already possible to grasp the purpose of the design. The count was delighted by what he saw, and his comments alert us to the refreshing novelty of the 'irregular' English style:

> For us, everyone sees and understands in the blink of an eye the plan of a vast garden. In English Gardens, on the contrary, a little area of terrain is multiplied and extended by frequent comings and goings and with every step changes the magic perspective… When the garden is finished it will be, thanks to the design, one of the most beautiful in Italy for the variety of its contents and for its views.

In 1787, when Caserta's *Giardino Inglese* was just beginning to take shape, Prince Marcantonio Borghese commissioned Jacob Moore to remodel the park of Villa Borghese in the 'English' style. Moore was a Scot, an expatriate inhabitant of Rome and a fashionable landscape painter. He was given a botanist and an architect to back him up, but the prince recognized the need for painterly skills in the creation of the new landscape picture. In a letter to Lord Cowper written in 1788, Moore says that Prince Borghese was 'highly pleas'd' with his design, and explained that he had 'caus'd them to plant Trees in Groups in a Picturesque manner which they were not acquainted with such as weeping willows &c.'

By the end of the eighteenth century the English landscape had become so fashionable that it was perceived by some as a threat to the traditional Italian garden, and there was scarcely a painter, philosopher, politician or poet who did not have an opinion on the matter. In 1792 Melchiorre Cesarotti, poet, intellectual and garden maker, invited Ippolito Pindemonte to present a dissertation on the English garden to the Academy of Letters, Sciences and the Arts in Padua. Cesarotti had an extraordinary knowledge of the literature and culture of every conceivable period and nationality. The garden of his own villa at

LEFT *Gaetano Salamone's expressive back view of Venus as she begs Adonis not to set out on a hunting expedition that is to end in a fatal encounter with a wild boar.*

Selvazzano, near Padua, was a homage to the poetry of James Thomson and William Shenstone. Ippolito Pindemonte was also a successful and very well travelled poet. In essence his *Dissertazione su i giardini inglesi* was critical of the English garden, which he defined as a means of 'beautifying vast areas to make them look like the work of nature', creating beautiful scenes 'by chance'. In his view nature was much better enjoyed in its virgin state, on a hillside or a riverbank. He begged his audience not to be ashamed of their love of geometry in the garden, and as a finale he pointed out that Torquato Tasso's description of Armida's garden in *Gerusalemme Liberata* predated Milton's *Paradise Lost* and the description of earthly paradise that was generally cited as the origin of the informal English garden.

In the face of so much foreign influence, it is important to remember that the traditional gardens championed by Pindemonte were still being built throughout the eighteenth century. In 1726 Marc'Antonio dal Re published a collection of images and descriptions of Lombard gardens entitled *Ville di delizia o siano palagi camparecci nello stato di Milano* (Delightful villas, or country palaces in the state of Milan). Many of the illustrations in dal Re's collection show sites that combine the traditional Italianate style with French canals and radiating axes. One of the most interesting gardens in the collection is that of Villa Comazzo, designed by Francesco Croce for Cristoforo Pertusati. The complex layout, which has long since disappeared, combined terraces, pools and canals with elaborate hydraulic effects, including cascades, pyramids and unearthly music. Dal Re's illustration shows the terrace below the villa furnished as a drawing room,

ABOVE *This view of the English Garden at Caserta is by Jakob Phillip Hackert, who began working in Italy in 1768 and became court painter to Ferdinand IV in 1786.*

RIGHT *Hubert Robert's impression of the Temple dedicated to Aesculapius, the Greek god of healing, on an island in the middle of the lake at Villa Borghese.*

with comfortable sofas, console tables and looking glasses on the retaining wall.

In the isolated and somewhat conservative region of Le Marche, gardens continued to be designed in the traditional idiom. In 1763 Marchese Francesco Mosca engaged Carlo Marchionni to enlarge the Villa Caprile on the slopes of the San Bartolo hill above Pesaro. Other Italian regions were embracing French, or even English landscape design by this time, but the gardens that took shape around Villa Caprile over the next twenty years were entirely traditional. Three terraces were constructed below the villa, and a green theatre was planted, with seats of clipped cypress. The first terrace was filled by parterres in box and myrtle. The retaining wall below it contains a number of grottoes. Elsewhere in Italy the passion for water-powered, practical jokes in the garden diminished during the eighteenth century, but at Villa Caprile the grottoes are riddled with elaborate and very effective *giochi d'acqua*, or 'water tricks'. Water-spouting dolphins flank the central grotto. Inside, the walls are richly decorated with shells and stalactites. Visitors are invited to press their eye to a peephole in the wall so that they can watch a tiny water-powered carousel revolving. As soon as they were settled, the marquis would nip into the grotto next door and flick the lever controlling the *giochi d'acqua*. Water sprayed from a star on the wall at the front of the grotto and cascaded from a metal flower in the ceiling. The entire length of the retaining wall was fitted with pipes, so that even spectators leaning over the balustrade above were in danger of a soaking. At the far end of the retaining wall the most elaborate grotto in the garden is flanked by small alabaster busts. Inside it is decorated with mosaics and delicate shellwork. Wooden shutters conceal a crude painted devil holding a pitchfork. Francesco Mosca encouraged his guests to touch the devil's face for luck and they, poor fools, were soaked once again by a jet from his mouth and more water from the floor and ceiling. Two stone seats on the terrace outside are fitted with metal clamps, a device that suggests force more than persuasion. It is all too easy to imagine Francesco Mosca holding a visitor down, forcing the clamps over his legs and rushing off to turn on the *giochi d'acqua* trained at eye level.

The garden of Villa Buonaccorsi is near Ancona, also in Le Marche. Its park was remodelled, but the eighteenth-century garden is virtually intact. Five terraces descend from the villa, and on the upper three the original planting of espaliered lemons survives, as do the elaborately carved obelisks lining the paths. The upper terrace is inlaid with the stone-edged compartments that were a common feature of the seventeenth and eighteenth-century garden (see Chapter 7). The third terrace consists of a narrow gravelled path lined with busts of the Roman emperors. Once again, grottoes, *giochi d'acqua* and other water-powered

generation in the Veneto. He lived in Vicenza, where he had direct contact with the steady stream of English gentlemen who came to study Palladio's buildings at first hand. In 1708 he was commissioned by Lord Twysden to make a series of drawings of Palladian buildings in Vicenza and of classical monuments in Rome. Despite his contact with Englishmen and their ideas, Muttoni continued to work in a full-blown Italianate style, and the garden at Trissino is a daring celebration of the rococo.

Francesco Muttoni's ingenious design for the *manège* at Villa Trissino has already been described (see Chapter 8). The garden occupies the south-facing slope below the *manège*, and today it links two separate villas that originally belonged to different branches of the Trissino family. The upper villa was remodelled by Muttoni from a medieval fortress belonging to the Trissino Baston and overlooking the Agno Valley that was once their fiefdom. Muttoni transformed the rough cliff on which the castle stood into a series of belvederes and promenades

devices are the salient feature of the garden. The nymphaeum at the end of the third terrace contains a statue of Flora, crowned with a water-spraying star. A life-size praying monk occupies the grotto beneath the villa. Another monk looks on in horror at the wooden Devil's head that pops out of the rock. *Giochi d'acqua* riddle the ceiling. On the lowest of the garden terraces there is a grotto that houses the garden's most extraordinary survivals – a collection of eighteenth-century water-powered automata. A wooden huntsman sits on a rock, his horn raised to his lips. In the niches behind him are a Turk, a harlequin and Vulcan and his blacksmiths at their forge. Their mechanisms are still intact and they are clothed in the faded tatters of their eighteenth-century costumes.

By the eighteenth century the Veneto had, like Le Marche, become slightly isolated. Three important baroque gardens were made in the region. The first was designed in 1722 by Francesco Muttoni who had been commissioned by the Trissino to renovate their villa of the same name in Trissino, near Vicenza, and to create a garden around it. Muttoni was the most accomplished rococo architect of his that were arranged on varying levels around the upper villa and interconnected by an audaciously complex web of terraces, hidden staircases, tunnels, courtyards and ramps. Muttoni's main objective was the creation of a garden frame for the magnificent panorama of the Agno Valley. On his original plans he marked each gloriously elaborate rococo gate, balustrade, belvedere, seat, fountain, statue and parterre. As building progressed, he annotated, dated and colour coded the design to show which parts had already been completed. Although he worked at Trissino for over twenty-five years, only a fraction of his original plan had been realized by the time he died in 1748. The garden's main features are the *manège*, the long south-facing terrace below it and the octagonal belvedere garden. The terrace was used as a lemon garden where the lines of pots were punctuated with statues by Orazio Marinali, the most distinguished Venetian sculptor of his day. Beyond the terrace, the belvedere garden was decorated with a geometric tracery of stone-lined beds incorporating the Trissino family crest. The beds were originally filled with coloured gravel. Today the trees surrounding the garden are overgrown, but originally Muttoni's belvedere garden was suspended in thin air above a breathtaking view of the Agno Valley.

The lower villa originally belonged to the Trissino Riale, a separate branch of the family. No archival evidence exists to link the garden with Muttoni, although the style of the flamboyant wrought-iron gates, the belvedere and the staircases linking the different levels of the garden all suggest Muttoni's hand in the design. The villa stands on a terrace overlooking a grassy, rectangular space with an octagonal pool at its centre. The belevedere is linked to the garden by a flight of steps. After the complexities of the upper garden, this simplicity is very pleasing. The only ornaments are the statues by Orazio Marinali and Giacomo Cassetti gathered around the pool and lining the balustrades on the garden boundary.

The Riale line became extinct in the nineteenth century and the lower villa passed to the Trissino Baston. There was a plan to link the two properties by extending the upper garden with a series of terraces. This was the idea of the architect Ottone Calderai, and when he died the plan was abandoned. In 1841 a fire destroyed the villa. It was rebuilt, but shortly afterwards it burnt down again. In the nineteenth century the burnt out carcass of the villa was transformed into a picturesque ruin, complete with battlements.

Francesco Muttoni's design for the garden of Villa Trissino was daring and inventive. Other eighteenth-century gardens in the Italianate

style were built on much more conventional lines. At Costozza di Longare near Vicenza, for example, the Trento family remodelled and extended the family garden of the building now known as Villa da Schio. The garden, which consists of five south-facing terraces cut from a rough slope in the Berici hills, was made to celebrate the marriage between Francesco Trento and Valeria Ferramosca at the beginning of the eighteenth century. It was very fortunate for the Trento that Marinali should have his workshop in a small building that stood against the upper boundary of the garden. This was a very convenient arrangement for Marinali himself, as the building was next to one of the largest quarries in the Veneto. Marinali often worked with his brothers, Francesco and Angelo, and their light-hearted statues of courtiers and their ladies, dwarves and characters from the *commedia dell'arte* were a vital element of any traditional eighteenth-century garden in the Veneto.

In 1783 Count Antonio Rizzardi commissioned Luigi Trezza to design a garden on the hill beside his villa at Pojega di Negrar, near

Verona. Trezza's career as municipal engineer in Verona spanned the eras of the Venetian Republic, the Napoleonic administration and Austrian rule. This history suggests a diplomacy that is also evident in the design of his garden, which incorporates something of both the Italian and the fashionable English tradition. The garden is laid out on a slope behind the Rizzardi villa. The Italianate element of Trezza's design consists of three terraces cut into the hillside. He used hornbeam hedges as screens between the three levels of the garden, which he linked with a steep flight of steps. Below the terraces he made an oval pool, which he described on his original plan as 'a little lake' with 'green perimeter walls and ornaments'. Trezza's perimeter walls were curved laurel hedges that opened out into a series of enclosed green rooms.

The 'English' element of Trezza's design consisted of a series of enclosed lawns and grand 'perspectives'. Three avenues give structure to this part of the garden. The first is more a tunnel than an avenue. It is planted in hornbeam and runs from the parterre garden in front of the villa. The trees are clipped to leave a narrow strip of sky between their arching branches and this effect is mirrored in a ribbon of grass between the trees. An avenue of cypresses runs at right angles from the end of the hornbeams and links the three levels of the garden. At the top of this avenue Trezza designed an intrinsically baroque, octagonal belvedere with a raised platform surrounded by a balustrade and decorated with statues of *putti*. The third axis of the garden leads from the mid point of the cypress avenue and links the green theatre (see Chapter 8) to the villa. It is this axis, also planted in cypress, that gives backbone to the more informal, though none the less geometric spaces of the English part of the garden. The area between the belvedere and the garden entrance is planted as a small informal wood. This might appear to be a nod to the English Romantic tradition, but Trezza's original plan showed a geometric design of tunnels cut through the trees to create a green cloister leading to six green rooms.

At the centre of this square layout Trezza built a circular temple without a roof. Inside, the curved wall is decorated with statues of Diana, Hercules and Minerva and encrusted with shells and stalactites. During the Austrian occupation of the Veneto the original wood was felled and later replanted in an informal style.

Villa Rizzardi's garden was complete by 1791. Despite Trezza's gestures to the English tradition, it is often cited, rather mournfully, as the last gasp of pure Italianate design. Although the fashion for English and French landscapes in the eighteenth century did result in the destruction of some Renaissance and baroque gardens, the influx of foreign influences on the Italian tradition should be a cause for celebration because it reinvigorated a waning garden culture.

LEFT *Half concealed by Virginia creeper, this statue occupies a niche in the retaining wall of the upper terrace of the Villa Trissino Reale.*

RIGHT *Neptune, the only statue to survive from the original sixteenth-century layout of Villa da Schio.*

ABOVE In spring beech leaves form a translucent, green roof for the circular temple in the wood at Villa Rizzardi. The walls are decorated with volcanic rock and Diana and Hercules occupy niches to each side of the door.

LEFT The terrace of the hexagonal belvedere overlooks one of the three axes in the 'English' part of Villa Rizzardi's garden.

RIGHT A classical figure stands beside the path in Villa Rizzardi's bosco. A nineteenth-century underplanting of Trachycarpus, the windmill palm, is just visible to the right of the picture.

Padiglione Chinese per un Giardino   Ⓐ.Ⓓ.

X | International style
European fashions 1800-1867

BY THE BEGINNING OF THE NINETEENTH CENTURY the story of the Italian garden merges and becomes part of the continuum of European garden history. The formal, or 'geometric' garden as it was known, had been finally rejected. In the words of Luigi Mabil, called on in 1796 to answer Ippolito Pindemonte's dissertation on the English garden (see Chapter 9), symmetry and uniformity eventually produces 'nothing but boredom'. Despite Napoleonic occupation, the English landscape continued to spread across Italian soil. At the beginning of the nineteenth century Napoleon's building programme altered the appearance of many cities. In Turin, for example, ancient city gates and fortifications were demolished to make way for new public gardens. Elisa Bonaparte Baciocchi represented her brother's administration in Tuscany. She made radical decisions about the gardens under her control, initiating plans to transform the gardens of Boboli, Poggio a Caiano and Poggio Imperiale into English landscapes. At her own home, Villa Reale near Lucca, she annexed a summer palace and garden belonging to the Bishops of Lucca to her own property, gaining a beautiful seventeenth-century grotto in the process. She preserved the original seventeenth-century part of her own garden (see Chapter 8), but in 1805 she commissioned Pasquale Poccianti to transform the remains of the bishops' land into an English landscape with a fine lake.

In 1801 Ercole Silva published *Dell'arte dei giardini inglesi*, the first Italian treatise on the English garden. Silva's work was a critical translation and adaptation of Christian Hirschfeld's *Geschichte und Theorie der Gardenkunst* (Theory of garden art, 1779), which was already well known and highly respected in Italy. It was Ercole Silva who advised

the modern 'artist-gardener' to abandon the architectural approach to garden making. In his words, the architect is 'hampered by rigid proportions, and worried by the inflexible rules of austere, geometric exactitude'. He defines the architect's approach as the 'enemy of impulse and genius', and says that it tends to 'paralyse anything subject to its calculations'. This was the atmosphere of the nineteenth century, and the gardeners who emerged from it were, above all, plantsmen and botanists, trained to satisfy the infinite demands of a massive influx of new and exotic plants.

During the nineteenth century India, the Americas and China became more accessible to merchant ships, and as a result a steady stream of new plants flowed into Europe. William Chambers's *Designs of Chinese buildings, furniture, dresses, machines and utensils* was published in Britain in 1757, but its impact was reflected all over Europe in a rash of Anglo-Chinese landscapes furnished with pagodas and planted with rhododendrons, camellias, azaleas and magnolias. There was no real market for these plants in early-nineteenth-century Italy, and the creators of *chinoiserie* in the garden had to obtain them through complex channels. Initially, new plants tended to be acclimatized in royal parks or in gardens built on a grand scale for aristocratic patrons.

One such garden surrounded the Villa Durazzo Pallavicini, at Pegli, overlooking the Bay of Genoa. It was designed and built for Marquis Ignazio Pallavicini by Michele Canzio between 1837 and 1846. Canzio was a set designer who worked in the Teatro Carlo Felice in Genoa. The theatrical nature of Canzio's design was immediately apparent to Sir George Sitwell when he visited in 1890. A paragraph in his essay *On the making of gardens* (1909) was devoted to the 'raised approach' to gardens. In it he describes the entrance to 'the modern Villa Pallavicini at Pegli, where huge retaining-walls of stone a quarter of a mile long and in places not less than sixty feet high lift up a roadway bordered with flowers and shaded by an ilex avenue.' Canzio's romantic landscape

LEFT *Chinoiserie entered the Italian garden in the nineteenth century as a consequence of a highly influential book by William Chambers. It brought with it a rash of pagodas, camellias, rhododendrons, azaleas and magnolias. This exotic 'Chinese' tent could provide shade anywhere in the garden.*

opens out as a series of pictures furnished with references to every period and nationality of garden history. There is a Chinese pagoda and a classical island temple on a lake, a hermit's hut, triumphal arch, Roman road, coffee house, mogul pavilion, rose arbour, a summer house with mirrored walls and a magnificent, heated glass house. The planting was equally eclectic. It included banks of camellias and weeping willows, camphor, cork and monkey puzzle trees, palms and Lebanese cedars. Ignazio Pallavicini had always intended the park to be accessible to the public, and as soon as it was completed in 1846 the gates were opened to the local population, and to an ever increasing number of northern European tourists drawn to the Italian Riviera by the mild climate. These visitors were free to wander along winding paths, to explore the lakeside grottoes in a boat – a dubious pleasure as many of the boats were fitted with *giochi d'acqua* – to soar above the water on an iron swing, lose themselves in the maze or picnic beneath weeping willows. In *Italian villas and their gardens* (1904) Edith Wharton was thoroughly disapproving of Canzio's creation. She described the gardens as 'a brummagem creation… to which guidebooks still send throngs of unsuspecting tourists, who come back imagining that this tawdry jumble of Chinese pagodas, mock Gothic ruins and exotic vegetation represents the typical "Italian garden".' Bitter words, but by the mid-nineteenth century, even 'unsuspecting tourists' were probably aware that there was no longer any such thing as a 'typical Italian garden'.

It became fashionable in the mid-nineteenth century for Italy's royal families to send their gardeners and landscape architects on educational voyages to northern Europe – a kind of Grand Tour in reverse. One of the earliest examples of this tradition was the journey made between 1783 and 1786 by Ercole Silva in the company of Archduke Ferdinand, the Habsburg ruler of Lombardy. Silva was a count and not a professional gardener, but their journey established the blueprint for similar expeditions. The archduke took Silva to see gardens in Austria, and then they travelled on to Germany and England. Sadly, all the records of this journey have been lost.

The best documented example of the phenomenon was an expedition organized by King Carlo Alberto of Savoy between 1840 and 1843 for the orphaned Roda brothers, sons of his head gardener at the royal park of Racconigi. Their journey took them to Lombardy and the Veneto, and then Austria, Germany, Holland, France and Britain, and the royal family asked very specifically that they should keep an accurate written and pictorial record of everything they saw. In Germany and England they had language lessons, and in each country they visited the most important gardens, met their head gardeners and learnt new techniques of floriculture and glasshouse cultivation. In Britain their tour included Windsor, Hampton Court, Kenwood, Gunnersbury Park, the Royal Botanic Garden at Kew and the Royal Horticultural Society Garden at Chiswick, Regent's Park and several nurseries. Expeditions outside London took them to Woburn

Abbey, Chatsworth and Holkham Hall. Both Holkham and Chatsworth were centres of agricultural experiment and improvement, and the brothers took English concepts of 'beauty' and 'utility' back with them to Italy, developing numerous horticultural schemes for generating income for the park, although the landscape that they designed behind the royal palace at Racconigi was in the French style.

From 1820 onwards glasshouse cultivation attracted enormous interest in Italy. This was an important element of the Rodas' education abroad, and shortly after they returned to Racconigi a monumental neo-gothic glasshouse was built on the north-west boundary of the park. Marcellino designed a heating system for the upper south-facing chamber, and this became a very productive pineapple house. A second chamber was built below and used as a fernery and orchid house, and for acclimatizing exotic plants.

The trajectory of Marcellino and Giuseppe Roda's careers reflects important changes in the place of the garden in Italian society during the nineteenth century. The brothers worked for the House of Savoy throughout their lives. Marcellino become director of all the royal parks and gardens and Giuseppe was director of the royal school of agriculture, founder of the Horticultural Society of Piedmont and of Lombardy. Both brothers were knighted for their services to the House of Savoy, and this gave them access to the highest echelons of Italian society, but in the latter part of their careers they chose to work on public projects, designing gardens for schools and railway stations, and taking on commercial work. The Unification of Italy in 1860 resulted in the emergence of a new middle class, and this in turn led to the popularization of horticulture. A mass of new gardens was built on a domestic scale in northern Italy. This was the gardenesque phase of Italian style. The Roda brothers responded to fashion by writing numerous gardening manuals, and monthly magazines full of advice about cultivation techniques, floriculture, ornamental gardening, design and hothouse cultivation. They were printed on cheap paper and written in a clear and accessible style.

The popularization of gardening generated an increased demand for plants, and as a result numerous new nurseries opened, particularly near Padua and Milan. Their catalogues reflect a huge increase in the range of species and cultivars available in the second half of the nineteenth century. They also reflect the popularity of trees and plants with striking leaf forms and colours. Purple or bronze-leafed or variegated plants were widely available, as were plants with composite or palmate leaves, or a weeping habit.

One of the first stops on the Roda brothers' voyage to the north had been Lake Maggiore in Lombardy, where they visited Isola Madre

RIGHT *This Chinese bridge and pagoda were designed by Michele Canzio for Villa Durazzo Pallavicini. A weeping willow adds another 'Chinese' element, but Canzio also designed neoclassical arches, temples and picturesque cascades, creating a landscape that could be drawn from any continent or century.*

and Isola Bella. Here they found a situation parallel to their own, for the Borromeo family employed the two Rovelli brothers as head gardeners. The nineteenth century was a very important period in the history of the two Borromean islands. Isola Bella had been transformed into an elaborate terraced garden by Count Carlo III Borromeo in the seventeenth century (see Chapter 6). It was clothed in lush Mediterranean vegetation and the sun-drenched terraces had proved perfect for citrus cultivation. During the nineteenth century the island underwent a radical transformation under the care of Count Vitaliano IX Borromeo and the Rovelli brothers. The count was a knowledgeable botanist, and

between 1825 and 1830 he introduced a vast new collection of exotic plants from China, New Zealand, India, the Himalayas, South America and Australia to Isola Bella and Isola Madre. During the seventeenth and eighteenth centuries Isola Bella was principally admired for its architecture. The heavily manipulated artificial landscape might have been expected to fall out of favour in the nineteenth century, but instead visitors subtly altered their perception, and Isola Bella's terraces began to be seen as a series of romantic follies set in a magnificent landscape garden. Sir George Sitwell encapsulates this romantic perception of Isola Bella, describing it as:

…a thing in itself, not a garden, but a mirage in a lake of dreams; a great galleon with flower-laden terraces and fantastic pinnacles which has anchored here against a background of purple mountains on its return to the realm of rococo.

Isola Madre is the larger of the two Borromean islands, and it had traditionally been used as an orchard, vineyard and hunting ground by the Borromeo. Two thirds of the island was covered in woodland. Between 1825 and 1830 Count Vitaliano IX had much of the native vegetation cleared to make way for his new collection of exotic trees

and plants. The camellia was one of the most popular plants in Europe during the nineteenth century, and Lake Maggiore offered ideal conditions for its cultivation. The Rovelli brothers became experts in cultivation and hybridization. In 1845 they published a catalogue of all the plants on the two Borromean islands, and the list included over 500 varieties of camellia.

Rather like the Roda, the Rovelli brothers straddled two worlds. They were retainers in the private and highly privileged milieu of aristocratic gardening, and they also operated in the commercial world of the mainland, where they opened a camellia nursery on the shore of the lake

in Pallanza. The boundaries between these two very distinct activities sometimes became confused, and on one deeply uncomfortable occasion Count Borromeo discovered that camellias grown in his own gardens were being sold in the brothers' nursery in Pallanza.

Nineteenth-century visitors were generally stunned by the combination of architecture and planting on Isola Bella. However, in 1852 two English brothers called Daniel and Thomas Hanbury visited Lake Maggiore. Thomas described Isola Bella in some detail in his journal. He lists cacti, opuntias, aloes, two specimens of *Chamaerops humilis*, cork and camphor trees, but nevertheless declares himself 'rather disappointed in the variety of plants the place afforded'. Thomas may have been echoing the words of his older brother, Daniel, who had followed their father into the pharmaceutical profession and become an exceptionally gifted botanist. The rare and exotic plants in the Borromeo collection would have interested him, but his vision of a garden was built upon systematic collections of plant genera and species, correctly labelled and arranged to create a living reference library for the botanist and an outdoor laboratory for the pharmacist. In 1867 Thomas Hanbury bought a dilapidated villa just inside the Italo-French border at La Mortola and 45 hectares of rough arid land plunging down to the sea. Thomas and Daniel were both involved in the creation of La Mortola. They shared the vision of a botanical garden where exotic plants would be persuaded to take root among the indigenous species. The Hanburys' reservations about Isola Bella had been entirely botanical. They recognized the extraordinary botanical potential of a garden in the micro-climate of Lake Maggiore, and they felt that it had not been fully realized. The Italian Riviera offered similar conditions, making La Mortola the ideal location for a truly ambitious plantsman's garden. The only real problems were lack of water and the poverty of the arid clay soil. These difficulties were addressed with the help of local labour. Several underground reservoirs and irrigation channels were built and the soil received intensive preparation.

By the autumn of 1867 Thomas Hanbury had already brought several cistus plants to La Mortola from his father's garden in London, and planted them alongside passion flowers, peonies, geraniums, roses and eighty varieties of acacia ordered from a nursery just over the French border in Hyères. In 1868 Ludwig Winter was appointed as head gardener. Winter had trained in Potsdam and worked in the royal

LEFT *A garden scene by Silvestro Lega conveying the informality of the nineteenth-century garden.*

RIGHT *Tranquillity infuses this painting by de Nittis entitled* Breakfast in the Garden.

gardens of the Tuileries in Paris until he was sacked for whistling the 'Marseillaise' in the presence of Empress Eugénie. Daniel had travelled all over Europe and to the Middle East to study the pharmacopoeia of different countries. He published articles in the *Transactions of the Linnean Society*, and the *Journal of the Linnean Society*. Through these activities he was linked to an international network of botanists and botanical gardens, and in this way he obtained the fascinating collection of seeds and plants that were to form the backbone of his brother's new garden. The first tree to be planted was a eucalyptus, a native of Australia, fast growing and drought resistant. By 1880 fifty different species of eucalyptus grew in the garden, swelling the woody framework of cypress and olive already on the site. Succulent plants could survive in near-drought conditions and this made agaves another favourite at La Mortola. Once again the aim was to build up as complete a collection as possible, and by 1871 there were already forty different species and subspecies of agave in the garden. It was Thomas's idea to plant the agaves in unbroken blocks, a style that was quite unknown in the nineteenth century but has since become common practice.

Daniel Hanbury died of typhoid in 1875, but Thomas was the guardian of his brother's ambitious vision, and the plant collection continued to grow. As it became more famous La Mortola received gifts from all over the world. The Bishop of Lebombo sent seeds from Delagoa Bay, and other consignments arrived from Mexico, Madagascar, Tenerife, Tasmania and Sierra Leone. The garden soon contained the best citrus collection in Italy, and the collection of succulent palms is still one of the finest in the world. By the end of the century Joseph Hooker, then director of the Royal Botanic Garden at Kew, declared that for richness and diversity La Mortola had 'no rival among the principal collections of living plants in the world'. In 1912 the third edition of the *Hortus Mortolensis* was printed and it contained entries for 5,300 different species of plants and trees.

At the end of the nineteenth century Italy contained a thriving cocktail of private gardens – great and small – public parks and successful nurseries. Several garden clubs and societies were formed, and from the middle of the century flower shows became common in many Italian cities. The most important of these was the Società italiana di orticoltura (The Italian horticultural society) which organized fruit and flower shows in the gardens of Florence. There was nothing in this vibrant picture to suggest the rapid decline that the twentieth century held in store.

XI | An open ending
The modern garden 1902-1968

THE FIRST WORLD WAR casts its long shadow over the history of the Italian garden in the twentieth century. However the brief pre-war period saw the creation of a number of new gardens. Their patrons belonged to a highly privileged and often intellectual group of English and American émigrés living in Florence, on the Italian Lakes or the Amalfi coast. *On the making of gardens*, Sir George Sitwell's essay published in 1909, conveys something of the psychology of expatriate garden culture in Italy at the beginning of the twentieth century. Sir George's own garden at Montegufoni in Tuscany was not made until 1926, but his essay was the fruit of a decade of visiting Renaissance and baroque gardens in Italy, and meditating upon their atmosphere and the qualities of their design. The essay is a vivid and elegantly written vignette of Italy's historic gardens at the beginning of the twentieth century, and an eloquent expression of their highly romantic appeal to the Edwardian imagination. In Tivoli, for example, Sitwell finds Villa d'Este's garden in the romantic state of near dereliction that he adores:

> Sleep and forgetfulness brood over the garden, and everywhere from sombre alley and moss-grown stair there rises a faint, sweet fragrance of decay… Deep drifts of withered leaves have gathered on the stairways, the fountain basins are overgrown with maiden-hair or choked with water weeds, the empty niches draped with velvety moss or tapestried creepers.

He is alive both to the physical experience of the gardens that he visits, and to the effect that they produce upon the mind, the 'subtle magic', the 'strange, elusive charm which must be felt, but cannot be wholly understood'. Expatriates living in Italy in the early twentieth century generally wanted to reproduce their own romantic – and often inaccurate – vision of the Renaissance or baroque landscape. By the time Sir George Sitwell published his essay, and with it his plea to the world to 'turn its back on Kent, Capability Brown and Horace Walpole, and … seek to learn the principles of garden design from Alberti, Michelozzo, Bramante, Vignola, Raphael, Michelangelo', many new gardens were already under construction in this retrospective style.

The first was created by Arthur Acton at La Pietra, a fifteenth-century villa near Florence. Arthur Acton and his wife Hortense first rented La Pietra in 1902. After six years Hortense bought the villa and the small estate that went with it. The original Renaissance and baroque landscape around the house had been destroyed in the nineteenth century to make way for a romantic English garden. The only surviving features were a large walled *pomario*, or orchard, dating from the eighteenth century, and a lemon house. Arthur Acton possessed all the necessary skills to transform this denuded landscape. Time spent at the École des Beaux Arts in Paris had trained his eye and improved his draughtsmanship. He was a close friend of the art historian and critic Bernard Berenson, and like him he was immersed in Renaissance and baroque culture. He dealt in fine art and amassed a large and distinguished sculpture collection of his own. Despite these qualifications, there has always been some doubt about the true source of the design. A survey survives, but the signature on it is obscure. There are also a number of scale models in plaster of Paris, presumably executed by the same hand. The design, which may have been the combined effort of Acton and several different friends and colleagues, was a brilliant pastiche of an Italian Renaissance garden that would double as an ideal open-air gallery for his sculpture collection. The first section of the garden was aligned with the long causeway that links La Pietra to the road. This was the main axis of Sir Arthur's layout, and

LEFT Senecio leuchostachys *provides a foil for 'Iceberg' roses in a typical example of the imaginative planting at La Landriana, where the* nucleus of the garden was designed by Russell Page before the owner, Marchesa Lavinia Taverna began to realize her own designs.

it fell away behind the villa in a series of steps and terraces. Cross-axes divided the land to each side of the main axis into small rooms. At this level of the garden the designer worked to a traditional mock-Renaissance layout, creating contrasts of light and shade, openness and enclosure. As he proceeded down the hillside the design became less traditional, more personal and unpredictable. He made long axial connections and controlled vistas, planting structured layers of foliage made up of cypress and stone pine at the highest level, followed by holm oak and yew, with box hedges at the bottom. He used the dense matt foliage of cypresses and the reflective leaves of holm oak and box to create different atmospheres, and contrasts in the quality of the light. In this way he generated the background lighting effects for the statues, arranging them in groups that would be illuminated by the sun at different times of the day. The Renaissance pastiche did not extend to garden iconography, and the statues were arranged to their best advantage, regardless of any symbolic message that they might convey. Photographs in the family archive reveal that Acton regularly moved the statues in the garden. Sometimes he sold them and sometimes he simply moved them to a better position. Sometimes he bought a statue and then designed a garden space to surround it. One of the main structures in the garden is a green theatre, perfect in every 'seventeenth-century' detail. It was specifically designed to accommodate a set of light-hearted eighteenth-century statues by Francesco Bonazza.

Acton understood the spirit of the Renaissance garden as well as the principles of its design. He made his own garden an essential part of daily life in the villa, just as it would have been in the sixteenth century.

It was an enormous open-air drawing room, and it became an essential port of call for every distinguished traveller passing through Florence and an elegant backdrop for the social life of the expatriate community.

In 1905 Sophie and Silvio della Valle di Casanova started work on another Anglo-Italian garden at Villa San Remigio, high above Lake Maggiore in Piedmont. Sophie and Silvio were first cousins. She was Anglo-Irish and he was Anglo-Italian. When they married in 1903 they renovated and enlarged a small chalet belonging to Sophie's family, transforming it into a handsome villa on the summit of the Castagnola, a promontory that reaches into Lake Maggiore and has spectacular views over the lake and the mountains. The garden that they made to surround the villa and then fall away to the shores of the lake is a highly romantic, northern European vision of the Italian baroque garden. Unlike Arthur Acton, Sophie and Silvio decided to continue the tradition of garden iconography. Again their approach is a romantic interpretation of the original language of iconography, and the garden became a very personal celebration of their love for each other, of Silvio's career as a professional musician and Sophie's skill as a painter.

ABOVE *This early twentieth-century watercolour is just one of hundreds of romantic views of Florence painted by the expatriate artists who flocked to the city from northern Europe.*

RIGHT *La Pietra's garden is densely furnished with statues. This is the side*

wall of the upper terrace – known as the Prima Vasca. The young cypresses in the foreground have been planted during the garden's restoration. They are part of the rich mixture of yew, holm oak, stone pine and box that form the background of the garden's vegetation.

LEFT Cascades of 'Dorothy Perkins' roses and a broken arch create a romantic background for this guest, a woman dressed in costume for an event in the garden of Villa La Pietra.

BELOW View from the villa of the Seconda Vasca, one of the two principal fountains in the garden, and the Corinthian peristyle beyond it. These early photographs have provided enormously useful reference for the garden restoration.

ABOVE RIGHT Looking back at the villa from the Seconda Vasca while it was being built in the early 1920s.

RIGHT Guests gathered for a lavish performance in the green theatre during the 1930s.

A plaque on the wall of the villa introduces the theme:

> We are Sophie and Silvio della Valle di Casanova, and this garden was born of the dreams that we shared in our youth. We planned it as children, and as man and wife we have created it.

Their personal iconography is spelt out with inscriptions like this throughout the garden, and in physical form. For example, Silvio built a high wall between the north façade of the house and the garden below as a symbol of the proper division between domestic life and romantic love.

The formal element of the garden plan consisted of two sets of terraces on the southern and eastern slopes of the Castagnola. The most dramatic of these were the six baroque terraces to the south. Sophie designed them, working up models made from wood and cloth, and then adjusting their design until she was happy with the effect at all times of day, and even on moonlit nights. They are set against the dramatic backdrop of the lake. The first is outside the villa, its balustrade decorated with eighteenth-century statues of the Four Seasons by Francesco Rizzi. The second is a little salon, furnished with an armchair cut from box and a series of rococo shell seats supported by dolphin pedestals. The retaining wall has a false façade of classical

columns interspersed with arches planted in myrtle. Between these decorations four masks pour water into shell basins. In the Casanovas' garden iconography, there was a reference to Silvio in the music of the fountains, and to Sophie in the colourful planting of the beds.

LEFT AND BELOW LEFT *The winter garden built into the retaining wall of San Remigio's third terrace, where Sophie della Valle di Casanova poses romantically among the ferns for a photograph taken by her husband.*

RIGHT *Sophie sitting on the terrace outside the villa to be photographed against the startlingly beautiful backdrop of Lake Maggiore.*

BELOW *Today Villa San Remigio's walls are bare, but this photograph of family and friends shows the villa romantically swathed in climbing plants.*

This appeal to sight and sound was completed with a camomile lawn, designed to satisfy the sense of smell.

Under the third terrace Sophie made a vaulted grotto. By glazing it on the outside, and channelling a small stream to run through it, she created a winter garden ideal for cultivating sub-tropical plants, ferns and orchids. Silvio took numerous photographs of Sophie in romantic poses among the ferns in this grotto. On the terrace outside the grotto Sophie made The Hour Garden. The circular sundial at its centre is a fine excuse for another inscription: 'Put here by Silvio and Sophie so that the new light of day may dispel the shadows of fled hours.'

A second winter garden stands above the lowest terrace. This was the Garden of Happiness, and it was planted with a series of broderie parterres laid out around a central pool. The climax of the terraces is a fountain at the centre of this garden. It was made by Riccardo Ripamonti, a contemporary Neapolitan sculptor who worked extensively in Milan, to represent the goddess Diana, riding triumphantly through the basin in a shell chariot pulled by two web-footed horses. Like much of the decoration in the garden, the fountain is made from a composite material unable to withstand the weather or the passage of time. This brought a romantic air of neglect to the garden quite soon, and has created some critical conservation issues.

Wrought-iron balconies overlook the lowest terrace – the Garden of Sadness. It is occupied by two pools set in lawns and surrounded by an iron fence. The Garden of Happiness on the terrace above was filled with roses and bright bedding plants. In the Garden of Sadness, the planting is restricted to mournful evergreens.

Between the terraces and the lake the sloping ground was cut into steps and winding paths, and informally planted with a mixture of rhododendrons, azaleas, exotic and native trees. Elegant shell seats were installed, where visitors might rest and enjoy long unbroken views over the water.

BELOW *San Remigio's garden terraces are set against a dramatic, mountainous backdrop.*

RIGHT *Riccardo Ripamonti's* Triumph of Diana *depicts the goddess charging through the Garden of Happiness in her chariot.*

The Amalfi coast in southern Italy also attracted foreign settlers, and in 1904 Ernest Beckett, later Lord Grimthorpe, spent a hundred lira on a ruined farmhouse, a wood, a vineyard, a walnut grove and an unbroken view over the Gulf of Salerno. Like Sophie della Valle di Casanova at San Remigio, he chose not to employ an architect. Instead, he recruited Nicola Mansi, a local man, a tailor and a great traveller and connoisseur, to help him. Together they spent fifteen years transforming the farmhouse of Cimbrone into a fortified palace with towers, battlements and a mixture of Arabic, Venetian and gothic details. The garden occupies the space between the house and the cliff edge, and the rocky slopes above the sea. It is composed of an eclectic and eccentric mixture of features, including formal flower gardens, winding woodland paths, classical temples, eighteenth-century statues, a picturesque grotto and a Moorish loggia. Grimthorpe is thought to have taken advice on the planting from Vita Sackville-West – although there is no archival evidence to prove this. An infinite view of the sea in one direction and the Cilento mountains in the other brings drama to every part of the garden. Grimthorpe fed the romantic atmosphere with a scattering of carefully selected inscriptions in English and Latin on the walls of the house and the garden buildings.

The site is divided into an upper and lower garden and an area of woodland intersected by narrow paths. The garden's main axis leads from the imposing 'medieval' gates to a terrace suspended high above the sea. The path is known as the Viale dell'Immenso – a reference to the boundless sea view at its far end. It is spanned by bridges and covered in part by a magnificent wisteria pergola. To the left the grassy lawn is scattered with fritillaries each spring. Beyond the walk a circular Doric temple -- the first of many classical structures – shelters a statue of Ceres that is silhouetted against the sea. The terrace beside it is the most dramatic feature in the garden. Suspended 300 metres (1,000 feet) above the Gulf of Salerno, it is bounded only by a balustrade decorated with eighteenth-century busts. Below the terrace a grassy slope leads down to a wood and the winding path to the Temple of Bacchus, its dome inscribed with a quotation from Horace. Lord Grimthorpe died in London in 1917, but his ashes are buried beneath the statue of Bacchus at the centre of the temple. Beyond the temple the path leads on to Eve's Grotto, a natural cave in the cliff face which gives shelter to an eighteenth-century statue by Tadolini.

The upper gardens were designed to frame views of the Cilento mountains. There are three gardens on this level. They are flower gardens, enclosed by walls of an eccentric design and furnished with classical reproductions, genuine archaeological remains, a sundial, a Moorish loggia and a melancholy inscription from the *Rubáiyát of Omar Khayyam*.

LEFT *A circular Doric temple occupies one end of Villa Cimbrone's beautiful terrace. The pale statue of Ceres is seen against the deep blue of the sea.*

RIGHT *Eighteenth-century busts break up the view across the Gulf of Salerno from Villa Cimbrone's terrace.*

The majority of expatriate gardens were made near Florence in the early twentieth century, and many of these were designed by Cecil Pinsent a young English architect who arrived in Florence for the first time in 1907. Pinsent had trained at the Architectural Association and the Royal Academy School of Architecture in London. At the Royal Academy Sir Reginald Blomfield taught him to admire formal garden design, rejecting the fashionable naturalism of William Robinson and his followers. This was the ideal stance for an architect intent on making a career among English and American patrons in the grip of nostalgia for the formality of Renaissance and baroque design. By 1911 there were 35,000 English-speaking expatriates living in Florence or on sunny hills overlooking the city, and it was among these patrons that Pinsent worked for forty years, making several new gardens and renovating or extending a number of old ones. His formal architectural training gave him a deep understanding of Renaissance and baroque style, enabling him to work with a light hand on historic sites.

Cecil Pinsent's first major commission came from Bernard Berenson, the American art historian and critic who was renovating a house called I Tatti in Settignano, outside Florence. In 1909 Mary Berenson commissioned Pinsent to help with the work. The peculiar social circumstances at I Tatti must be explained as they were to have a considerable effect upon Pinsent's immediate future. Berenson and his wife Mary had a relatively 'open' marriage, but he had finally lost patience with his wife's infatuation for a young Englishman called Geoffrey Scott. For two years Scott had been acting as secretary to Berenson, but now his employer wanted to be rid of him and announced that there was no longer any work for him to do. Scott had spent a term at the Architectural Association in London, and Mary suggested both to him and to Pinsent that they should form a business partnership. In this way she could keep Scott at I Tatti for the duration of the renovations. Pinsent was to be the architect, and Scott the consultant on interior design. In 1910 Pinsent accepted her suggestion – which may have become something of an obligation – and the two men rented an apartment together in Via delle Terme in Florence where they lived and had their studio. Much has been written about Geoffrey Scott's foibles, and there can be no doubt that his eventful emotional life often distracted him, leaving Pinsent to do more than his share of the work. However Scott's life work, a book called *The architecture of humanism* (1914), cannot be so lightly dismissed. It was extremely influential, and it is a key to understanding the neo-baroque formula of Pinsent's gardens. It is a book on the aesthetics of architectural style, written while the two men were working together, and dedicated to Pinsent. Although Scott abhorred the accepted forms of the picturesque, which transform the garden landscape into 'a

ABOVE *Villa I Tatti's* giardino pensile *is enclosed by a decorative, neo-baroque wall and planted with geometric blocks of clipped lavender.*

RIGHT *The old* limonaia *at I Tatti is swathed in ivy and roses. Below the steps that link the building to the garden Pinsent created a miniature nymphaeum.*

"prospect" of little holes and hills', he identifies 'all that is unexpected, wild, fantastic, accidental' in nature as its proper constituents, and bemoans the absence of these qualities from Renaissance architecture. Scott's ideal of architectural style was the baroque, because 'it intellectualised the picturesque'. He argued his case very eloquently:

> To give the picturesque its grandest scope, and yet to subdue it to architectural law – this was the baroque experiment and it is achieved. The baroque is not afraid to startle and arrest. Like Nature, it is fantastic, unexpected, varied and grotesque. But, unlike Nature, it remains subject rigidly to the laws of scale and composition.

LEFT *A pebble mosaic decorates the steps that intersect the terraces below Villa I Tatti. Screens cut from holm oak hide the lowest terrace.*

ABOVE *The* giardino segreto *at Villa Le Balze, overlooked by the pergola. The garden and villa are beautifully maintained by Georgetown University, who use it as their European campus.*

The laws of scale and composition governed Pinsent's own approach to garden design. The only article that he ever published appeared in *Il giardino fiorito* in 1931, and in it he named order and symmetry as the vital constituents of a garden. He also advised the reader to partially cover walls with climbers such as wisteria, clematis and jasmine. At I Tatti he recreated the enclosed spaces, the hidden details and the element of surprise characteristic of the baroque garden. To the west of the house he designed a *giardino pensile* or hanging garden, enclosed by a decorative neo-baroque wall that is swathed in wisteria. The old *limonaia* to the south of the villa became a screen to shield the main garden from the house, so that Pinsent's formal terraces were revealed as a delightful surprise to the first-time visitor. Four narrow terraces descend the hill, intersected by a central staircase. On the terraces to either side of the steps Pinsent planted neat squares of box. That is the overview of the garden, but as one descends the steps, the details of Pinsent's design unfold. The steps that form the main axis of the garden are decorated

with an elaborate pebble mosaic, and inside the box hedges there are low geometric parterres, invisible from above. On the lowest terrace he made an oval pool, flanked by tiers of box. Beyond it was a wood of holm oaks that were already over twelve metres (40 foot) high when they were planted so that Berenson could enjoy them in his lifetime. Nicky Mariano, who became Berenson's long-term assistant, saw the garden in its infancy. In her memoir, *Forty years with Berenson* (1966), she describes the new terraces, as looking, '…out of proportion, the statues in the new, formal garden ridiculously large as compared with the tiny box and cypress hedges'. The hedges grew, of course, but the scale of the garden worried Pinsent himself in later life. When he returned to I Tatti to visit Berenson after the Second World War, he remarked that if he were able to build the terrace garden again, he would make it wider.

I Tatti was the fulcrum of intellectual expatriate society in Florence – an ideal place for the Pinsent-Scott partnership to find new clients. Their next commission came when the American philosopher Charles Strong visited I Tatti. Strong studied with Berenson at Harvard and made his home in Italy after the death of his wife. He was impressed by the renovation work at I Tatti, and by the new garden. In 1911 he commissioned Scott and Pinsent to design a new villa and garden on an extremely steep and unpromising tract of ground in Fiesole. The first two years were spent designing and building the villa on a narrow shelf of land cut into the hillside overlooking Florence and the Arno valley. Pinsent designed a first-floor loggia to the east and a library on the ground floor to the west. In 1914 he turned his attention to the garden, creating a series of rooms to east and west of the villa. Wrestling with a difficult and restricted space, Pinsent made one of the finest gardens of his career. He was unable to impose strict symmetry on the site as it was too narrow and irregular. Instead he made a series of interlocking but enclosed spaces linked by long views. At the end of each perspective he placed an eyecatcher – an urn, perhaps, or a statue. In this way he emphasized the length of the garden, drawing attention away from its restricted breadth. The graceful first-floor loggia of the villa was outside Strong's bedroom. His window overlooked the *giardino segreto*, a 'secret' garden enclosed to the south by a high wall concealing the view over Florence. The simple layout of box-lined, grass parterres around a central pool is densely furnished with pots of lemons, and the air is full of the scent of the jasmine that Pinsent planted to cover the walls. In the narrow space to the north of the villa Pinsent built an elaborate grotto against the hill, cladding it in shells and pebble mosaics and decorating it with busts of classical philosophers. Beside the grotto a handsome baroque staircase leads up to a raised pergola. The pergola, with its stone piers,

became one of the hallmarks of Pinsent's style. At Le Balze he used it to claim the dead space above the garden, creating a new north-south view over the garden and the valley beyond. Charles Strong's library was designed to overlook the garden to the west. Here the window frames a sober enclosed space. Beyond it Pinsent made the Philosopher's Walk, lining the path with iris and lavender backed by holm oaks.

In 1915 Pinsent and Scott were called next door to Villa Medici, Fiesole, by Lady Sybil Cutting for a commission that eventually brought their partnership to an end. Lady Cutting had owned the villa since 1911. Its garden, which commanded the same view over Florence as Le Balze, was originally designed by Michelozzo Michelozzi in the mid-fifteenth century (see Chapter 1). At the end of the seventeenth century the villa was sold by Cosimo III de' Medici to Vincenzo del Serra, who added a pretty, pebble-encrusted nymphaeum to the upper terrace. Although many changes were made to the villa, the garden remained intact until the end of the eighteenth century. At this point modern flowerbeds were made on the lower south-facing terrace and a glasshouse was built against the retaining wall. Pinsent liberated this space and restored the integrity of the Renaissance garden by creating a simple geometric

LEFT *Steps lead up from the grotto to the pergola at Le Balze. They are decorated with rocaille, the pebble mosaics that were a traditional Tuscan feature of the Renaissance and Baroque garden.*

RIGHT *A carefully placed bench beyond the Philosopher's Walk, where the garden is open to the stunning view over Florence.*

layout of parterre beds and lawns around a circular pool. The greenhouse was replaced by a raised pergola – a similar structure to the pergola at Le Balze. This linked the two garden terraces to the *giardino segreto* – or secret garden – to the west of the villa. Here Pinsent made a sombre design of lawns gathered around a central pool. He planted a magnolia in the centre of each lawn.

It is always said that Scott was more interested in finding a rich wife to support his intellectual life than pursuing a more practical career. His work at Villa Medici brought him into close contact with Lady Cutting, who was a wealthy American widow. She became Scott's wife and released him for the duration of their marriage from the need to earn. This was the beginning of a new and exciting era for Pinsent. After the interruption of the war he could hardly wait to get back to the task of developing his own architectural practice. A letter written in January 1919 captures this sense of excitement:

> I shall bang the door on the war on the 31st, and go back to beloved Via delle Terme, to pick up the strings of work again – my own work this time. It seems like getting near the gates of Heaven.

When Pinsent returned to Florence after the war he found no shortage of clients. Before long he had a large and sophisticated client base of Anglo-American expatriates, Florentine aristocrats and even European royalty. Sir George Sitwell was among Pinsent's post-war clients. He had bought the Castello di Montegufoni near Florence in 1898, and in 1926 he commissioned Pinsent to design a small garden. Pinsent created his usual sense of enclosure with tall cypress hedges, and planted simple box parterres on a grassy lawn. Many of Pinsent's clients commissioned him to make alterations to existing villas or gardens. In 1928, for example, he was engaged by Henry Clifford to make a swimming pool at Villa Capponi. The villa's beautiful garden was a combination of sixteenth-, seventeenth- and eighteenth-century elements made by successive generations of the Capponi family. At some time after 1882, when the villa was bought by Lady Scott of Ancrim, a new rose garden had been added below the *giardino segreto*. The architect, whose name is not recorded, copied the original intricate design of the baroque walls, and made traditional stone edges for the flower beds. Pinsent designed a new space below the rose garden, enclosing it with cypress hedges. The rectangular pool inside this discreet garden room resembles a simple baroque fish pool. The only decoration is the shell fountain at one end of the pool and the statues and stone benches that line the hedges.

Cecil Pinsent's most important post-war garden was La Foce, which he designed for Marchesa Origo (better known as the author and historian Iris Origo) near Chianciano Terme in southern Tuscany.

Pinsent first met Iris Origo when he was employed by her mother, Lady Sybil Cutting, to work on the garden of Villa Medici in Fiesole. By the time she commissioned him in 1924, Iris was a young woman, engaged to Marchese Antonio Origo. The couple were very idealistic. They had rejected the comfortable privileged environment of Iris's childhood and bought a derelict inn, a range of buildings and 3,500 acres of poor and neglected land on the western slopes of an arid exposed ridge of hills that form the watershed between the Val d'Orcia and the Val di Chiana. Beyond the house the land fell sharply away to the valley of the Orcia river, and the long view was stopped only by the dramatic profile of Monte Amiata. Erosion had stripped the topsoil from much of the land on the estate, creating the lunar landscape of clay and bare rock, known as the *crete senesi*. In winter the farm was often battered by the freezing Tramontana wind, and in summer it was scorched by the sirocco. The landscape was huge, empty and barren, quite unlike the gentle fertile hills that surround Florence. In her autobiography, *Images and shadows*, Iris Origo described her first view of the house:

> … surrounded by these desolate hillocks: no tree, no patch of green, no trace of human habitation, except against the sky a half-ruined watch tower… Suddenly an overwhelming wave of longing came over me for the gentle, trim Florentine landscape of my childhood… and most of all, for a pretty house and garden to come home to in the evening. I felt the landscape around me to be alien, inhuman – built on a scale fit for demi-gods and giants, but not for us.

LEFT *Cecil Pinsent's lower terrace at Villa Medici where, once again, he built a raised pergola which is swathed in Rosa banksia.*

ABOVE *Antony Beevor, future historian, presents flowers to Iris Origo during her birthday picnic.*

Pinsent and Iris were firm friends. The creation of a 'pretty house and garden' was only one of a myriad of different projects that kept him at La Foce for months at a time over the next fifteen years. Iris and Antonio devoted their energy to restoring fertility and productivity to the bleak, barren landscape, stopping soil erosion by building retaining walls and planting trees, and improving the lives of their tenants and labourers. Most of the buildings that they commissioned Pinsent to design reflected the philanthropic nature of their work. In 1933 he designed a first aid clinic and a chapel, in 1935 he returned to build a kindergarden and a primary school, and in 1936 he built the *dopolavoro* – an 'afterwork' club for labourers on the estate.

Pinsent began work on the garden in 1926, restricting himself initially to the 'inner garden' an area immediately outside the house. Here he created an intimate room enclosed by the villa on one side and tall hedges on the others. At the centre he placed an eighteenth-century dolphin fountain and designed a boat-shaped bowl to surround it. The fountain was then enclosed with lozenges of box, creating a sheltered and densely furnished landscape in miniature, a perfect antidote to the vast spaces beyond the garden, and the *crete senesi* that Iris perceived 'as bare and colourless as elephants' backs, as mountains of the moon'.

In 1930 Pinsent extended the garden beyond the tall hedges of this inner sanctum. This was the site of the Lemon Garden, a gently terraced hanging garden that embraces the view across the valley to Monte Amiata. Pinsent planted box hedges along the edges of each terrace, just as he had done at I Tatti. Here, however, both the hedges and the terraces are broader and this gives a more generous feeling to the design. The garden takes its name from the pots of lemons that are arranged on stone plinths inside the hedges, leaving the broad paved paths free. At the base of the walls that enclose this serene geometric layout on three sides Iris planted a riotous herbaceous border. In 1938 Pinsent added his usual raised pergola, a rose garden and a *limonaia*. The wisteria-covered

ABOVE *The double staircase and nymphaeum in the lower garden at La Foce. Pinsent brought unity to his design by using this serene travertine stone throughout the site.* Magnolia grandiflora *occupy the box compartments in the garden beyond.*

pergola strikes out to the west from the house before curving around the shoulder of the hill. At its far end it opens into the woods, where Pinsent had already built a small chapel and a cemetery. In 1939, just before Italy joined the Second World War, Pinsent embarked on the final addition, the Lower Garden which projects like the prow of a ship over the valley below. It was linked to the Lemon Garden by a mighty double staircase with a nymphaeum beneath it. The space is entirely enclosed by tall cypresses and filled with wedge-shaped double box hedges that taper towards a pool at the far end of the garden. Once again, Pinsent had created a mathematically controlled, enclosed landscape built on a human scale. It was the perfect foreground for the view over the wide wild spaces of the Orcia valley, and the perfect antidote for any nostalgia that Iris may have felt for Florence and her gentle hills.

La Foce is a serene garden, and part of this serenity comes from the continuity of Pinsent's design. He loved the travertine stone quarried in Rapolano, and he put it to architectural use all over the garden for walls, stairs and balustrades. He used the same stone for smaller decorative details, such as the vases on the walls of the Lemon Garden and the stone basins at its base, the vases that flank the steps to the cypress avenue scaling the hill and the fountain basins in the nymphaeum and the Inner and Lower Gardens. Travertine is a porous stone and plants were quick to root themselves on the small pockets in its surface, rapidly softening the contours of the hard landscaping.

Pinsent's work at La Foce took place against the background of Mussolini's Fascist government. Many of the improvements made to the estate – such as the new agricultural buildings, the schools and the clinic – received state subsidies, as did the reforestation and road building. The Fascist regime also encouraged gardening, which it perceived as an important element of Italy's national identity – its *italianità*. In 1926 Mussolini launched a campaign to revive Italian garden culture, which had been in decline since the beginning of the twentieth century – despite the activity of Pinsent and his expatriate clients. The government organized competitions and awarded prizes for the most beautiful balcony and the best station garden. New public parks and gardens were built and planted with the native plants and trees that Fascists referred to as the *flora classica*. All the plants in the *flora classica* were mentioned in the classical poetry of Virgil, Horace, Tibullus and Propertius, or depicted in frescoes at Pompeii and the Villa Livia. In the new parks holm oaks, bay trees and Italian pines predominated, with an underplanting of oleander. The Italian pine, *pinus italicus*, became a national symbol, and it was used to line the edges of main roads.

In 1931 the government organized the *Mostra del giardino italiano* in Florence's Palazzo Vecchio. This was an exhibition devoted to the history of the Italian garden. Three floors and fifty-three rooms of the palace were filled with paintings, photographs, prints and drawings. Among the most popular exhibits were ten model gardens composed from a patchwork of features drawn from literary sources, paintings and real gardens, and installed in the Salone dei Cinquecento.

In 1938 plans were launched for an International World Exhibition (Esposizione Universale Romana, or EUR), scheduled for 1942. In 1940 Maria Teresa Parpagliolo was made head of the exhibition's planning department for parks and gardens. There were very few landscape architects in Italy in this period, and no opportunities for formal training. Parpagliolo was largely self trained. She had read all the garden literature that she could find, and travelled extensively to visit gardens in England, Holland, France, Belgium and Germany. In 1931 she spent seven months working for Percy Cane's office in London. In 1938 she grasped the opportunity offered by the Fascist government, compromising her own international style to create the plans for a seven-hectare (17-acre) site composed of features taken from all of Italy's most famous historic gardens. The drawings show a scaled-down version of Caserta's canal, an imitation of the amphitheatre at Boboli, Villa Reale's green theatre, the terraces from Villa d'Este and a section of the Botanic Garden in Padua. Italy joined the Second World War in 1940 and by 1941 plans for the exhibition had been abandoned.

As Italy's political climate darkened, one garden became a refuge for artists and intellectuals. Iris Origo gives an evocative description of the parties that her friends Roffredo and Marguerite Caetani, the Duke and Duchess of Sermoneta, gave in the garden of Ninfa, on the edge of the Pontine Marshes, south-east of Rome:

> Here, on Sundays, Roffredo and Marguerite kept open house for an extremely varied collection of guests: foreign diplomats and men of letters, elegant Roman ladies and Englishwomen with stout boots and an expert knowledge of gardening, bearded young painters or musicians and classical scholars from the American Academy, eminent foreign statesmen and rising young politicians.

These were informal events. Marguerite is described 'in faintly shabby country clothes, with her gardening gloves – just drawn off – on the grass beside her'. In this relaxed and friendly atmosphere, 'even the shyest visitor and the youngest child were at once as much at ease as the French Ambassador and the President of the Republic'. Marguerite Chapin Caetani was the American wife of Roffredo Caetani, Duke of Sermoneta. She was the founder and editor of two literary magazines, *Commerce* and *Botteghe Oscure*, a literary journal publishing poetry and fiction from England, Germany, Italy, France, Spain and the United States in the original languages. In the course of a long career Marguerite published a wide variety of authors and poets, including André Malraux, Albert Camus, James Joyce, T. S. Eliot, Paul Valery, Ignazio Silone, Robert Graves, Archibald MacLeish, e.e. cummings, Dylan Thomas and Marianne Moore. The garden that she used as her editorial office and literary salon was made in the ruins of the medieval town of Ninfa. The property had belonged to the Caetani since the thirteenth century, when it was given to Pietro Caetani by his uncle, Pope Boniface VIII. The little town thrived under Caetani rule. At the height of its prosperity it had a double wall surrounding six churches,

150 houses, a castle, a town hall, and numerous bakeries, smithies and watermills on the river than runs through it. These ruined structures became the ghostly skeleton on which successive generations of Caetani made a garden in the nineteenth and twentieth centuries. By the time Ada Bootle-Wilbrahim Caetani, the English wife of Duke Onorato, rediscovered Ninfa in the 1870s it had been ruined and virtually abandoned for five centuries. Its downfall came in 1382 when it was caught up in the civil wars surrounding the Great Schism of the Catholic church. An army amassed by another branch of the Caetani sacked Ninfa, razing its buildings to the ground, and killed its inhabitants. Over

the years a few people returned, but malaria was endemic in the Pontine Marshes, and a particularly bad outbreak emptied Ninfa for good. The ruined buildings, swamped in vegetation and wild flowers were periodically visited by travellers, and they had a particular appeal to the romantic, nineteenth-century imagination. In 1874 Augustus Hare wrote:

> …There is something unearthly about Ninfa which possesses and absorbs every sense. …. The only inhabitants are the roses and the lilies and all the thousands of flowers which grow so abundantly in the deserted streets, where honeysuckle and jessamine fling their garlands through the windows of every house, and where the altars of the churches are thrones for flame-coloured valerian. Outside the walls you would hardly believe it was a town, so encrusted in verdure is every building that the houses look like green mounds rising out of the plain.

Ada began to take her six children on outings to the ruined town from their summer house on the coast at Fogliano. She would pack a picnic

BELOW *There are over 200 different species of rose at Ninfa. They thrive in the gentle climate, rampaging over fallen rocks and hurling themselves up walls and through the branches of trees.*

RIGHT *The only place in the garden where the water lies still is this limpid, pool at the centre of a towering grove of bamboo, Phyllostachys sulphurea var. viridis.*

and a bundle of rooted rose cuttings. She stuck the cuttings in against the ruined walls of the buildings and they took root and thrived in the peculiar microclimate created by the river that cuts the town in two. The river flows from the spring-water lake behind Pietro Caetani's castle. It is completely clean, ice cold and fast moving. Its presence prevents the temperature dropping too far in winter, or soaring too high in summer.

On the death of Onorato Caetani in 1917, Ninfa was left to Ada's eldest son, Gelasio. He was in America at the time, where he had trained and practised very successfully as an engineer. When he returned to Italy in 1922 he was engaged in the huge government project of draining the Pontine Marshes. He also worked with his mother at Ninfa. Between them Ada and Gelasio had both the skill and the knowledge to impose a formal Italianate structure on the chaotic ruins of the town. There was an abundance of water to feed pools and fountains, and enough space to create an axial layout of long vistas. Ada had already created a garden at Fogliano – a period piece of palms and Eucalyptus rising out of a sea of bedding plants. Ninfa would have been an ideal site for another exotic garden of tender plants. However they both responded to the *genius loci*, allowing the garden to emerge from the existing structure of the ruins. Its evolution was site specific. Tender plants found shelter within the ruined walls of houses or churches – some of them still decorated with the remains of Byzantine frescoes – and robust ones scrambled over

LEFT *In late spring arum lilies, Zantedeschia aethiopica, pack the banks of the stream at Ninfa, apparently receding into infinity among the silver trunks of the birches.*

ABOVE *Marguerite created groves of silver birches in the damp areas of the garden, and underplanted them with irises.*

them. Ada and Gelasio planted strategic groups of holm oak, cedar and plane trees, and marked the main street with an avenue of cypresses. They restored the keep of Pietro Caetani's castle and rebuilt the town hall as a house. Gelasio brought the sound of water to every part of the garden, creating underground channels and surface streams that crossed over themselves in miniature aqueducts.

Together, Ada and Gelasio established the bones of Ninfa's garden. When he died in 1934, Gelasio bequeathed Ninfa to his nephew, Camillo. During the Second World War Camillo was killed in Albania. This left Ninfa in the hands of his parents, Marguerite and Roffredo Caetani.

Marguerite engaged with the garden in 1933, and continued to work in it until her death in 1958. She developed another layer to the planting, adding swathes of ornamental cherries to flower in April, when Ninfa seems to float on a raft of blossom, magnolias and thousands more roses. In the damp areas of the garden she created groves of silver birch, and packed the banks of the streams with arum lilies. Marguerite gardened with her daughter, Lelia, who took Ninfa's Anglo-American connections into a third generation by marrying Hubert Howard, another member of Rome's Anglo-Italian nobility. After Marguerite's death, Lelia and Hubert continued to work with the legacy of three

LEFT *The voluptuous flowers of Wisteria floribunda 'Macrobotrys' trail from a medieval bridge that spans the Ninfa river.*

RIGHT *Il Roseto, one of Porcinai's best-known domestic designs, where a circular hedge conceals the top of a spiral staircase leading to an underground garage.*

generations of Caetani gardeners, skilfully adding to the planting and safeguarding Ninfa's future by setting up the Caetani foundation.

Despite the efforts made by the Fascist government to revive garden culture, there was little interest in gardening in Italy, and very few plant or tree nurseries. In 1942, when Italy was already at war, Maria Teresa Parpagliolo contributed an article to the architectural magazine *Domus*, in which she focused on the problem of buying plants:

> In Italy up until now we have suffered a vicious circle; the nurserymen have not expanded and developed their activities further because of lack of demand, and the public does not ask for special plants and varieties because they lack know-how and knowledge.

Marguerite was generally compelled to order the plants and trees she wanted from abroad, and the majority of her new plants were supplied by Hilliers in England. *Domus* was founded in 1928, and it rapidly became a platform for Italy's sparse community of landscape architects. In the inaugural issue Tommaso Buzzi, architect and designer, wrote an article on garden architecture in which he bemoaned the 'general lack of interest in garden art'. In 1937 Pietro Porcinai, who became the most important landscape architect of his generation, criticized the 'little oval beds' and 'torturous paths' that had characterized the design of new Italian gardens for 150 years and, like Buzzi, he bemoaned the stasis of garden culture. Porcinai was a self-trained landscape architect. After receiving a diploma in agriculture in 1928 he had left Florence on a motorbike, intending to travel to England to study garden architecture. He only got as far as Germany and Belgium on this occasion, where he learnt modern cultivation techniques by working in commercial nurseries. On subsequent journeys Porcinai met Europe's leading landscape architects, among them Geoffrey Jellicoe, Russell Page, Gerda Gollwitzer, René Pechère, Karl Foester, Gustav Lüttge and Fritz Enchk. By 1938, at the age of only twenty-eight, he was a well established architect, with an office in Florence and a portfolio of commercial clients, many of them developers. His style was generally international and much of his high-profile work was done on public projects abroad.

In 1956 he worked on Hansavirtel Park in Berlin, in 1973 he was engaged in the landscaping around the Pompidou Centre in Paris, and from 1975-76 he designed a series of city parks in Saudi Arabia. In Italy his best-known private gardens are the Villa Riva at Saronno and Il Roseto near Florence.

Porcinai campaigned tirelessly for green spaces in Italy's newly urbanized, post-war landscape, and for better educational facilities for horticulture and landscape architecture. This was particularly important after the war, when Italy's rapid urbanization coincided with the removal of landscape architecture from the university syllabus. In 1960 he tried to set up his own landscape education centre in Fiesole. He was unable to get the support that he needed, but a few years later his ambition was realized when the university of Genoa opened its own department of landscape architecture. Other universities soon followed Genoa's example.

Cecil Pinsent left Italy shortly before the outbreak of the Second World War. In a letter written to Mary Berenson in October 1938 he explained his motives in the following words: 'What I have offered is not congenial to the time, and what the times want is not congenial to me'. Had Pinsent remained in Italy after the war he would have found his client base of English and American expatriates severely depleted.

Pinsent's place as Italy's English garden architect was taken by Russell Page, who began to visit Italy in the 1950s in order to study its Renaissance and baroque gardens. By this time Page was already internationally famous as a landscape architect and plantsman. His work ranged from small domestic sites to projects on a grand scale, such as the Festival Gardens in Battersea Park, London, that earned him an OBE in 1952. When Page began to work in Italy his clients were Italian

ABOVE *Lady Susana Walton has an intimate and expert knowledge of the plants in her garden. Here she is seen against a backdrop of tree ferns – Dicksonia antarctica.*

RIGHT *Russell Page's Orange Garden at La Landriaia formed the nucleus of a layout that eventually incorporated thirty-two separate rooms and covered ten hectares.*

rather than English or American. His first commission came in 1955 from Giovanni and Marella Agnelli, who asked him to redesign and extend the gardens of the family house in Villar Perosa, near Turin. The house was surrounded by a crowded, nineteenth-century garden which Page opened up to the views and 'the light and atmosphere' of the surrounding countryside. This involved felling several trees – a painful process as each one seemed to have associations either with an Agnelli ancestor, or with the gardener of fifty years' standing. He went on to extend the garden into the wooded valley below the villa, where he designed a wild garden of rhododendrons, azaleas and magnolias, underplanted with bluebells and lily-of-the-valley. He dammed the stream to create a series of eleven ponds, filling the small valley with the sound of water cascading from one pool to the next.

In 1956 Page was engaged by Sir William Walton to design a garden at La Mortella on Ischia in the Bay of Naples. The site was a steep hillside covered in holm oak, neglected olives and chestnut trees, and a narrow gulley strewn with chunks of weathered lava. Page stayed with the Waltons for three days, drawing up plans that would keep Lady Susana

Walton occupied for the next decade. On this first visit, Susana Walton recalls, 'Russell drew a handsome plan for us to follow and, in 1956, blissfully ignorant of the difficulties that lay ahead, we started to build the garden.' Although the house was not built until 1962, work on the garden began immediately. Page had established a single axis for the site that ran straight as far as possible, and then made a dramatic, right-angled turn. The Waltons employed a team of men for seven years to build layer upon layer of drystone walls across the steep hillside, and link the levels with flights of stone steps. They imported peat, installed underground collection tanks for rainwater and planted Californian tulip trees to provide shade. Page's planting plan was largely composed of silver-leafed Mediterranean ground-cover plants. However even these native plants struggled to survive the heat and drought until the Waltons devised a system for giving them shade. For three summers they suspended straw matting from a framework of wooden poles over the cultivated areas in the valley.

By the time Page returned to Ischia twelve years later, the island had been connected to the Naples water mains by an undersea pipe.

Page celebrated this event by designing three pools with fountains. The first was an egg-shaped pool among the rocks below the house, the second a smaller oval pool on the slope opposite it, and the third consisted of two concentric basins at the eastern end of the valley. Page also devised a planting list of palms, cycads and Mexican aloes that were arranged in thick belts to bring architectural structure to the view from the house. Susana Walton added her own selection of exotic trees and plants to the valley, many of them native to her home in Argentina.

When Russell Page paid his final visit in 1983, he added a fourth pool and fountain to the garden. The octagonal bowl was set in an octagonal terrace, and linked to the egg-shaped pool by a glittering ribbon of water. Susana Walton has continued to expand the garden, and to add layer upon layer to its rich and exotic planting.

In 1964 Russell Page returned to Italy to meet Count Donato and Countess Maria Sanminiatelli at San Liberato, an isolated hill overlooking Lake Bracciano that Maria Sanminiatelli had inherited from her father. The hillside was covered in chestnut woods, and below the trees the ground formed a natural amphitheatre enclosing a gently sloping field of rough grass and a few olive trees. The fourth-century church of San Liberato stood on one side of this field. It was half buried in soil that had washed off the hillside and accumulated over the centuries. Below the hill the great open plain of the lake opened out.

When her father died Maria Odescalchi was already married to Donato Sanminiatelli, a well-known art historian. After only one visit to San Liberato they decided to build a house on the site. The new house stood with its back to the hill. It was not long before Count Sanminiatelli began to plant more trees along the edge of the woods. He also excavated a single terrace to break the slope below the house, but here work came to a halt. The sheer size of the site was intimidating, and so was its spectacular position above the lake. The Sanminiatellis spent several weeks studying landscape books, and then they decided to engage Russell Page.

Page began by advising the Sanminiatellis to plant more trees. Experience in the north of the country had shown him that trees from China, Japan and North America could thrive in Italian soil. He had no idea if the same species would take to the hotter conditions of central Italy. Any doubts soon proved unfounded, as the slightly acid conditions on the hillside and the microclimate created by the lake turned out to be a winning combination, creating growing conditions that Page described as 'something radioactive'.

A rhythm was soon established at San Liberato. Page would visit the site every three or four months to monitor progress and discuss the next phase of work. When he returned, he would find his instructions carried out to the letter. Count Sanminiatelli and Page collaborated on the position of every tree in the arboretum. When they had reached an agreement about the site, the count would plant the sapling himself. This level of co-operation gave Page particular pleasure. In a diary written towards the end of his life he said, 'If I consider this garden especially good it is because we, its owner and myself, were always alert to the nature of the place; in placing every plant.' Today the garden is enclosed by a dense grove. There are cherries to herald spring, acers to set it all ablaze in autumn and liquidambar, camphor, black walnut, cedar, sequoia, and tulip trees of an extraordinary height.

The countess was keen to have a rose garden, and Page made this on the lowest of three terraces. The roses are planted in formal beds arranged around a small fountain. Their scent is trapped between the retaining wall and a hedge of grey-leafed *Teucrium fruticans*. A generous flight of steps leads to the upper terraces, where the formality of the defined beds falls away to a blazing herbaceous border. A 'Rambling Rector' rose has made its way to the top of an ancient olive, its flowers cascading down among peonies, gigantic alliums, lupins and white campion. Valerian has seeded itself in the retaining walls, softening the edges of the beds.

In 1968 Page was contacted by Lavinia Taverna, a prospective client who was soon to become a firm friend. In 1956 Lavinia Taverna and her husband, Marchese Gallerati Scotti, had bought a derelict dairy farm 40 kilometres (25 miles) south of Rome. Their principal interest was in the pastureland and at first they gave little attention to the ugly house and derelict barns that had been thrown in with the sale. In retrospect Taverna was surprised that they put down roots in such an inhospitable place. The land lay only four kilometres from the sea and it was full of unexploded mines left over from the war. The fields were raked by sea winds and over the years they had been stripped of any natural vegetation.

Gardening infiltrated Lavinia Taverna's life slowly, taking her almost by surprise. At first she was interested in alpines and other rock plants. Then she focused on plants from Australia, South Africa and California. She found that she could acclimatize exotic plants in the gentle coastal climate of La Landriana. By 1968 she already had a sizeable collection of exotics, and it was at this point that she met Russell Page and commissioned him to create a framework for her large but somewhat disparate plant collection.

The Orange Garden was the first of Page's 'rooms'. He originally planted the square beds with roses, but after six years the soil was exhausted. Lavinia Taverna devised a new planting scheme. She put bitter orange trees at the centre of four of the beds. Severely clipped to resemble glossy green lollipops, the trees are studded with brilliant fruit throughout the year. Globes of Cape myrtle (*Myrsine africana*) mark the corners of the beds, and an underplanting of *Pratia pedunculata* provides a splash of violet-blue each spring. The garden is given a less formal dimension by the softer shapes of the *Acer platanoides* 'Globosum' that Taverna planted in the centre of the remaining beds.

Beyond the first room is Page's Olive Garden, its entrance marked by a majestic cork oak. The space is enclosed by olives and has beds arranged around two stone fountains. Page invited Lavinia Taverna to concoct her own planting scheme for this area. The beds became

wonderful densely woven carpets in which the shades of violet and yellow were repeated again and again.

Taking courage from Russell Page's design, Lavinia Taverna began almost at once to make the garden her own. She was a passionate plantswoman and a fearless gardener. She would plant mature trees and shrubs to create instant effects, and if a new design fell short she would not flinch from reducing it to bare earth. Failure to thrive was never tolerated for long at La Landriana. Operating on the scale of

a Renaissance prince, it took her little more than four decades to create one of the largest and most important modern gardens in Italy. By the time she died in 1998 it encompassed thirty-two separate rooms and covered an area of ten hectares (25 acres).

Russell Page chose his clients with care. They were genuine gardeners and, left to their own devices, almost all of them worked like Lavinia Taverna to develop and enlarge his original design. Page came to Italy to learn from its great Renaissance and baroque gardens. What he gave in return was a clutch of exceptional gardens designed in an international and site-specific style. This international approach is Italy's future, a future that must bring any history of the Italian garden to a close.

ABOVE *There are over 500 different species of rose at La Landriana. Many of them grow in the Valley of* *the Roses, which Lavinia Taverna described as the most important part of her garden.*

Epilogue

THE HISTORY OF THE ITALIAN GARDEN begs a question: What happened? Why did Italy appear to abandon horticulture and garden design in the twentieth century? Although the issue is complex, certain factors undoubtedly played a significant role in undermining Italian garden culture. During the twentieth century Italy engaged in two world wars that wrought radical changes in the country's social, political and economic climate. Between the wars Cecil Pinsent made several new gardens in Italy, but he worked with an expatriate élite whose enthusiasm for garden making had no equivalent in contemporary Italian culture. Despite Fascist attempts to rekindle popular interest in gardening, landscape architects like Pietro Porcinai and Maria Teresa Parpagliolo were forced to look abroad both for training and employment. After the Second World War political uncertainty and the threat of communism were accompanied by rapid urbanization. Those affluent enough to commission gardens no longer wanted to draw attention to their properties in this uneasy political climate. Unpaid apprenticeships became illegal, and this put an end to the traditional training route for a young gardener. Almost simultaneously landscape architecture was excised from university curricula. A vast proportion of the population moved into cities, where their only outdoor space might be a small balcony. Finally, Italy's low rainfall had always been a problem for gardeners and garden designers, and now there was neither the means nor the will to build the hydraulic systems that had traditionally been used to irrigate gardens.

These were the factors that contributed to the twentieth-century crisis in Italian garden culture. However the past twenty years have seen the formation of a small but determined nucleus of Italian landscape architects, designers, garden archaeologists and conservators. By their efforts the concept of conserving historic gardens as well as buildings has gradually entered Italian culture and the discipline has found its place on the university curriculum. Investment in conservation and restoration has been made both by local authorities and by the private sector. Outstanding among the privately funded projects are those of Villa Barbarigo at Valsanzibio, Poggio Torselli near Florence and Giardino Giusti in Verona. The investment of public money in both palace and park has resulted in Caserta being listed by UNESCO as a World Heritage Site. It has also funded the restoration of Villa Pisani's gardens in Stra, Boboli's magnificent Grotta Grande in Florence, the gardens of Villa Medici, Villa Torlonia and the Secret Gardens of Villa Borghese in Rome, of the hydraulic machinery at Villa d'Este in Tivoli and the Giardino del Principe at Palazzo Doria Pamphili in Genoa. Italian gardens have always attracted the attention and admiration of foreigners but, as the bibliography attests, Italy has distinguished garden historians of her own. The future holds more hope than fear.

LEFT *A gardener at work at Villa da Schio, near Vicenza in the Veneto.*

Bibliography

CHAPTER ONE

James S. Ackerman, *The Villa: Form and Ideology of Country Houses*, Thames & Hudson, London, 1995

Leon Battista Alberti, *Opere Volgari*, ed. C. Grayson, Bari, 1972

Leon Battista Alberti, *On the Art of Building in Ten Books*, translated by Joseph Rykwert, Neil Leach, Robert Tavernor, MIT Press, Cambridge Mass. and London, 1992

David R. Coffin, *The Villa in the Life of Renaissance Rome*, Princeton University Press, Princeton, 1988

Giorgio Galletti, 'Una committenza medicea poco nota: Giovanni di Cosimo e il giardino', in *Giardini Medicei*, a cura di Cristina Acidini Luchinat, Federico Motta Editore, 1996

Christopher Hibbert, *The Rise and Fall of the House of Medici*, Penguin, London, 1979

Georgina Masson, *Italian Gardens*, Antique Collectors Club, Woodbridge, 1987

Pius II, *Commentaries*, vols I–II, ed. Margaret Meserve and Marcello Simonetta, Harvard University Press, 2003

The Letters of the Younger Pliny, ed. Betty Radice, Penguin, London, 1963

Pierre de la Ruffinière du Prey, *The Villas of Pliny: From Antiquity to Posterity*, University of Chicago, Chicago and London, 1994

Alessandro Tagliolini, *Storia del giardino italiano, Gli artisti, l'invenzione, le forme dall'antichità al XIX secolo*, La Casa Uscher, Firenze, 1988

Vasari, *Lives of the Painters, Sculptors and Architects*, Everyman, London, 1996

Villa Medici a Fiesole, Leon Battista Alberti e il prototipo di villa rinascimentale, Villa Medici, Fiesole, Leon Battista Alberti and the prototype of the Renaissance Villa, ed. Donata Mazzini, Centro Di della Edifimi, Florence, 2004

G.F. Young, *The Medici*, Random House, New York, 1930

CHAPTER TWO

Francesco Berni, *Rime*, a cura di Danilo Romei, Mursia editore S.p.A., Milan, 1985

David R. Coffin, *The Villa in the Life of Renaissance Rome*, Princeton University Press, Princeton, 1988

Vincent Cronin, *The Flowering of the Renaissance*, Pimlico, London, 1992

Francesco Guicciardini, *Storia d'Italia*, a cura di Silvana Seidel Menchi, Collezione: I millenni, Giulio Einaudi editore, Turin, 1971

Christopher Hibbert, *The Rise and Fall of the House of Medici*, Penguin, London, 1979

Claudia Lazzaro, *The Italian Renaissance Garden*, Yale University Press, New Haven and London, 1990

Agostino del Riccio, 'Del giardino di un re', in *Il giardino storico italiano*, Atti del convegno di studi, ottobre 1978, a cura di Giovanna Ragionieri, Olschki, Florence, 1981

Pierre de la Ruffinière du Prey, *The Villas of Pliny: From Antiquity to Posterity*, Chicago and London, 1994

Roy Strong, *Art and Power, Renaissance Festivals 1450–1650*, Boydell Press, Woodbridge, 1984

Vasari, *Lives of the Painters, Sculptors and Architects*, vol.2, Everyman, London, 1996

D.R. Edward Wright, 'Medici Gardens of the Florentine Renaissance', in *Italian Gardens*, ed. John Dixon Hunt, Cambridge University Press, 1996

CHAPTER THREE

Riguccio Galluzzi, *Istoria del Granducato di Toscana*, 1781

The Origins of Museums : the cabinet of curiosities in sixteenth- and seventeenth-century Europe, ed. Oliver Impey and Arthur MacGregor, Clarendon Press, Oxford, 1985

A.G. Morton, *The History of Botanical Science*, Academic Press, London, 1981

Lucia Tongiorgi Tomasi, *An Oak Spring Flora, flower illustration from the fifteenth century to the present time*, The Oak Spring Garden Foundation, 1997

Luigi Zangheri, *Storia del Giardino e del paesaggio: il verde nella cultura occidentale*, Leo S Olschki, 2003

Luigi Zangheri, 'Curiosities and marvels of the sixteenth-century garden' in *The History of Garden Design: the Western Tradition from the Renaissance to the Present Day*, Thames and Hudson, London, 1991, pp59–67

CHAPTER FOUR

David R. Coffin, *The Villa in the Life of Renaissance Rome*, Princeton University Press, Princeton, 1988

Fons Sapientiae, Renaissance Garden Fountains, Dumbarton Oaks Colloquium on the History of Landscape Architecture V, ed. Elisabeth Blair MacDougall, Dumbarton Oaks, Washington DC, 1978

Claudia Lazzaro, *The Italian Renaissance Garden*, Yale University Press, New Haven and London, 1990

Claudia Lazzaro, 'The Villa Lante at Bagnaia: An Allegory of Art and Nature', PhD dissertation at Princeton, published in *The Art Bulletin*, 59, 1977

Elisabeth Blair MacDougall, *Fountains, Statues and Flowers, Studies in Italian Gardens of the Sixteenth and Seventeenth Centuries*, Dumbarton Oaks, Washington DC, 1994

Ovid, *Metamorphoses*, trans. Ted Hughes, Faber & Faber, London, 1977

Agostino Ramelli, *The Various and Ingenious Machines of Agostino Ramelli*, 1588, trans. Martha Teach Gnudi, Scolar Press, London, 1976

Agostino del Riccio, 'Del giardino di un re', in *Il giardino storico italiano*, Atti del convegno di studi, ottobre 1978, a cura di Giovanna Ragionieri, Olschki, Florence, 1981

CHAPTER FIVE

Ludovico Ariosto, *Orlando Furioso*, Einaudi, Turin, 1966

Margaretta J. Darnall and Mark S. Weil, 'The Itinerary of the Sacro Bosco', in *Journal of Garden History*, Vol.4, no.1, January–March 1984

Ovid, *Metamorphoses*, trans. A. D. Melville, Oxford University Press, 1987

Arturo Sandrini (ed.), *Villa della Torre a Fumane*, Banca Agricola di Cerea, 1993

John Shearman, *Mannerism*, Penguin, Harmondsworth, 1979

Roy Strong, *Art and Power, Renaissance Festivals 1450–1650*, Boydell Press, Woodbridge, 1984

Jessica Wolfe, *Humanism, machinery and Renaissance literature*, Cambridge University Press, 2004

CHAPTER SIX

Margherita Azzi Visentini (ed.), *Il Giardino Veneto*, Electa, 1988

Gilbert Burnet, *Voyage de Suisse, d'Italie et de quelques endroits d'Allemagne et de France, fait és années 1685 et 1686*, A.Acher, Rotterdam, 1687

Giovanni Campana / D.Rossetti, *Le fabbriche e i giardini dell' Ecc.mz Casa Barbarigo posto in Val San Zibio*, Verona, 1702

Malcolm Campbell, 'Hard Times in Baroque Florence', in *The Italian Garden*, ed. John Dixon Hunt, Cambridge University Press, 1996, pp.160–201

Paolo Bartolomeo Clarici, *Istoria e cultura delle piante*, 1726

David Coffin, *Gardens and Gardening in Papal Rome*, Princeton University Press, 1991

Paolo Cottini, *Giardini di Lombardia*, Edizioni Lativa, Varese, 1994

John Dixon Hunt, *Garden and Grove. The Italian Renaissance Garden in the English Imagination: 1600–1750*, J.M.Dent, London and Melbourne, 1986

Georgina Masson, *Italian Gardens*, The Antique Collectors Club, Woodbridge, 1987

Lionello Puppi, ' "Hell and Paradise are Here": The Garden of Villa Barbarigo at Valsanzibio, Padua', in *The History of Garden Design*, ed. Monique Mosser and Georges Teyssot, Thames & Hudson, London, 1991

John Raymond, *Il Mercurio Italico. An itinerary contayning a voyage made through Italy in the yeare 1646, and 1647*, 1648

J. Salomonio, *Inscriptiones patavinae sacrae et prophanae*, 1696

CHAPTER SEVEN

Alberta Campitelli e Alba Costamagna, *Villa Borghese, L'Uccelliera, la Meridiana e i Giardini Segreti*, Ministero per i Beni e le Attività culturali, Rome, 2005

David Coffin, *Gardens and Gardening in Papal Rome*, Princeton University Press, Princeton, 1991

Giovanni Battista Ferrari, *Flora ovvero cultura dei fiori*, Leo S. Olschki, Rome, 2001

Giovan Battista Ferrari, *Hesperides, sive, de malorum aureorum cultura et usu*, 1646

David Freedberg, *The Eye of the Lynx, Galileo, His Friends, and the Beginnings of Modern Natural History*, University of Chicago Press, Chicago and London, 2002

The Origins of Museums : the cabinet of curiosities in sixteenth- and seventeenth-century Europe, ed. Oliver Impey and Arthur MacGregor, Clarendon Press, Oxford, 1985

J. Manilli, *Villa Borghese fuori di Porta Pinciana descritta da Iacomo Manilli Romano Guardaroba di detta Villa*, Lodovico Grignani, Rome, 1650

D. Montelatici, *Villa Borghese fuori di Porta Pinciana con l'ornamenti, che si osservano nel di lei Palazzo. e con le figure delle statue più singolari*, Gio Francesco Buagni, Rome, 1700

A.G. Morton, *The History of Botanical Science*, Academic Press, London, 1981

Lucia Tongiorgi Tomasi, *An Oak Spring Flora, flower illustration from the fifteenth century to the present time*, The Oak Spring Garden Foundation, 1997

Lucia Tongiorgi Tomasi, *Flora e Pomona: l'orticoltura nei disegni e nelle incisioni dei secoli XVI–XIX*, Leo S. Olschki, Rome, 1990

CHAPTER EIGHT

Leon Battista Alberti, *Opere Volgari*, ed. C. Grayson, Bari, 1972

Leon Battista Alberti, *On the Art of Building in Ten Books*, translated by Joseph Rykwert, Neil Leach, Robert Tavernor, MIT Press, Cambridge Mass and London, England, 1992

Alberta Campitelli and Alba Costamagna, *Villa Borghese, L'Uccelliera, la Meridiana e i Giardini Segreti*, Ministero per i Beni e le Attività culturali, Rome, 2005

David Coffin, *Gardens and Gardening in Papal Rome*, Princeton University Press, Princeton, 1991

Il Luogo teatrale a Firenze, a cura di Mario Fabbri, Elvira Garbero Zorzi, Anna Maria Petrioli Tofani, Electa, Milan, 1975

John Hale, *The Civilisation of Europe in the Renaissance*, Fontana, London, 1993

John Dixon Hunt, *Garden and Grove, The Italian Renaissance Garden in the English Imagination: 1600–1750*, J. M. Dent & Sons, London, Melbourne, 1986

Georgina Masson, *Italian Gardens*, Antique Collectors Club, Woodbridge, 1987

D.R. Edward Wright, 'Some Medici Gardens in the Florentine Renaissance: An Essay in Post-Aesthetic Interpretation', in *The Italian Garden*, ed. John Dixon Hunt, Cambridge University Press, 1996

CHAPTER NINE

Margherita Azzi Visentini (ed.), *Il Giardino Veneto*, Electa, 1988

Margherita Azzi Visentini, *Il Giardino Veneto tra sette e otto cento e le sue fonti*, Edizioni il Polifilo, Milan, 1988

Margherita Azzi Visentini, 'Gardens and Villas in the Veneto', in *The Italian Garden*, ed. John Dixon Hunt, Cambridge University Press, 1996

George L. Hersey, *Architecture, poetry, and number in the royal palace at Caserta*, MIT Press, Cambridge, Mass., 1983

Carlo Knight, *Il Giardino Inglese di Caserta: un' avventura settecentesca*, Sergio Civita, Naples, 1987

Richard Pommer, *Eighteenth-century Architecture in Piedmont, the open structures of Juvarra, Alfieri and Vittone*, NYU, London, 1967

Charles Quest-Ritson, *The English Garden Abroad*, Viking, London, 1992

Alessandro Tagliolini, *Storia del giardino italiano. Gli artisti, l'invenzione, le forme dall'antichità al XIX secolo*, Usher, Florence, 1988

CHAPTER TEN

Alasdair Moore, *La Mortola, in the footsteps of Thomas Hanbury*, Cadogan, London, 2004

Charles Quest-Ritson, *The English Garden Abroad*, Viking, London, 1992

Ercole Silva, *Dell'arte dei giardini inglesi*, Leo S. Olschki, Rome, 2001

Sir George Sitwell, *On the Making of Gardens*, reprint David R. Godine, Jersey, New Hampshire, 2003

Alessandro Tagliolini, *Storia del giardino italiano. Gli artisti, l'invenzione, le forme dall'antichità al XIX secolo*, Usher, Florence, 1988

CHAPTER ELEVEN

Katie Campbell, 'Cecil Pinsent and the Anglo-Florentine Garden', in *Hortus*, 73, Spring 2005

Ethne Clarke, 'A Biography of Cecil Ross Pinsent, 1884–1963', in *Garden History*, 26:2, Winter 1998

Sonja Dümpelmann, 'Maria Teresa Parpagliolo Shephard (1903–74): her development as a landscape architect between tradition and modernism', in *Garden History*, 30:1, Spring 2002

Giorgio Galletti, 'Il ritorno al modello classico: giardini anglofiorentini d'inizio secolo' in *Il giardino storico all'italiana*, a cura di Francesco Nuvolari, Electa, Milan, 1992

Benedetta Origo, Morna Livingstone, Laurie Olin, John Dixon Hunt, *La Foce, A Garden Landscape in Tuscany*, University of Pennsylvania Press, Philadelphia, 2001

Iris Origo, *Images and Shadows: Part of a Life*, John Murray, London, 1998

Iris Origo, *War in the Val d'Orcia*, Allison and Busby Ltd, London, 2001

Russell Page, *The Education of a Gardener*, Harvill, London, 1994

Mariachiara Pozzana, 'Il giardino e il suo doppio: la ricerca del giardino all'italiana', in *Il giardino storico all'italiana*, a cura di Francesco Nuvolari, Electa, Milan, 1992

Charles Quest-Ritson, *The English Garden Abroad*, Viking, London, 1992

Geoffrey Scott, *The Architecture of Humanism, A Study in the History of Taste*, Constable and Company Ltd, London, 1947

Sir George Sitwell, *On the Making of Gardens*, reprint David R.Godine, Jersey, New Hampshire, 2003

Gabrielle van Zuylen, *The Gardens of Russell Page*, Stewart, Tabori & Chang, New York, 1991

Gardens to visit

It is advisable to check opening times as they may change.

VILLA ALDOBRANDINI
Via G Massaia 18
Frascati
Lazio
Contact: 06 9420331
Opening: All year: Monday to Friday
9.00–13.00 and 15.00–18.00; closes 17.00
in winter

VILLA LE BALZE
Georgetown University
Via Vecchia Fiesolana
50014 Fiesole
Tuscany
Contact: 055 59208; info@villalebalze.org
Website: www.georgetown.edu/villa
Opening: By appointment

BARBARIGO
Valsanzibio
Veneto
Contact: 049 8059224
Website: www.valsanzibiogiardino.it
Opening: From beginning of March to end
of November: every day (Saturday, Sunday
and Holidays included) 10.00–13.00 and
14.00 to sunset

BOBOLI GARDENS
Piazza Pitti 1
Florence
Contact: 055 218741
Website: www.firenzemusei.it/boboli
Opening: November–February: 8.15–16.30;
March: 8.15–17.30; April, May, September and
October: 8.15–18.30; June–August: 8.15–17.30.
Entry is permitted up to an hour before
closing time. Closed on the 1st and the last
Monday of each month, New Year's Day, May
1st and Christmas Day.

The Grotta Grande is open for accompanied
visits, depending on the opening hours of the
Gardens: 11.00, 13.00, 15.00 all year round.

VILLA BORGHESE
Piazzale Flaminio
Rome
Contact: 06 85304242
Website: www.villaborghese.it
Opening: February–December: guided tours
of the *giardini segreti* Saturday and Sunday,
book on 06 85304242

VILLA BUONACCORSI
Via Giardino 9
Potenza Picena
Contact: 0733 880355
Opening: By appointment

VILLA CAPRILE
Via Caprile 1
Pesaro
Contact: 0721 21440;
ita.cecchi@provincia.ps.it
Opening: 15 June–15 September:
Monday–Sunday 15.00–19.00

VILLA CAPPONI
Via Pian dei Giullari 3
Florence
Contact: 055 2298609
Opening: By appointment

VILLA CETINALE
Sovicille
Siena
Tuscany
Contact: 0577 311147; cetinale@libero.it
Opening: 10.00–13.00, not weekends

VILLA CIMBRONE
Via Santa Chiara 26
Ravello
Campania
Contact: 089 857459; info@villacimbrone.com
Website: www.villacimbrone.com
Opening: 9.00–dusk

VILLA DURAZZO PALLAVICINI

Via Ignazio Pallavicini 13
Pegli
Liguria
Contact: 010 666864;
villapallavicini@astergenova.it
Opening: autumn/winter months: 9.00–17.00;
spring/summer months: 9.00–19.00
Botanical gardens: 9.00–12:30.
Closed: Mondays, Christmas Day, Boxing Day,
New Year's Day, Easter

VILLA D'ESTE

Piazza Trento 1
100019 Tivoli
Contact: 0424 600460
Website: www.villadestetivoli.info
Opening: 8.30, closes one hour before sunset.
The ticket office closes one hour before the
closing of the monument. The hydraulic
organ of the Organ Fountain is active daily at
the following times: 10.30, 12.30, 14.30, 16.30,
18.30. The Fontana della Civetta functions at
the following times: 10.00, 12.00, 14.00, 16.00,
18.00 The Monument is closed all Mondays, 1
January, 1 May, and 25 December. If Monday is
a holiday, the monument will remain open
and the weekly closure will fall on the next
working day.

VILLA LA FOCE

61, Strada della Vittoria
53042 Chianciano Terme
Tuscany
Contact: 0578 69101; info@lafoce.com
Website: www.lafoce.com
Opening: By appointment

VILLA GAMBERAIA

Via Rossellino 72
Settignano
Tuscany
Contact: 055 697205; villagam@tin.it
Opening: Monday–Friday 9.00–13.00,
14.00–18.30

VILLA GARZONI

Piazza della Vittoria 1
Collodi
Tuscany
Contact: 0572 429590
Website:
www.provincia.pistoia.it/MuseiEValdinievole/
ing/m_garzoni.htm
Opening: Monday to Sunday, summer:
9.00–sunset; winter: 9.00–12.00/14.00–17.00

VILLA GEGGIANO

Pianella
Siena
Tuscany
Contact: 0577 356879
Website: www.villadigeggiano.@tin.it
Opening: By appointment

GIARDINO DEI SEMPLICI

Via Micheli 3
Florence
Contact: 055 2757402; e-mail ortbot@unifi.it
Opening: Monday, Tuesday, Thursday, Friday
9.00–13.00, Wednesday 9.00–12.00

ISOLA BELLA

Lake Maggiore
Piedmont
Contact: 0323 30556
Website: www.borromeoturismo.it
Opening: April–October 9.00–17.30

LA LANDRIANA

Tor San Lorenzo
Via Campo di Carne
Ardea
Campania
Contact: 039 6081551; info@landriana.com
Website: www.giardinidellalandriana.it
Opening: April–May every weekend
10.00–12.00, 15.00–18.00; June, July,
September, October every first and third
Sunday of the month and holidays (including
2 June) 10.00–12.00, 16.00–19.00. August,
weekend of the 15th (the Assumption)
10.00–12.00, 16.00–19.00

VILLA LANTE

Via J Barozzi 71
Bagnaia
Contact: 0761 288008
Opening: Monday–Friday 9.00–one hour
before sunset

SAN LIBERATO

Via Settevene Palo 33
Bracciano
Lazio
Contact: 06 9988384; info@sanliberato.it
Website: www.sanliberato.it
Opening: By appointment

VILLA MADAMA

Via di Villa Madama
Rome
Contact: Ministero degli Affari Esteri, Piazzale
della Farnesina, 1–00194 Rome; Tel: 06 36911
Opening: By appointment

VILLA MEDICI

Via Beato Angelico 2
Fiesole
Contact: Signora Anna Marchi Mazzini 055
59417 / 055 2121116; Fax 2398994
Opening: By appointment, mornings only,
not weekends

VILLA MEDICI DI CASTELLO

Via Castello 47
Castello
50141 Florence
Contact: 055 454791
Website:
www.polomuseale.firenze.it/english/musei/villacastello/
Opening March, April, May, September and
October 9.00–17.30; November, December,
January and February 9.00–16.30; June, July
and August 9.00–19.30. Closed on the first
and the last Monday of each month, New
Year's Day, 1 May and Christmas Day.

LA MORTELLA

Via Francesco Calise 39
Forio
Ischia
Contact: 081 986220; mortella@pointel.it
Website: www.lamortella.it
Opening: Easter–November, Tuesday,
Thursday, Saturday, Sunday

LA MORTOLA

C.so Montecarlo 43
Ventimiglia
Imola
Contact: 01842 29507
Opening: March to September 10.00 to 17.00;
winter, daily, except Wednesday, 10.00–16.00

NINFA

Via Ninfina
Doganella di Ninfa
Cisterna
Latina
Contact: Fondazione Caetani 06 6873056
Opening: April–November first weekend of
each month

ORTO BOTANICO
Via Orto Botanico 15
35123 Padua
Contact: 049 8272119
Website: www.ortobotanico.unipd.it/
Opening: Monday–Friday April–October
9.00–13.00, 15.00–18.00; November–March
9.00–13.00

ORTO BOTANICO
Via Luca Ghini 5
I-56126 Pisa
Contact: 050 2215350; Fax +39 050 551345;
direzione@dsb.unipi.it
Website: www.dsb.unipi.it/
Opening: 8.30–13.00. Closed Sunday

PALAZZO PICCOLOMINI
Piazza Pio II
Pienza
Tuscany
Contact: 0587 748503; Fax 0587 748379, La
Società Esecutori Pie, Siena
Website:www.cultura.toscana.it/architetture/
giardini/siena/palazzo_piccolomini.shtml
Opening: 10.00–12.30, 15.00–18.00. Closed
Monday

VILLA·LA PIETRA
Via Bolognese 120
Florence
Contact: 055 5007210; villa.lapietra@nyu.edu
Website: www.nyu.edu/lapietra/
Opening: By appointment only, villa and
garden Friday afternoon, garden only Tuesday
morning

VILLA PISANI
Via A Pisani
Stra
Veneto
Contact: 049 502074
Website:
http://sbmp.provincia.venezia.it/mir/musei/str
a/home.htm
Opening: Tuesday to Sunday from 1
October–31 March 9.00–16.00; from 1
April–30 September 9.00–19.00

CASTELLO DI RACCONIGI
Racconigi
Cuneo
Contact: 0171 261467
Website: www.ilcastellodiracconigi.it
Opening: 27 March–6 November. Closed
Monday

PALAZZO REALE
Piazza Castello
Turin
Contact: 011 436 1455
Opening: Tuesday and Thursday–Sunday
15:30–19:30; Wednesday and Friday
8.00–14.00

VILLA REALE
Via Villa Reale
Marlia
Tuscany
Contact: tel/fax 0583 30108
Opening: March 1st to the end of November.
In July the park is only open on Tuesdays,
Thursdays, and Sundays. Visits are always
guided and visiting times are as follows: 10.00,
11.00, 15.00, 16.00, 17.00, 18.00. Closed on
Mondays

LA REGGIA
Viale Dohuet 2/a
1-81100 Caserta
Campania
Contact: 0823 321400; reggiacaserta@tin.it
Opening: January, February, November,
December 8.30–14.30; March 8.30–16.00;
April 8.30–17.00; May and
September 8.30–17.30; June, July, August
8.30–18.00; October 8.30–16.30
The English Garden closes one hour before
the park. Guided tours every hour 9.30–13.00

VILLA RIZZARDI
Pojega de Negrar
Verona
Veneto
Contact: 045 7210028; pojega@guerrieri-
rizzardi.it
Opening: 1 April–31 October, Thursdays
15.00–19.00

SACRO BOSCO
Bomarzo
Lazio
Contact: 0761924029
Opening: 9.00–dusk

VILLA SAN REMIGIO
Verbania
Piedmont
Contact: 0323 503249;
turismo@comune.verbania.it
Opening: By appointment

PALAZZINA DI STUPINIGI
Piazza Principe Amedeo, 7 –
Stupinigi
Turin
Contact: 011 3581220
Opening: Winter 9.00–12.30, 14.00–17.00,
closed on Mondays. Summer
9.30–12.30,14.00–18.00, closed on Mondays

VILLA I TATTI
Via di Vincigliata 26
Florence
Contact: 055 603 251; fax: 055 603 383;
info@itatti.it
Website: www.itatti.it
Opening: By appointment, Tuesday and
Wednesday afternoons only

VILLA DELLA TORRE
Fumane
Veneto
Contact: Address all enquiries to Giuseppina
Cazzola Savio
Via San Vitale 7
37129 Verona
045 8033204
Opening: By appointment

VILLA TORRIGIANI
Camigliano
Lucca
Contact: 0583 928041
Opening: March to the second Sunday in
November: 10.00–12.30 and 15.00–18.30.
Closed Tuesday

VILLA TRISSINO
Piazza Trissino 2
Trissino
Veneto
Contact: 0445 962029; Fax 0445 962090
Opening: By appointment

Picture acknowledgements

The publisher would like to thank the following individuals, galleries, and picture archives for permission to reproduce their illustrations. Every care has been taken to trace copyright holders. However, if we have omitted anyone we apologize and will, if informed, make corrections in any future edition.

KEY
AA = The Art Archive, London
BAL = The Bridgeman Art Library, London
Scala = Scala Archives, Florence

All photographs by Alex Ramsay unless listed below.

Page 5 Accademia, Venice/BAL; 8 Palazzo Schifanoia, Ferrara/AA; 9 Uffizi, Florence/BAL; 10 British Library, London/BAL; 11 Biblioteca Riccardiana, Florence/Scala; 12 Palazzo Medici Riccardi, Florence/BAL; 13 Sta. Maria Novella, Florence/Scala; 17 Uffizi, Florence/BAL; 18 Piccolomini Library, Siena Cathedral/BAL; 22–3 Musées Royaux des Beaux Arts de Belgique, Brussels; 25 Uffizi, Florence/BAL; 28 Uffizi, Florence/BAL; 30–1 Museo Storico Topografico Firenze com'era, Florence/BAL; 36 Private Collection; 38 Uffizi, Florence/BAL; 38–9 Museo Storico Topografico Firenze com'era, Florence/BAL; 40 Uffizi, Florence/Scala; 42 Castello Buonconsiglio, Trento/AA; 43 Biblioteca d'Ajinda, Lisbon/AA; 44–5 Musée du Château de Versailles/AA; 47 Engraving from Guida all'Imperial Regio Orto Botanico di Padova, 1854, Private Collection; 48–9 Kew Gardens Library, London; 52 Villa d'Este, Tivoli/BAL; 54–5 Villa La Pietra, Florence/AA (detail); 60 Private Collection/BAL; 62 (above) Private Collection ; 62 (below) Private Collection/BAL; 63 Private Collection ; 64 Villa Lante/BAL; 66 Private Collection; 74 National Gallery, London/BAL; 88 Angelo Hornak, London; 89 Museo Storico Topografico Firenze com'era, Florence/AA; 92–3 Biblioteca Estense, Modena/AA; 95 Didier Boguet (1802–c.61), View from the Upper Loggia of the Villa Aldobrandini at Frascati, Musée Granet, Aix-en-Provence/BAL; 102 Private Collection/BAL; 105 (above) Engraving from J.C.Volkamer, Continuatio der Nürnbergischen Hesperides, 1714, Private Collection; 108 Kew Gardens Library, London; 109 Richard Mervyn/Skyworks, London; 110 Private Collection/Christie's Images, London; 114b Private Collection/BAL; 116 Private Collection/BAL; 118 Uffizi, Florence/Scala; 119 Museo Botanico dell'Università, Florence/Quattrone, Florence; 120 Frontispiece from Ferrante Imperato's catalogue, Dell' historia naturale, 1599, Private Collection;

121 Private Collection/BAL; 122 Christie's Images, London/BAL; 123 Private Collection; 124 Private Collection; 125 (both) Private Collection; 126 Ca'd'Oro, Venice/Akg-images, London; 127 Private Collection (AR); 128 The Royal Collection © 2006, Her Majesty Queen Elizabeth II; 129 Private Collection/BAL; 130 Museo Civico Luigi Bailo, Treviso; 131 Society of Antiquaries of London; 132 The Royal Collection © 2006, Her Majesty Queen Elizabeth II; 133 Musées des Beaux Arts, Rouen/AA; 134–5 Private Collection/AA; 136 Villa Medici, Rome/BAL; 137 (above) By courtesy of Andrea Bianchi Bandinelli; 138 Stefano della Bella, Open air theatre, Florence. Uffizi, Florence/Scala ; 139 Orazio Scarabelli, Naumachia. Uffizi, Florence/Scala; 141 (above) Engraving by Teresa del Po from Carlo Fontana's design for Allestimento del giardino Chigi alle Quattro Fontane per la festa del ferragosto, 1668. Private Collection; 142 By courtesy of Andrea Bianchi Bandinelli; 145 Accademia Carrara, Bergamo/Scala; 146–7 Giovanni Reder (1693–1764), Fair for the return of the grape pickers in the garden of Palazzo Rospigliosi on the Esquiline Hill, Rome (detail), Museo di Roma, Palazzo Braschi/AA; 148–9 G.B.Falda, Le Fontane di Roma, c.1675. Society of Antiquaries of London; 150 Claude Joseph Vernet (1714–89), The Gardens of the Villa Ludovisi, Rome, 1749 (detail). Hermitage, St Petersburg/BAL; 151 The Bodleian Library, University of Oxford (Ms d'Orville 539, fols Vv-VIr); 156 (left) Bosco sacro ad Apollo can trono e tempio, engraving of set design by Juvarra from Act III of 'Ciro', 1712. Private Collection; 162 Engraving from G.Carboni, a Villa di Stra, collection of prints, Paris, 1782. Private Collection/BAL; 164 Private Collection; 166–7 Engraving by Carlo Nolli after Luigi Vanvitelli, Palazzo di Caserta; 1756, from 'Dichiarazione dei Disgni del Reale Palazzo di Caserta. Private Collection/BAL; 172 Museo di Capodimonte, Naples/AA; 173 Napoleonic Museum, Rome/AA; 180 Bibliothèque des Arts Decoratifs, Paris/AA; 184 Q. Wasmann, The Ottmansgutes Flower Garden at Merano, c.1840. Hamburger Kunsthalle, Hamburg/BAL; 187 Private Collection/© Robert O'Rorke, London; 188 Palazzo Pitti, Florence/BAL; 189 Museo de Nittis Barletta, Bari/AA; 192 Ernest Rowe, A View of Florence from the surrounding hills, 1904. Private Collection/BAL; 194–5 Acton Collection, Villa La Pietra, New York University, Florence; 196–7 By courtesy of Silvia Bonacossa Sella; 209 By courtesy of the Beevor family; 217 Karl-Dietrich Bühler; 218 John Ferro-Sims, London

The photograph on page 224 was taken at Villa Buonaccorsi; on page 228 at Villa d'Este; on page 232 at La Landriana and on page 234 at Villa da Schio.

Index